AUTOPSY
OF
WAR

ALSO BY JOHN A. PARRISH, M.D.

12, 20, & 5: A Doctor's Year in Vietnam

Playing Around: The Million-Dollar Infield Goes to Florida

*Between You and Me: A Sensible and Authoritative
Guide to the Care and Treatment of Your Skin*

AUTOPSY
OF
WAR

A PERSONAL HISTORY

JOHN A. PARRISH, M.D.

THOMAS DUNNE BOOKS
St. Martin's Press
New York

THOMAS DUNNE BOOKS.
An imprint of St. Martin's Press.

AUTOPSY OF WAR: A PERSONAL HISTORY. Copyright © 2012 by John A. Parrish, M.D. All rights reserved. Printed in the United States of America. For information, address St. Martin's Press, 175 Fifth Avenue, New York, N.Y. 10010.

Copyright © Piet Hein Grooks: THE NOBLE ART, page xv. Reprinted with kind permission from Piet Hein a/s, DK-5500 Middelfart, Denmark.

www.thomasdunnebooks.com
www.stmartins.com

Map design by Paul J. Pugliese

Cover design by Steve Snider
Cover photograph by Sami Sarkis/Getty Images

Library of Congress Cataloging-in-Publication Data

Parrish, John A. (John Albert), 1939–
    Autopsy of war : a personal history / John A. Parrish.—1st ed.
        p. cm.
    ISBN 978-0-312-65496-2 (hardback)
    ISBN 978-1-4299-4104-4 (e-book)
    1. Vietnam War, 1961–1975—Personal narratives, American.   2. United States. Marine Corps. Division, 3rd. Medical Battalion, 3rd—Biography.
3. Physicians—United States—Biography.   4. Vietnam War, 1961–1975—Medical care.   5. Vietnam War, 1961–1975—Psychological aspects.   6. Vietnam War, 1961–1975—Veterans—United States—Biography.   7. Post-traumatic stress disorder—Patients—Biography.   8. Combat.   I. Title.
    DS559.5.44.P35 2012
    959.704'37—dc23
    [B]
                                                                            2011050610

First Edition: June 2012

10   9   8   7   6   5   4   3   2   1

To war fighters and their families

ACKNOWLEDGMENTS

Characters in this story are acknowledged throughout the book—possibly in more detail than they wish. I survive and thrive because of some of them.

When I could not reach the core of war within me, I turned to books to guide me and help me recognize and disclose my failures. On occasion I found rich ore containing insights, perspectives, affirmations, or a passage that expressed something I knew to be true, but said with more authority, grace, and intellect than I could muster. I also found fully processed gems with naked power I could recognize but would never have found within myself. My own language was inadequate.

I boxed the three hundred war books stacked on my desk for years, making a bunker that left just enough room for my laptop and pads of paper. These books are filled with stickies and scraps of paper with handwritten scribbles. Most have dog-eared pages and pages marked by paper clips, notes in the margins, circled paragraphs and underlining in pencil, red ink, black ink, and green Magic Marker. Two are swollen and stiff from a basement flood. Others have smudges from coffee, food, sand, dirt, sunscreen, and sweat. They are worn and wounded by my frenetic search for the meaning of the American War in Vietnam or wars in general. Hundreds of authors have shared with me, and their books are still in my head and on various bookshelves. I'm sure I have read more about war than all other topics combined. This includes the journals and textbooks I have read in the course of my professional efforts.

Although I never found exactly what I was looking for, I often found comfort, especially in books or passages written by infantrymen. Some of the books made me weep. Others caused rage—at myself, my society, and unknown beasts. I learned and relearned a great deal. I am grateful for the authors' unknowing contributions to this book. We are comrades in arms.

The description of my mother's death in chapter 21 is modified from a commentary written by me and published in the *Journal of the American Medical Association* (*JAMA*): "An Unquiet Death," December 6, 2006, Vol. 296, No. 21, pp. 2531–2532. Copyright 2006 American Medical Association. All rights reserved.

In my professional life, I have been fortunate to surround myself with people much more talented than I. At present, this is especially true in the Boston-based Center for Integration of Medicine and Innovative Technology (CIMIT) and the Red Sox Foundation–Massachusetts General Hospital Home Base Program. These people bring me great joy and sense of purpose. I am grateful and honored. They create a pathway to my future professional success and emotional stability, and I am learning to follow. I am especially grateful for the decades of friendship and collaboration with Ron Newbower, Ph.D. He joined me in forming CIMIT. In fact, the words I use to describe CIMIT are mostly his.

I will limit my individual acknowledgments to those who actually crafted the book itself.

Over forty years the leadership of MGH trusted me to take a very unconventional career pathway. I was only offered one job, Chief of Dermatology; the other five or six responsibilities I created myself. I could not have been successful without the support, reputation, and intellectual riches provided by HMS and MGH.

ACKNOWLEDGMENTS

While managing a large part of my private and professional life, my assistant, Mary Beth Nolan, has typed and retyped hundreds of drafts of letters, chapters, notes, poems, confessions, and essays. She was always ready to tackle my messy, scraggly, disorganized hand-written pages with inserts and inserts into inserts. If I was in a frenzy, she not only worked nights, weekends, and holidays but also main-tained a steady nonjudgmental, pleasant tone that kept me calm and confident that all the scattered pieces would eventually come together. I could not have completed this book without her skill and support.

During early clumsy attempts to reduce my chaotic thoughts to writing, my good friend of forty years, David P. Simmons, M.D., carefully edited my work in a thoughtful way that helped me better understand what I really meant to say.

As therapy for me and a project for himself, Dr. James Groves in-terpreted and improved many drafts over many years. I am grateful for his scholarship and support, wisdom, and sense of humor.

Dr. Barbara Gilchrest had substantive influence on the content and structure of this book.

More recently, Glenn Stout was my coach, partner, interpreter, counsel, editor, cowriter, and friend. He made order out of hundreds of pages of thoughts, letters, and narratives. He interviewed me for many hours in order to help me fill in places I had omitted or forgot-ten or, in some cases, was unwilling to face.

I am grateful to my literary agent, Ike Williams, for his expertise, advice, good work, and friendship.

The editing by Rob Kirkpatrick and Nicole Sohl was excellent, au-thoritative, and friendly despite working with the range of ways my personal history invaded the writing of my story, including childlike vocabulary, unsophisticated narrative style, the harsh language of the foot soldier, and the hyperbole of an angry soul.

This book does not describe my children. I regret I was too dam-aged and selfish to make them more central in my life. Because I love them so, that breaks my heart and fills me with regret.

ACKNOWLEDGMENTS

I take full responsibility for all content. *Autopsy of War* is a report of "seeing for myself" the causes of my spiritual near-death experience.

I am most grateful to the warriors who taught me what I need to know to come home from war.

PREFACE

This is a war story. It describes my experiences in the American War in Vietnam in 1967–68 and how that year has overshadowed my life ever since. Despite numerous attempts, for more than forty years, I have not been able to stop writing and rewriting my war story. I don't know why. Primarily I persist because I can't get it right. With a wide spectrum of emotions, I scribble, edit, and move passages around. I describe the same events over and over again from different perspectives. I forget things I have written before, discovering old manuscripts that seem at first like someone else's stories. After forty years, I still remember war scenes for the first time.

Within a few months after entering the war zone, my social, religious, ethical, and psychological foundations were shattered. I no longer knew my place in the world. Upon my return, the 1969 America was different from the '50s and '60s society that formed me, and I was a different person. I reacted to inner pain in a way that inflicted pain on others—pain twice suffered. I became distant, selfish, and inconsiderate in my personal life and poured all my angst and energy into my professional life in academic medicine. Success in the latter stole further from my family. At all times I was either working, acting out harmful behaviors, or writing about the American War in Vietnam.

About twenty years ago, I began to analyze psychological factors molding my adult life—a complex mixture of intrinsic depression, and reactions to childhood experiences, and war-related exposures to carnage and death. I considered the possibility that a growing number of disturbing symptoms and destructive behaviors could be framed by what has been called post-traumatic stress disorder (PTSD). My story begins before the term existed.

Leaders within the Departments of Defense and Veterans Administration suggest the term "post-traumatic stress" to describe the normal reactions to extraordinary circumstances and reserving use of "Post Traumatic Stress Disorder" to describe the "medical condition" or cluster of persistent behaviors that adversely impact normal activities of life. Even then, the use of the word "disorder" may add to the stigma preventing warriors from seeking help. "Stigma" is typically the perception that help-seeking behavior will be detrimental to career (e.g., prejudicial to promotions and leadership positions) and/or reduce social status among peers. Mental health experts know that stigma is a general societal issue. In large comprehensive studies, the Institute of Medicine of the National Academy of Sciences and the RAND Corporation use the term "invisible wounds of war" to describe the overlapping symptoms of PTSD, mild traumatic brain injury (TBI), and depression. I find this term useful.

This book reflects an attempt to understand my journey over the past forty years. There are elements of confession and search for absolution, forgiveness, catharsis, atonement, and redemption. Because I am embarrassed by the weaknesses I expose, I also write to justify, explain, and defend myself. Finally, I am motivated by a lingering determination to see myself as a warrior.

I need to create a part of me outside myself, safe and apart from my physical self: a permanent record, a communication with my ancestors and future generations. I write as a means of reexperiencing horror and failure. I do this to gain control and diminish fear. At the same time I want to be jolted, shocked, lifted out of apathy and sameness. I want to pick at scabs and cut myself with my own sword. I must demonstrate through pain that I am still alive. I also write to lash out and express anger.

I submit my testimony because I believe that coming forward is the right thing to do—possibly the brave thing to do. I do this with considerable anxiety, remorse, fear of failure, and shame. Although it might be considered in poor taste, I describe unattractive behavior. I want to be authentic and thorough, and I wish to break my unspoken contract with men who celebrate themselves and each other as ideal family people while hiding their infidelities beneath winks, nods, and intentional blinders.

I accept that there will always be war, but I need to believe more can be done to help its victims, specifically the warriors who have left the battlefield but not their personal war. This book is witness to the power of time, acceptance, self-discovery, hard work, and love in belatedly diminishing one man's psychic war. Even so, I cannot experience the rewards of inner peace without guilt, knowing that for many others their war continues. Still, perhaps my healing is a helpful message.

I have very limited and mixed expectations about the impact of this work. My story may be a bothersome fly passing by the eye of the enormous bull of our defense industry and American militarism. A condescending or angry blink may be all I deserve. My professional colleagues may be surprised, shocked, or amused by my revelations. Most will judge me, and I will become fodder for hallway gossip and jokes at the conference room table, as well as an opportunity for self-congratulatory expressions of righteousness. Others may examine the lengths to which they go to be in the inner circles of power, and their need for control. My family may wish that I had left some things unsaid, but I hope they understand me better.

I was a U.S. Navy physician who served with the U.S. Marine Corps. Therefore, in this story I usually use the word "marine" to describe the infantry in the war zone in Vietnam. I am aware that some veterans and active duty personnel feel strongly that the word "soldier" should be used only to describe army personnel. However, in this manuscript when I speak of "soldiers" I am often referring to servicemen and servicewomen in the U.S. Army, Navy, Marines, Air Force, Coast Guard, National Guard, and Reserves—and enemy forces. No disrespect to the U.S. Army is intended. My choice of words stems primarily from the toy soldiers and Christian soldiers of my childhood. Recently, in public speaking, to be in step with the Department of Defense, Department of Veterans Affairs, and many veterans organizations, I use the word "warrior" to mean all men and women who have served in the U.S. military and "war fighter" for those who have been or will be in battle. The word that most easily comes to my mind for infantrymen (I never served with women) is "grunt." I use the term with respect, admiration, and gratitude.

By telling my story, I wish to bring no dishonor to warriors. I hope they interpret my story as an acknowledgment of their service and sacrifice—and proof that they are not alone. I hope warriors and their families will be motivated to seek help for invisible wounds of war.

This following story is true, and I have made every effort to maintain its accuracy and authenticity. However, given the passage of time and the nature of my experience, it is entirely possible that my recollection and interpretation of events and those of others may not be identical. That is the nature of the process. Some names have been changed to protect the privacy of individual persons.

Some portions of this book in which I describe events I experienced and witnessed during the Vietnam War appeared in somewhat different form in my 1972 memoir, *12, 20, & 5: A Doctor's Year in Vietnam.*

I write to share my grief and to acknowledge that all the enabling attitudes toward war are in me. Had I not been to war, I would want to go. I resist submitting this manuscript because it is not finished. It may never be finished. I still haven't gotten it right. Publication is an act of surrender.

—JOHN A. PARRISH, M.D.
Boston, Massachusetts
April 2011

The noble art of losing face
May someday save the human race
And turn into eternal merit,
What weaker minds would call disgrace.

—PIET HEIN

The willingness with which our young people are likely to serve in any war, no matter how justified, shall be directly proportional to how they perceive the veterans of earlier wars were treated and appreciated by their nation.

—ANONYMOUS, OFTEN ATTRIBUTED TO GEORGE WASHINGTON

"Whom shall I send? And who will go for us?" And I said, "Here I am. Send me!"

—ISAIAH 6:8

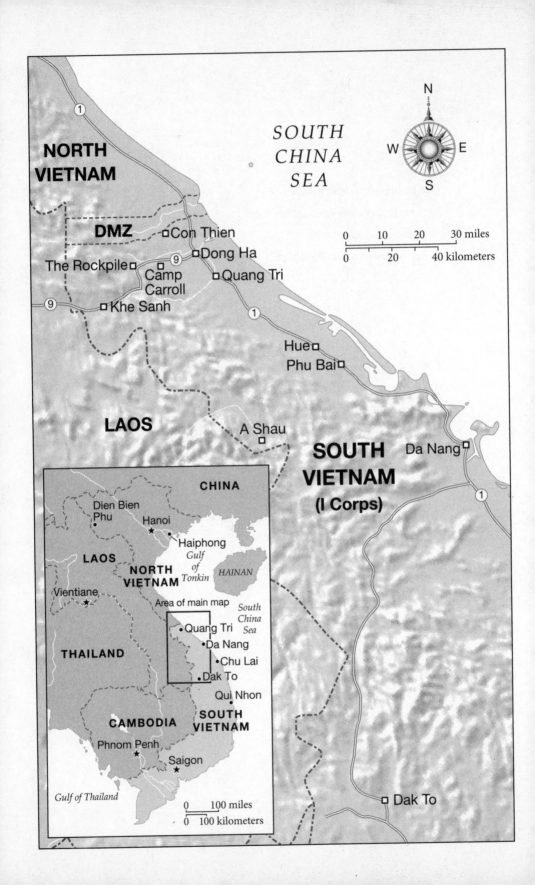

AUTOPSY
OF
WAR

PROLOGUE

The bed of a large truck is overflowing with a jumbled pile of bodies—desperate, terrified marines had heaved the dead and the wounded together in a heap without battle dressings, tourniquets, splints, or first aid of any kind. Corpsmen and other doctors are already sorting through the pile in the bed of the truck, untangling the living from the dead, and lowering them onto litters.

I climb up one side of the truck and lower myself in among the pile of bloody bodies. One marine with a large wound in his neck tries to stand up and take a step toward me. As he grabs my shirt, he steps on a dead man with no head and falls backward, pulling me onto the pile of flesh. From beneath us, I hear screams of agony. To right myself, I place my arm behind me. My hand enters a gaping, feces-filled tear through a marine's rectum and pelvis. The marine next to him vomits blood and begins to gag. I try desperately to turn him over so he can breathe, but he is pinned to the pile by a leg—not his own—that prevents me from flipping him over.

I reach down and tug at the leg. It suddenly flops free, and I almost tumble again. All I have in my hands is the leg—there is no body attached.

The vomiting marine stops moving and is no longer breathing. I start to resuscitate him and then see brains matted in his black hair.

I let him go. My hands are slippery with blood, and I have his brains under my fingernails . . .

Decades later, I am in Washington, D.C., sitting at a large, heavy polished mahogany table ringed with large leather chairs in a lavish conference room. I am attending a meeting of the Defense Science Board, a committee that advises the U.S. Department of Defense (DoD) on scientific and technical matters. Today the group includes about twenty people—retired generals, experienced, high-level DoD advisers, CEOs and board members representing various defense and weapons industries. The room is rimmed with aides, chiefs of staff, and eager, well-groomed male and female military officers in dress uniforms.

I am a new member of a group that already seems to know each other well, yet no one introduces me or makes note of my presence. For the past several months I have been receiving briefing reports and packets of classified background information to prepare me for the meeting. I had been interviewed by the FBI and had undergone a thorough background check. Even my high school classmates had been interrogated. The only medical professional in the room, I was invited to join the meeting because of my work with the Department of Defense in developing new ways to treat casualties.

With no formal introductions, the members start to speak, and soon the discussion centers on how best to defeat or coerce the enemy while causing the least "collateral damage." The generals, consultants, and former defense industry executives discuss the relative merits of stealth weapons, unmanned aircraft, snipers, Special Forces, image-guided bombs, and other kinds of high-tech hardware and strategy. At one point, the conversation veers off onto a discussion of tactics, the selection of military targets, the most efficient ways to destroy specific structures, and how best to target select populations and individuals.

On a large screen we watch video clips that demonstrate the high-precision weaponry used in Iraq and Afghanistan. A truck slowly rumbling down a dirt road passes through superimposed crosshairs and explodes in a cloud of smoke—a precise hit from a jet fighter. A cluster of men in loose pants and flowing robes evaporates when struck with a small bomb launched from a drone. Some in the group laugh out loud and cheer as if they are witnessing a sporting event.

Foreign civilian casualties are weighed against American civilian intolerance of their own dead and wounded soldiers. Tables and charts of costs, hearts and minds, kill zones, quantification of civilian casualties, ratios of dead women and children to total dead civilians, soldier morbidity and mortality, combat casualty care, and medical evacuation time are used to compare the present wars with the American War in Vietnam and other U.S. military actions. The conversation goes on and on and on.

I think about what I know of war, what I have learned after witnessing its human cost for a year and examining its carcass for nearly forty years. During a lull in the discussion, I speak softly to the defense contractor sitting next to me. "Try diplomacy," I say. "Try peace."

Several men nearby overhear me. They look my way and scowl. No one asks my opinion after that, and I keep silent. Forgetting where I am, I drift . . .

The door flies open, and two soldiers rush in carrying a Vietnamese woman with both legs missing at midthigh. She is naked, and her stringy, jellied stumps are no longer bleeding. "No need to stop here," I say. "She's dead."

"What do we do with her, sir?" asks one of the marine stretcher-bearers. "Take her to Graves? Throw her away?"

Before I can answer, other soldiers carry a Vietnamese woman with a missing right hand and several flank and thigh wounds past me. With her good arm she holds a baby to her breast. Both are covered with dirt and blood. As the mother loses consciousness, the baby slides away from her grasp and begins to cry. It falls to the floor and then becomes still and quiet.

A steady stream of women and children blown apart and badly

burned flows through the door as the conference room becomes a makeshift hospital emergency room. A dead baby, charred black, is still warm to the touch. A six-year-old girl with a missing leg refuses to let go of her unharmed but bewildered two-year-old brother. Mourning mothers cling to dead children, and terrified children cling to dead mothers. Women of all ages wail, and babies and children scream. The conference room is further transformed to a forward triage center. The smell of burned flesh causes my eyes to water, and I start to gag. I know these sounds and smells are penetrating my brain, there to stay, and I fear they will rear up when I least want them.

I cannot keep up. I have no control over the flow of casualties. As I try to push a growing mound of bowel back into a small boy's abdomen, I become aware that another doctor has joined me and is inserting a tube through the boy's thin chest wall. The semiconscious boy moans loudly. The doctor explains to me that more than twenty Vietnamese have been wounded by "friendly fire." In the ville, another dozen still lie dead where they fell.

"Today is February 14," he says bitterly "We could call this our St. Valentine's Day Massacre." I work on in silence, frantically and frenetically at first, but then I begin to pace myself with unemotional efficiency. Ignoring the surrounding flesh and suffering, blame and shame, I focus on one life, one limb, one wound at a time . . .

Slowly the carnage retreats. Once again I begin to absorb the calm male voices around me talking about the ways to wage war. Eventually the discussion shifts to the growing number of suicides among veterans and soldiers on active duty. Accidents and suicides cause almost half of all fatalities in DoD. Recently, suicides outnumber combat deaths. Historically, the age-adjusted suicide rate has been significantly lower in the military than among the civilian population, but beginning in 2004 that pattern changed, and in 2008 the suicide rate in the army exceeded the rate in the civilian population.

No longer am I rendered speechless in this room lined with generals and defense industry executives. I open my mouth and put forth ideas about using social media to reach out to veterans and active-duty soldiers with stress-related psychological wounds and make suggestions about how to treat them. "Maybe," I say, "we could get more of them back to duty." Heads around the table nod in agreement.

Although never invited to another meeting, I am on the team.

BOOK ONE

THE GOOD BOY

CHAPTER 1

My first memory of my father is seeing him in a white dress military uniform, standing at the pulpit in his church, parishioners fanned out before him and looking up in adoration, as he spoke of sin, Jesus, and love. I was four, perhaps five years old.

War frames my earliest memories, and war was a major force that lifted my extended family from the poverty and ignorance of the Deep South in the years surrounding the Great Depression. By the time I began school all the men in my extended family had "gone to war." I would follow them. Service in the military was the single event we all shared that determined the future course of our lives.

My mother's father was an itinerant farmer in Tennessee, and although he never served, during World War I he left the farm to work at a munitions plant in Spring Hill, just south of Nashville. There he learned a trade, becoming a brick mason, and earned a steady wage for the first time in his life. Soon after the war ended, so did his job. In 1923, during the Florida building boom, he hitchhiked to West Palm Beach to look for work. A year later, he sent for his wife and four children: the identical twins, Jack and Earl, age ten; Claude, age six; and my mother, Lucile, who was still an infant.

They took the train to Florida and arrived with no possessions except the clothes they wore and moved in with my grandfather in one room of a boardinghouse. The three boys slept in the attic, and my mother slept with her parents. My mother's strong-willed mother, my grandmother Mama Blair, worked as laundress, secretary, bookkeeper, or housekeeper, raised four children, and saw that they went to church. Staying just ahead of bill collectors, the family moved a dozen times over the next five or six years. The day after they fled one apartment to avoid overdue rent payments, the building was destroyed by the 1928 hurricane. My mother's father did not often have steady work. When he did, he usually left most of his paycheck in a bar.

The twins never enrolled in school in Florida. Instead, they worked various odd jobs to help the family. Handsome, charismatic, and athletic, they became motorcycle policemen in the winter and in the summer played semipro baseball. In 1942, when the twins were in their late twenties, both boys and their younger brother, Claude, were drafted. Soon afterward my grandfather got drunk and left home for good.

Claude was the good boy. He joined the Boy Scouts, helped rescue victims of the 1928 hurricane, got involved in the church, and stayed in school. He graduated from high school as president of the student body and valedictorian and lettered in four sports despite working twenty hours a week with AT&T, first as a lineman and then in an office job. Even though he had no military experience, AT&T arranged for him to be an officer in the Army Signal Corps. He thrived in the military, eventually becoming an intelligence officer. In between military stints he returned to AT&T and simultaneously earned a law degree. Recalled to the service during the Korean War, he left active duty in 1953 as a major and rejoined AT&T. In rapid sequence he became vice president in charge of the Telstar Satellite Program, then president of Ohio Bell, president of Pacific Northwest Bell, and finally president and chairman of the National City Bank Corporation. He died at age ninety-seven. The headline of his obituary in the *Palm Beach Daily News* referred to him as "bank chairman and veteran."

The twins, Jack and Earl, received formal training as military policemen and, although both had stateside assignments, were separated for the first time in their lives. After the war, they returned to the Palm

Beach police force and reunited, their reputations enhanced and burnished by their service for their country. They always worked together and provided security for the growing number of extremely wealthy and powerful residents with winter homes in Palm Beach, families like the Woolworths, Rockefellers, Astors, and Kennedys. The Blair twins were very close to the Kennedys, especially Joe Sr. and, before he was killed in World War II, Joe Jr. On more than one occasion they acted as "watch-out" or helped provide cover for a Kennedy when he cavorted with a married woman.

To show real class, one could display the twins as "security" for very small dinner parties, and the rich and famous often planned social events around the availability of the Blair brothers. Standing next to their shiny giant motorcycles on either side of a mansion's front entrance, they were treated more like guests than workers. Increasingly, however, they acted as private detectives and personal secret agents, cultivating contacts to arrange anything legal or illegal for a growing list of clients.

Eventually they bought a large hotel and started a rental car business as a legitimate front for one of Palm Beach's largest gambling and prostitution rings. For decades the twins were powerful enough to keep major rental car companies and organized crime out of Palm Beach. A small band of men without last names was always around when needed, and Mama Blair was hired as a bookkeeper for a gas station they operated on the rental car lot. Executives from all over the United States and Europe could place discreet phone calls to one of the twins and by the time they arrived at the West Palm Beach airport whatever they wanted would be waiting: a car, a driver, women, hotel rooms, drugs, other entertainment, and gambling options. When clients were returned to the airport, their bill would be scrubbed to simulate a business trip, or there would be no paperwork at all showing that the client had ever been in Palm Beach.

My father, James Parrish, grew up in the poverty, ignorance, and bigotry of the Deep South in Sylvester, Georgia. His mother bled to death when she delivered her third child. As was the custom in his clan, his father, also named James, an alcoholic who occasionally worked as a fireman, actor, salesman, or barber, married the sister of his deceased wife. As the oldest (age five) child, my father assumed responsibility for the care and feeding of his family and tried to protect his two younger siblings from their genuinely evil stepmother. Doing odd jobs and stealing, my father provided the only steady source of food. He worshipped his father, who was most generous, attentive, and loving when he was sober and working and was dramatic, entertaining, and demonstrably affectionate when he was drinking. His frequent binges lasted days or weeks.

Crawling under porches and going through trash to find cigarette butts, my father began smoking at age six. He also joined his father, and further bonded with him, in binge drinking by the time he was ten years old. Because Prohibition started when my father was six years old, the liquor he made or stole was not only illegal but sometimes downright poisonous. During binges he would sometimes be deathly ill.

He went to school just enough to keep the truant officers at bay but forced his siblings to attend regularly and do their schoolwork. He swept streets or cleaned buildings before school, stocked groceries after school, and worked in a drugstore in the evenings. Although he was tough and easily provoked, his strong work ethic endeared him to his growing list of employers.

His father died when he was thirteen, and he became the official head of the household.

After school one day, to defend his brother from harassment, my father took on the school bully, who was two or three years his senior and considerably bigger. He beat him so severely that classmates pulled him away. For money or any reason, he could fight anyone anytime and most often won by sheer will. At 130 pounds, five feet nine inches, he was the starting offensive center and defensive nose guard on the high school football team. His teammates called him "pissant." After his siblings' needs were met, my father spent his time drinking, smoking, moving with a tough gang, and chasing girls. Secretly he was sleeping with at least one older married woman.

The summer after he finally graduated from high school, he had his first serious depression and suicidal thoughts. He was awarded a football scholarship to a small college but was too drunk to matriculate.

To get closer to one particular girl, he attended a Southern Baptist church and was soon "adopted" by a deacon who took particular interest and, by overpaying him for odd jobs, provided enough money for my father's siblings and stepmother. My father had long talks with this man, began to attend church regularly, and became close to the fire-and-brimstone preacher. After a powerful conversion experience, my father was "saved from sin" by the grace of Jesus Christ and committed his life to God's will. He stopped drinking completely, stopped volunteering for fistfights, and left his gang to be in the church community. His church mentors and hard work made it possible for my father to become the first of his generation to go to college, attending Stetson University, a Baptist school in DeLand, Florida. He was elected president of the student body, not because of his athletic prowess or classroom performance but because he was an effective orator, giving speeches at school events, civic organizations, churches, and anywhere else he was invited. He met and fell in love with my mother, a gentle, quiet, attractive classmate who had a part-time job playing saxophone in a local dance band. She gave up her music because my father associated it with sin—dancing and alcohol.

They married, and after graduation he earned a doctor of divinity degree at the Southern Baptist Theological Seminary in Louisville, studying and practicing oratory by preaching at local churches. My older brother, James, was born while my father was in college; I was born during his years in the seminary; and my sister, Mary Blair, was born while he was the minister of a small church in Florida. He claimed to be in ecstasy when he was preaching. He was loved by his flock, who provided housing, a small salary, and a black maid to do housework and child care. The local car dealer gave him a car, and all the storekeepers gave him special deals on groceries, clothing, appliances, haircuts, and baseball tickets.

An American dream was launched. Every two or three years my father was "called" by bigger churches and Jesus to move us to different cities in the Deep South. He began to travel all over the South to conduct revivals—a week of daily evening services designed for the already saved to celebrate with singing, testimonials, and a powerful, emotional fire-and-brimstone sermon designed to bring new converts into the church. My father was apparently very good at creating the emotion and energy required to bring people to accept Jesus as their personal savior. When Jesus concurred, in 1940 my father accepted the invitation to become pastor at a small church in Plant City, Florida.

He proudly never helped with household chores or family care— we were there to care for him and serve as decoration, brought out for "show and tell" before my father's friends and acquaintances from church, but otherwise left alone. If I happened to be around, to demonstrate what a great parent he was he would pull me close to him and pinch my cheek and say, "This is my little Bubba, this is my little John Albert." Prefaced by "Gimme some sugar," my father was always kissing the preschool children of his congregation, signs of affection that were withheld from the rest of us.

Except for my older brother, James W. Parrish Jr., the firstborn child, called "Little Jimmie." Even when it seemed inappropriate, my father took Little Jimmie with him to civic meetings and adult gatherings, publicly smothered him with kisses, and wore him as a badge of family and fatherly love.

In 1942, when I was three years old, with great drama and patriotic virtue, my father announced to his congregation that when a certain number of church members joined the war effort, he, too, would go. He did. My mother was stunned. My father had never discussed this with her, but in our household, all decisions were his alone to make.

After attending chaplain school at William and Mary in Virginia, my father became a navy officer on active duty from early 1942 until

Jimmie and Lucile Parrish, 1943.

V-J Day in 1945. As chaplain, he served aboard the USS *Hampton* troop transport ship, was temporarily assigned to the Seabees in Iwo Jima, and was stationed at bases in Hawaii and the Great Lakes Naval Base. He was once assigned as the chaplain to a black military unit stationed at Norfolk, Virginia, and founded a black Southern Baptist church in the community. His love of preaching was stronger than his strong racism.

While my father was caring for "our boys overseas," his home billet frequently changed. Although my father was never with us, my mother faithfully moved us by car to five different military bases in five different states. California, New England, Michigan, and other places I cannot remember.

I loved being in the crowded car with my mother, my younger sister, my older brother, and all of our possessions. We had an old car, and my mother drove very slowly. If it was a long trip, we would sleep together in one room in a cheap motel. Usually, when the manager discovered my father was in the military he lowered the rate or gave us the night for free.

On these trips we had a tire malfunction almost every day—a gradual flat, a large blister, or a blowout. My mother would pull over, stand passively next to the car, and wait for someone to stop. She was stately, almost regal—tall and thin, very beautiful, with dark hair that was always perfectly in place. Inevitably some nice man would stop and change the tire, and then we would find a gas station and wait again while the torn tire was resealed or replaced.

One day while she was driving, a cow walking alongside the highway suddenly decided to cross the road. We struck the cow broadside, and I was thrown against the back of the front seat and cut my lip. I liked the salty taste of my blood.

Although I always thought of my mother as fragile, on this occasion she took total charge. She told us to stay in the car while she talked to people who had stopped in the road. Apart from my split lip no one was hurt, although the car was badly damaged. She finally let us out of the car to see what was going on. The cow made terrible groaning moos as it lay injured on the road, unable to stand. When a policeman arrived, my mother ushered us back into the car so we could not see what happened next.

The policeman stood next to the cow, took out his gun, and fired it. The blast hurt my ears, and I could feel a shudder in my chest. Sudden death dealt by the gun of a uniformed man branded me. I had never known such violence before, and it made a strong impression. Men in uniform had the authority to kill.

A farmer attached heavy chains to our car and towed us with his truck. My mother had to steer and brake to keep the car from rolling into the back of the truck, but she couldn't quite get the timing right. The ride was very jerky; if the truck went too fast our heads would jerk back, and if my mother got too close to the truck she would put on the brakes and we would bolt forward. She started laughing, and I can still hear her laugh punctuated by our high-pitched squeals. I wanted the ride to last forever.

After several cross-country moves, my father returned briefly and moved us to Albany, Georgia to be near his brother and sister. Then he left my mother with three small children living through two winters in a tiny old house heated only by a single potbellied furnace. My dad's brother was a soldier stationed nearby, and he came home most nights and weekends to be with his wife and two infant boys. My father's sister had a small child, and her socially challenged husband repaired tires. He was the only male member of my family who did not join the military. My father never considered allowing my mother to live in West Palm Beach, Florida, where her mother and three brothers could provide support and comfortable living conditions.

In our one-room house my mother cooked on an electric hot plate and maintained a coal-burning fire in the stove. One day my little sister was severely burned when she sat on the hot plate thinking it was a potty. For days, she lay on her stomach with her butt uncovered. When my mother let me apply the ointment, it was the only time my sister didn't cry. I had the job from that point on.

When the adults were together, my mother was very quiet as the others spoke nonstop about food, the past and all its people, or the weaknesses and sins of others. At these times, children were ignored, and we learned about the world by listening. Even the often repeated jokes contained lessons. I learned that blacks were stupid, dirty, and smelly and would eat anything and that the "white-only" water fountains and bathrooms were to keep us safe from social and biological contamination. By nature, women were inferior to men and boys, and their purpose was to raise children and serve men. Divorce was a major sin that ruined all members of a family forever. The men constantly made references to my aunt's enormous breasts. The comments made them laugh and caused me to feel a forbidden pleasure when she hugged me.

We were taught that Jews had a highly unfounded sense of entitlement, a relentless work ethic, and a selfish and manipulative gift for making money at the expense of others—it was no wonder the Germans were killing most of them. Otherwise, Germans and the "Japs" were the embodiment of evil and found great pleasure in torturing and killing Americans. Catholics were to be distantly tolerated even though they were pagan worshippers of Jesus's mother. Africans and Asians, if they did really exist, were pitiful, weird, ignorant people who were doomed to hell. Missionaries tried to save a few by telling them about Jesus, but it was a pretty hopeless task. Even though we were poor, our white, Christian privileged status was obvious to all, and only we had the comfort of being in God's grace.

I learned that God knew everything and was all-powerful and that America was history's most impressive combination of might and right. America sometimes had to go to war to protect innocents, free the oppressed, and defeat evil. In death and in life, American soldiers were heroic and honorable, even though they sometimes drank or cursed or touched girls in private places. Touching one's own private parts was evil, and God knew when one did it—one was physically and mentally compromised for the remainder of the day after playing with genitals. Romantic love with only one predetermined special person could lead to fulfillment on this earth, and death, through temporary and dramatic grief, transitioned into an everlasting life of peace and joy in heaven.

Some truths were not taught directly but had to be figured out through observation and trial and error. For instance, parental approval and love was earned by being quiet, good, industrious, and reliable and rubbing adults' feet whenever asked to do so. One way to manipulate others and to take a break from the boring routines and monotonous conversations was to act wounded by some phrase uttered by a family member. Dramatic pouting and poorly disguised anger could last for hours.

Except to my mother, belching and farting were always funny, the loudest ones getting the best and longest laugh and commentary. All the adults, except my mother, smoked, and prolonged laughing-coughing spells were frequent, with the best entertainment being farting caused by coughing. Even when it made them cringe inside, children and women were to appear to be sweetly tolerant of physical displays of affection from adult males. On the other hand, women should never willingly initiate public displays of affection. My mother never touched me except to rub my back at bedtime. Yet we had an unspoken deep bond that required little verbal or physical demonstration or reinforcement.

While still in the navy, my father was recruited by the First Baptist Church of Laurel, Mississippi. Offered a bigger salary and a free place for us to live in the "pastorium," next to a stately new church, he left the church members of Plant City, Florida, who had patiently awaited his return, without hesitation. My father came home for a few weeks when we moved into what I thought was an enormous house. For five dollars a week and leftover food, a black woman prepared all meals, cleaned house, washed and ironed, and took care of my older brother, my younger sister, and me.

When Little Jimmie was seven or eight he began to lose his vision. For weeks he suffered from severe headaches, pain that would leave him alternately screaming and whimpering. My mother took him to a military hospital, where the eye doctor explained that there was swelling in the back of both eyes. I would learn later that he had a brain tumor and was losing his vision due to swelling of the brain and pressure on his optic nerves.

Over the next year or two, as my brother's vision continued to deteriorate, I became his caretaker, darkening the lines in his coloring book with a black crayon and holding his hand when we ventured outside the house. When his vision was almost gone, I pulled him around the neighborhood in our red wagon. Within a few months, probably due to increases in growth hormone caused by the influence of the tumor on his pituitary gland, my brother grew to be bigger than most adults. He was taller and much heavier than my parents, and his head became disproportionately large. He could barely fit into the wagon, and pulling him became hard work.

Little Jimmie began to vomit every night. After sleeping for a while, he would suddenly sit up and spew vomit into his bed and mine and onto the wall and floor. Sometimes it seemed a long time

In late 1945, Little Jimmie's head started to enlarge. Here he is with me and our sister, Mary Blair.

before my mother would come to clean up. I usually pretended to be asleep so she would give Little Jimmie all of her attention. In order to fall asleep again I would focus on protecting three dolls: Boy, Dog, and my teddy bear Goody. They needed me very much. I always made sure I was touching all three of them when I went to sleep. I needed them to feel safe. I needed them to need me.

As Jimmie's health deteriorated, my father suddenly returned from war to take him to a military hospital in Jacksonville, Florida. Wearing his military khakis, my father drove away with one hand on the steering wheel and the other on my brother, who lay in the back-seat writhing in pain and having seizures.

The next day, three older couples, wealthy, loyal parishioners who were big donors to the church and thought my father was wonderful, arrived at our home. One couple drove my mother to the hospital in Jacksonville. Without explanation my sister and I were each taken by one of the other couples. I was taken to an enormous house with expansive, manicured lawns. The next morning the old woman informed me that my brother had gone to be with Jesus and was to be planted in the ground. She asked me if I wanted to pray or go out in the yard and play. I elected to go outside, and as I tried to sort through what was happening, I wrapped myself in a protective fog.

My mother and father did not contact me for days, and I did not go to school. The quiet old couple sat and read most of the time, so I was essentially alone. I did not know where my sister was. I spent my days wandering about in the biggest backyard I had ever seen. It had no boundaries and blended into a golf course. There were no balls, toys, swing set, sandbox, or children's books. When I asked questions about my brother and sister and parents, I only got empty comforting answers and invitations to pray. I soon stopped asking. I overheard phone conversations about flowers and church services and "viewings." The old woman repeatedly shared with callers that my nine-year-old brother was so large he required an adult casket. He was to be buried on his tenth birthday.

These events and concepts were difficult to comprehend and made me afraid and angry. How could I be out of my mother's thoughts for such a long time? Why would all-powerful, loving Jesus, who owned the whole world, want my brother? Why would my brother choose to be with Jesus? Why put my brother under the ground? Why was I in a stranger's house while all this was happening?

After what seemed an eternity, my father returned. Instead of his uniform he now wore a suit and tie, and he invited me and the older couple to kneel and pray. The prayer was about his sadness and unfailing faith and the love the couple had provided me. He told me I should be happy because I would see my brother again in heaven. Then he put me in the car and sobbed without speaking while we drove to pick up my sister at another house.

Suddenly, I was back in the room I had shared with Little Jimmie. I had never seen the room so clean, and it smelled like a disinfected bathroom. I could not find any of Little Jimmie's clothes or belongings. When I returned to school the teachers and students seemed extra nice to me but kept their distance. At home, my father and sister often cried. I never saw my mother cry, so neither did I. I was a quiet, good boy, and I sought no attention.

At night, before going to bed, I would kneel and say my bedtime prayer, "If I should die before I wake, I pray thee, Lord, my soul to take." Then I would lie awake, paralyzed by fear. Maybe if I didn't fall asleep I wouldn't die. Boy, Dog, and Goody needed me.

Although I never saw Little Jimmie again, for the next few weeks daily trips to the grave with my father reinforced the notion that he was in the ground. My father stood or knelt by my brother's grave. I stood next to him not knowing what to say or what to do when he started sobbing. We would then walk the main streets of Laurel, stopping in stores or places of business as my father greeted, told jokes, prayed, and chatted. He would often introduce me as "Bubba," "Little Bubba," or "John Albert" and then add that I was his "second son" or his "oldest living son."

I would stand in silence. I felt pressure to perform, and my bashfulness upset him, but I had no talents, no clever quips or practiced phrases to deliver. He would then ask me to pray. In a panic, and with great difficulty, I would stumble through the few phrases I could remember from his public prayers. I grew to dislike the main street of Laurel, and I felt my father grew to dislike me. I felt I was being unfairly compared to my saintly older brother, whose virtues became more remarkable with the passage of time. I was constantly reminded in private and public that Little Jimmie lived and died.

A few weeks after Little Jimmie went into the ground, I was carried flailing and screaming into a local hospital for "elective" removal of my tonsils and adenoids. My older brother had gone into a hospital and ended up both in the ground and in heaven with Jesus. I fought and screamed from the car to the waiting room, and when my time came I fought and screamed some more. I was convinced that I was actually fighting for my life, protecting my body from a planned invasion, an intrusion to cut out a part of me. The nurses asked three soldiers who happened to be nearby to carry me into a room. They took me from my mother, lifted me by the arms and legs as I kicked and twisted, then pinned me down on a table while ether was dripped onto a cloth covering my nose and mouth.

When I awoke, the pain from having living tissues of my throat ripped out through my mouth and nose quickly gave way to bigger trauma. The tip of my penis had been cut, rolled back, and sewn into the shaft. It looked distorted and disfigured. I felt invaded, insulted, betrayed, and brutalized. My mother must have been in collusion with my father and the doctors. She had failed to protect me or at least to warn me. How could I ever trust my parents again, or trust anyone? Even doctors and soldiers threatened my life, made me unconscious, and cut off the end of my penis. I couldn't even trust Little Jimmie—he had left me to be with Jesus.

Two days later on my first day back at home, in the room previously shared with my missing brother, I began to bleed profusely from deep within the back of my nose. I thought I was simultaneously bleeding to death and choking. Wearing his formal white military dress uniform, my father was at church stroking the meek and saving the wicked. My mother waited for what seemed like hours until a neighbor came to be with my younger sister, and then she took me to a doctor. After many failed attempts to pack my nose with gauze, a doctor shoved a giant instrument up my nose and cooked the back of my throat. I tried to be still but made the uncontrollable frenzied movements of a drowning boy.

Then my father went back to war, to be with "our boys overseas." My mother told me there was a baby inside her.

Shortly after my little brother, Gil, was born, my mother began to bleed and was taken to the hospital. Her femaleness, the organs of her fertility and my origin, was removed, and she returned a pale, sickly, weak, exhausted woman who clearly needed my protection. I was determined to protect us both but did not know if I could. Jimmie was in the ground, my father was at war, and my penis was partially gone.

I had only my little sister, and she stayed in her own world of dolls and dresses.

There was an enormous weeping willow tree with a trunk three or four feet across that stood in the center of our backyard. Its branches hung in a protective shroud over virtually the entire yard. Walking or playing beneath it in the shade and mottled sunlight, I felt safe and secure.

One day a crew of men showed up in a truck with chain saws and other equipment. I watched as they began to hack the tree to pieces. I ran to my mother, screaming and crying, pleading with her to make them stop, but she explained to me that my father had ordered it be done for safety reasons and I was never to openly challenge his reasoning or authority.

I watched from the back steps in tears as piece by piece the limbs were cut off, and then finally the trunk was cut down and removed. The backyard was flooded by sunlight. My little sister and I sat crying near the stump for hours. I could not protect anything I loved.

My father, doctors, soldiers, and Jesus had all the power.

CHAPTER 2

Jesus led my father to accept an offer of a significant salary increase and a large rent-free home in a nice residential area, to pastor the Riverside Baptist Church in Miami, Florida, a moderately large church close to the center of town. This was a definite step up for our family. The church was larger and the congregation much wealthier. The war was over, and "our boys overseas," like my father, had returned.

Despite serving for several years, my father talked to me only once about his war experience. I cannot recall why he chose to speak or precisely when, but I remember it vividly. He told me he held a flashlight so a dentist could identify dead soldiers by their dental records, because nothing else about the body was identifiable. I was left to fill in the details.

Although he may well have been in a sterile, stateside morgue, at the time I pictured him and the dental officer in combat uniforms on a pitch-black battlefield, bravely crawling from one torn-apart body to another, shells exploding in the distance, the air acrid with smoke. I was luridly fascinated by the romantic, patriotic scene I conjured up, envisioning my father heroically flaunting danger as bombs rained down and he absorbed grief and saved souls.

That was all. He never mentioned the war again, and this silence seemed a great loss to me. I resented his not sharing. Did he witness unmentionable horror and the dark side of men? Of himself? Was his pain too great? His guilt too massive? The fact that my father did not speak about the war added to its mystery and wonder. I was completely infatuated. Secretly, I hoped war would be my path to manhood and hoped my father would prepare me for the day it was my turn to go. The might and righteousness of my country, the power of God and man to take life, and my longing for heroism swallowed me.

In my childhood fantasies and backyard play, I refused to be a phony singing cowboy, a savage Indian, a policeman, or a robber. I only wanted to be a soldier. All of my preadolescent fantasies about women were in the context of saving them or protecting them during war. While playing war, I was frequently wounded but still carried on with great resolution and focus. When I did elect to die, I did so in a slow and dramatic fashion while remaining unselfish and silent. I knew that war would make me immortal in the minds of men.

Occasionally, I would be lost in a jungle or on an island with a beautiful woman. We would fall in love romantically, yet I would not succumb to her relentless lust. I had to be ready should the enemy find us. In my fantasies I never actually killed anyone, but my mere presence made the enemy tremble and retreat. In war, the quiet, timid, unathletic, thin boy would be revealed to be sturdy, daring, and impetuous. War would make me a man in the image of John Wayne. If my father had been broken by war, I would be formed and released to fulfill my full potential. My father and all other men would love and respect my bravery, strength, cunning, intelligence, nobility, and invincibility.

Only war could contain all that I was, or wanted to be. The Old Testament God, Christian soldiers, mythology, my people, salvation, might, righteousness, democracy, manhood, romance, sexual conquest, and physical prowess could all come together in war. War could bring all the contradictions, mysteries, anxieties, phoniness, and pettiness of my life to a shocking and permanent resolution.

My family, my church, my country, and mankind needed me to go to war. I would respond, at first quietly reluctant, but then with a force never known before. I hoped my war would come before the human race was ended by nuclear destruction or pollution. I had every confidence it would. I would surprise everyone by being ready.

Because my father loved to emote and to use public emotion as a means of power and control, I was especially perplexed about his silence; war stories seemed a wonderful opportunity to demonstrate his skill and fill his need to dominate every encounter he had with my family or friends or his congregation. Yet all I knew was that he held a flashlight, and nothing else about what he saw or what he did or what impact it had on him. Between my brother's death and war, though, something had come loose inside him.

After he returned from the war my father took up all the emotional space in our home. He was unpredictable, at times distant and unavailable, and often stayed in his study. At other times, he would be overly physical, suddenly demanding kisses and hugs. He would cry at the slightest hint of sadness in his life.

My father resented the care and love my mother gave to Gil, my new baby brother. He ignored the infant except for overbearing, overly dramatic public displays of affection. For no apparent reason, particularly when they were alone, he constantly poured emotional abuse onto my mother. She was very stoic and didn't express her emotions. I remember her having tears on her cheeks and trembling lips, but I don't remember her crying, and as far as I knew he never struck her.

I dreaded holidays, which were all twisted into something more like a funeral or memorial service for my brother. For years, I received Christmas and birthday presents "To John from Little Jimmie," written in my father's hand, and I had to give presents to family members in honor of Little Jimmie, who was present at every Christmas, every holiday. I used to hate holidays because they were so sad.

I could always feel my father's anger seething just beneath the surface, and I was paralyzed and petrified. The most frightening scenes happened at the dinner table after especially long prayers of gratitude to bless our food and thank the Lord for our bounty. If my father burned his lips on coffee, he would smash the cup against the wall. When my younger brother reached for a piece of meat out of turn, my father lashed out, socking him backhanded in the chest, sending him crashing backward onto the floor. Once he felt that my sister used too much ketchup and emptied the entire full bottle onto her plate. He kept pounding the bottom of the bottle as ketchup overflowed onto the table and the floor and my sister ran away in tears.

To keep his anger at bay I used perfect manners and only spoke when addressed. I was a very good, quiet boy because I knew how emotionally explosive he was. The only time he actually physically punished me was when he struck me with a belt for some minor infraction of household rules. As he struck me over and over I remained totally still and completely, utterly silent. He hit me until he was out of breath, exhausted, and then stopped and never touched me again. We had completed an unspoken passage. I never mentioned the incident to my mother or siblings.

Yet none of my father's mood swings or emotional violence was visible when he was in public or in the pulpit. Outside our home he insisted that everyone, young and old, call him "Brother Jimmie." A powerful orator, he could move his congregation at will. He was very charismatic, and he loved playing to the crowd. His time at home was spent planning and scheming and positioning himself for his next performance, like an actor studying for a part. He often included references to Little Jimmie in his sermons and told powerful stories of his intrinsic goodness and intelligence. He quoted Little Jimmie, and every word he uttered was like a parable, endowed with wisdom. Little Jimmie could sing like an angel, recite passages from the Bible from memory, and pray with profound eloquence. I could do none of these things.

My father sometimes took me with him to visit his hospitalized parishioners. If the patient was alone and unconscious, we would leave quickly, but if family members were present, he would say prayers that seemed to last forever and were filled with descriptions of the faith, love, and commitment of each person there. He told the sick people I wanted to see them to show my concern. He would even say I loved these people I did not know. After finding a subtle way to tell me their names, he would ask me to offer a prayer asking Jesus to make them well.

Even as a boy I noticed that the frequency of our bedside appearances correlated with the wealth of the patient. I deduced that only the wealthy got sick enough to be hospitalized. We always parted with tears, hugs, and squeezing of hands before my father rushed to the car for a cigarette.

My father's sermons were tightly planned with a clear beginning, middle, and end. He told stories and jokes and never used notes. Members of the congregation of all ages hung on his every word. He made them laugh. He made them cry. He taught the theology of the Bible and threw in a few phrases in Hebrew or Greek. I could tell that the people in the congregation were extremely impressed, but I did not know what to make of that because it seemed that our church had a large proportion of people who did not seem to be successful in the bigger world.

Standing on his toes, his face red, my father scolded sinners and pleaded for righteousness. Then the closing of each sermon was about love. "Love conquers all. Give love. Accept the love of God. Surrender to the love of Jesus and commit to him. Manly, worldly men do it. The meekest of victims do it. Get a better life and everlasting life in Heaven." And do it now!

I was moved by the sermons and testimonials I heard in church. In Sunday school I participated in a nonassertive manner and was tolerant of the fact that I knew more about the lesson content than my adult teachers. I was afraid not to believe what I was taught because my father was the authority, the Bible was a bestseller, and I didn't want to go to hell more than I didn't want to be blown up by an atomic bomb.

Every service ended with an emotional call for parishioners to come to the front of the assembly of the church and be "saved." While the congregation sang hymns of salvation, Brother Jimmie loudly moaned over a microphone, pleading for sinners to show themselves. I always thought it went on much too long and worried that my father would be disappointed or embarrassed or angry if no one came forward. Usually two or more souls were saved, and my father would welcome them into the church and congratulate them for choosing a blessed and committed life as a soldier of Jesus.

One Sunday morning after a particularly moving sermon about "serving the Lord," I was moved to come to the front of the church and dedicate my life to becoming a minister. My father was surprised and very emotional as he publicly announced that I was the joy of his heart. His son was following his mission. It was clear he saw the event as something that was about him and not about me or Jesus. The adults in church rejoiced and were very supportive.

My church friends thought it was a brave but somewhat weird thing to do. The next day at school I said nothing about Jesus or the ministry. I returned to my classes and was the same quiet boy I had been before. In church I did nothing to remind anyone of the demonstrative dedication of my life to Jesus and soon blended back into the flock.

Over time I saw more of the forbidden inner darkness of my father. At home I noticed that he seemed simultaneously frightened and driven and insecure. He barely slept and ate very little during the day but would drink ten or fifteen cups of black coffee. At night after dinner until long after I went to bed, he ate nonstop: peanuts, sardines, candy, and assorted junk food, always topped off with a pint or two of ice cream. Unknown to his congregation, he smoked three packs of cigarettes a day. Each day he called on the sick and dying, cultivated the rich, and practiced a contrived mix of being both a "good old boy" and civic-minded "Mr. Wonderful." His investment in his congregation and civic activities at the expense of his family increased in Miami as he recruited enough souls to transform a neighborhood church into a large, successful operation. He preached on the radio, became the "governor of governors" in the national Kiwanis organization, and was known in the press as "the most loved man in Florida."

In the eyes of many, my father was a great man building houses of worship, orating at weddings and funerals and civic events, and min-

Rev. Dr. James (Jimmie) W. Parrish in his church office reading the Bible.

istering to the rich and poor. Damaged as he was in his childhood, I am sure he was doing his best. In trying to allow him to be a complex person, I try to see him as a good man, but I cannot think of a single fun or loving interaction with him. Possibly I never did my part.

During all my own traumas and small triumphs, my father was always away on a mission: war, my brother's hospitalization, preaching the gospel of Jesus, or any one of a hundred other manly and important things he did. He was either not at home or in his study at his desk surrounded by cigarette or pipe smoke. There, alone in his room each night, he read his Bible, self-help books, and hidden pornographic magazines and prepared sermons, after-dinner speeches, funeral and wedding comments, and public prayers. He was not to be interrupted.

My father used the drama of trauma and the theater of grief to control others and had enough narcissism to believe all tragedies were his own. When I broke my leg he became a martyr. Even though I was the one in pain who had to wear a cast, the emphasis was on his inconvenience and sorrow. He preyed on the grief of others as he prayed for their souls.

His best friends were funeral directors. He enjoyed hanging out with them as they embalmed his parishioners. He often brought me with him. In some of my earliest childhood memories I am standing next to naked corpses while my father tells racist and sexist jokes, enjoying a few cigarettes with the embalmers, the only members of his congregation who knew he smoked.

One or more naked corpses always lay on metal tables. A plastic block behind their heads made it seem like they were trying to look through their closed eyes at their own dead bodies. From them I learned that women had hair around their genitals, penises came in various sizes, and breasts flattened and sagged off to each side of the chest. The bodies smelled like a mixture of onions, peppers, rotten hot dogs, vinegar, and cigarette smoke.

As an insecure, skinny kid with jutting ears, I was a threat to no one in my school, the church, or my neighborhood. At the end of each school day in fifth grade, my teacher had us line up in the coatroom according to height from shortest to tallest. When we were perfectly still and quiet, we were allowed to march out of the school in a single line. At the beginning of the year I was the shortest in the class. By the end of the year I was the tallest, but so thin I was embarrassed to take off my shirt to play sports or go swimming. You could count my ribs. I paid for and followed the advice of Charles Atlas and a host of other strong men who advertised in comic books. I lifted weights; I pushed and pulled and stretched contraptions made of springs or rubber. I drank awful-tasting powdery substances mixed in water or milk. Nothing made any difference. On several occasions I overheard my father making fun of me or making comments to my mother about how sad it made him that his oldest living son was heartbroken because he was so thin.

There was not a world where I was anywhere near the center of attention. To gain some degree of popularity, I worked hard at contributing something to childhood chatter and adult conversations, and as

John Parrish, age ten.

I grew older discovered I had a gift for sensing the needs of adults and meeting them with ease and steadiness. The cost of these survival skills was my own sense of self. Any hint of ambition or passion was buried in my stoic passivity.

I spent most of my private indoor time playing with building blocks, Erector Sets, Lincoln Logs, and toy soldiers, fighting wars in my mind. Never a good athlete, I nevertheless loved to play ball. My father never taught me anything about sports or outdoor activities. Occasionally I convinced him to play catch with a football. He threw underhand and seemed bored and unhappy. I always asked him to make it difficult for me to catch, causing me to reach, leap, or dive. He usually got distracted and lobbed the football right at me.

In sixth grade I was bold enough to accept my teacher's invitation to become a "patrol boy." Proudly wearing a white belt angled across my chest and a badge, I helped adult crossing guards stop traffic to allow younger children to cross the street, and I kept watch over the bicycle racks. In uniform, I felt important and powerful. By my actions I could save my peers from danger. Yet when my classmates teased me I was careful not to be too authoritative and agreed with them that I looked and acted silly. They soon lost interest in pestering me, and I could continue my fantasy.

While I was a patrol boy on the side of justice, Gil, now in school, revolted. He began to slip out of school about midmorning and go home. Although he was repeatedly scolded and bribed by our parents and his teachers, at some point every morning he would disappear.

My father tried his best to convince him to stop his truancy. He gave the schoolteacher permission to tie my brother to his chair, but he always managed to escape. One day my father lost his temper and when he found my brother at home beat him with his belt. This initiated a sick ritual. By noon my brother would escape from school and run home. My father would find him there, then make him face the wall and beat his buttocks repeatedly with his belt. Played out five days a week for months, the ritual escalated to longer and longer beatings that would make Gil scream out and leave him crying for hours. In an attempt to embarrass Gil, I was sometimes forced to be a witness. If my father did not come home until late afternoon, the beating was postponed, which only increased the anxiety. If my father's anger escalated into a frenzy, I could successfully intervene by quietly stepping between them. My father would suddenly snap out of it and stop. A strange look would come over his face and, still breathing heavily, he would suddenly turn quiet, as if he were suffering, then silently walk away, leaving me to tend to my brother.

The way my father would abruptly change without warning reminded me of an incident that took place in seventh grade. My shop teacher was said to have "shell shock" acquired during World War II. It was rumored that unexpected loud noises made him jumpy and nervous. One day, as a prank, one of the larger, more confident, and more popular students whistled loudly, as if to mimic an incoming shell, then swung a long 2 × 4 through the air, slamming it down across a wooden workbench.

At the sharp sound our teacher dove under his desk. He cowered for a few moments in a fetal ball with his arms wrapped tightly about his head as the class turned silent, shocked by his unexpected reaction. When he climbed out and stood, he seemed dazed and embarrassed and quickly and quietly left the room.

A few boys began snickering and then laughing out loud as they repeatedly acted out his fear, mocking his reaction. I joined my classmates in their amusement. Yet I knew we had seen something profound that I didn't really understand, and part of me felt shame. From that time forth, our teacher was seen as a clown and constantly ridiculed, losing all respect from his students.

My classmate who swung the 2×4 achieved the status of class hero. As a quiet, frail boy, when I entertained new audiences with the story of the prank I basked in some of the temporary, reflected glory of my childhood war story.

CHAPTER 3

When Addie Moorman knew what she wanted, she usually got it, and what she wanted changed my life. She was a tall, thin, moderately unattractive, middle-aged, gray-haired schoolteacher who pinned her hair up in a bun and wore simple light-colored dresses that had very long skirts and seemed slightly too big. A member of my father's church, but one who rarely attended services, she was a divorcée with no social life. It was rumored that between 4:00 P.M. and midnight she sat alone drinking and smoking a pack of cigarettes. In high school, in addition to being the teacher for some of my classes, Mrs. Moorman was my homeroom teacher for three years. I usually spent at least two periods a day in her classroom.

By high school I was virtually invisible, a student who came to school each day and left without leaving an impression, like a foot stepping into a puddle and then withdrawing. Then, in the tenth grade, as part of a fitness evaluation, all boys were timed in the hundred-yard dash, the quarter mile, and the mile run. In the blazing sun, many of my classmates, including football players, walked a portion of the mile run. When I saw them slow, I saw a chance to stand out. I pushed myself into a zone of pain and fear I had never known was accessible and breathlessly finished the run in less than six minutes. One of the physical education coaches suggested I try out for the track team.

John Parrish, age sixteen, in Orange Bowl
Stadium watching T and his teammates
scrimmage.

I was thrilled and told my family and friends I had been invited to
join the team. For the first time in my life, I was being recognized for
something. Over the next three years I was the third-fastest miler on
our track team, placing second or third in one or two small meets but
never earning a letter. Yet being on the team became part of my identity. At the end of the school day, Mrs. Moorman dismissed the athletes
fifteen minutes early so they could prepare for after-school practice. She
was kind enough to include me in that group, and I was proud to be
selected, leaving class with the athletes while our less fortunate classmates looked on in envy.

Still, I had no ambition and was making average grades. When it
came time to select courses I chose things like shop and chorus, classes
I felt might be fun and easy, the same classes that my friends did. I had

no concept of intellectual growth. I never said, "Boy, that would be challenging, I'd love to know more about that." One year I took two periods of chorus.

My parents neither knew nor cared about my choices in school or how I spent my time at home. I doubt if I talked to them about it. I still expected to become a minister. I didn't share the idea with people because I thought it might bring attention to me, but I was a true believer. I was always moved by church music and sermons, and I had a personal relationship with Jesus, albeit a very childlike relationship. I followed the rules because they came from God.

Early in my junior year Mrs. Moorman suddenly decided I was a bright underachiever. I am not sure why, but I think that being the minister's son had something to do with it. Everybody in Miami knew of my father because he was a very popular civic figure. Maybe she thought that because I was the son of this revered figure I was somehow expected to be more than I was. Her own son, Claude T. Moorman, known to everyone as T, didn't have a father around, and that also may have had something to do with it. From her perspective she probably thought I had the world's most perfect father.

Several weeks into the first term of eleventh grade, she abruptly pulled me out of shop, chorus, geography, and world history. Although I did not have the required prerequisite courses or even a high grade average, she convinced the teachers of advanced math and science and college-prep English and literature to accept me in their classes. As the quiet, good boy, I did what she requested.

The advanced classes were already in the third or fourth week, and I was lost. In my math class I had no idea that letters could stand for numbers. Apart from basic biology and simple arithmetic, I had never studied science. In English I was a slow reader because I had never tried to read rapidly and had never read challenging material. Although I did not understand much of the new classwork, I never asked questions for fear of slowing down the progress of others and standing out as stupid.

At first I was driven much more by fear of failure than by love of learning. I was terrified of being publicly embarrassed or appearing "dumb." By doing my homework, reading textbooks over and over again, and listening carefully to everything the teachers said, I survived. I virtually stopped every other activity as I struggled mightily to catch up with my elite classmates and then put even more energy into being among the best. Besides, when I was studying, the rest of my life did not matter.

I began to like figuring things out and liked knowing the answers. Within a few months I became an A student. My parents never acknowledged any of these changes. I signed up for summer school and decided to prepare myself to take a large number of advanced courses in my senior year.

My father had different plans. Work trumped academics. The chairman of the board of a chain of banks was one of my father's parishioners, and he did my father a favor by getting me work in construction, although I had no experience and was not very strong. My father saw physical labor as a retreat from idleness. At a "sitting" job the devil would have access to my mind, but if I was doing physical labor it was just the opposite. I would have no idle time. Besides, he always reminded me, we needed the money.

I became the youngest laborer on a construction crew building a new bank in downtown Miami. My first assignment was to walk the steel girders to bring things to and from the skilled steelworkers. I was expected to spend all day, every day, fifty to one hundred feet above the ground walking the beams. Instead of walking the steel girders, I straddled them and scooted along on my butt, terrified. Before I could resign from the task, or get killed, the foreman saw that I was too slow, clumsy, and afraid and gave me another assignment.

I was sent to the giant hole in the ground to help reinforce the foundation and build two underground floors. I was the only white unskilled laborer and was clearly the weakest man on the crew. Basically, there were two jobs to be done. Two or three men spent all day picking up debris, carrying supplies, pushing wheelbarrows, stacking lumber and concrete blocks and bricks, raking, watering to hold down dust, and distributing handwritten messages among various foremen. The second job required experience with a jackhammer. Although I had no such experience, I was assigned the second job.

I was in survival mode, never sure if I would make it through the day. The temperature must have been over a hundred degrees, there was no breeze in the hole, and it seemed as if we were always working in bright sunlight. All parts of my body hurt as the jackhammer rattled my bones. My hands were swollen and tender, and my lower back felt as if it were breaking. I worked constantly, getting very short of breath, light-headed, and overheated. My neck and face were always sunburned.

It was a miserable summer. I felt unusually oppressed and depressed. As September approached I realized I had not learned anything significant all summer. I was furious about that and felt like a victim and a failure—I might never learn all there was to learn.

I had begun the painful discovery of knowing how much I didn't know. Any achievement was immediately dwarfed by new challenges that loomed over me. Each bit of new wisdom almost immediately lost its shine because it revealed new worlds I had yet to explore, and I worried that I would never have the opportunity to do so.

At the start of my senior year, Addie Moorman decided to change my life a second time. This time it was more personal. As a single mother her main focus had always been upon T, her only child. T was Miami High's superstar in football and basketball and the state champion shot putter. He was also the class president, the president of the student council, an Eagle Scout, and recipient of numerous awards for scholarship, popularity, leadership, and general wonderfulness. Big, muscular, and handsome, T dated the most beautiful and popular girls and was king or Mr. Whatever at all school functions and a frequent honoree at civic events. I imagined that he was also having sex with all the cheerleaders.

Mrs. Moorman decided that T and I would be best friends. I did not really understand why I was chosen but did not examine the forced dynamics too closely. To this point I had been largely invisible to T and to all my other classmates. My only school friends were from my church, and they were not in any elite group by any criteria. Despite his elevated status, T was cheerful and friendly and accepted the worship of his peers in a calm, understated manner. He wasn't at all arrogant. He accepted me immediately and became a good friend who just happened to be intrinsically wonderful.

Up to this point my whole social life had been built around the church. Every Sunday morning I went to church, and every Sunday evening we had Bible school, followed by an evening church service. Wednesday night was prayer meeting, and a crowd of probably a hundred people would come to the church for an evening meal and then go into the auditorium for special prayers. If I went to other things like birthday parties or outings or camping, it was always with the church crowd, not the school crowd or neighborhood crowd.

That all changed when T publicly befriended me. It instantly elevated my image. Even the football players treated me with respect. I was elected president of the National Honor Society even though I was newly inducted.

T invited me to parties and dances, although I didn't dance, partly because I had been taught in the church that dancing was evil but mostly because I was bashful and ungraceful. T arranged double dates, and because I had never dated, he often provided my date. On one occasion, late at night, at T's request, we parked our car in a quiet residential neighborhood in Coral Gables. I was in the front seat with a girl from my church that I had mustered up the courage to ask out. T and his girl were in the back.

I convinced myself that this would be a good time to kiss my girlfriend, and bravely I did. She was delightfully receptive.

Then I heard a great ruckus in the backseat. T and his date were fucking. I was both intensely curious and mortified. I pinned my date in a position where she could not look back, turned on the radio, and began to talk loudly. T and his date took notice but didn't stop. They just spilled out of the car onto someone's front lawn, loudly finished their business, and climbed back into the car.

My date was silently crying as I drove her home, while T and his date made small talk and told jokes in the backseat. I can't remember how I brought that evening to an end. Jealousy and shock and the collision of righteousness and sin produced new and uncomfortable feelings in my chest, my forehead, and the back of my throat. A crack had been exposed in my foundation. I had failed to protect my girlfriend from sin. More importantly, I was unable to protect myself from my own attraction to evil. Righteousness, heroism, stoicism, and purity of thought and deed had always been expected of me, but a larger force, lust and desire, consumed me and with it delivered fear and shame. I never spoke of the event to anyone.

I never fully understood Mrs. Moorman's motivation, but about a month after I became best friends with T, she told us we were going to college together and began working on our applications. At this point she may have thought that I was a good influence on T, but this created a problem for me. T was such a good football player that he could go wherever he wanted—almost every school in the country was willing to offer him a full football scholarship. He planned to see who had the best offer and would provide him with the best platform for a career in professional football. He was very motivated and confident and planned to simultaneously play professional football and go to medical school.

My plans, on the other hand, were much less ambitious. I had a vague notion to go to either a state school or to Stetson University, the Southern Baptist school my parents had attended. After that I had always assumed I would go to a seminary and become a minister.

Addie Moorman changed all that in a relatively short period of time by exposing me to the world of ideas and learning. She inspired a lifelong need to achieve and helped create a foundation for my professional success. In my senior year I skyrocketed to near the top of my class and suddenly began to think of attending an Ivy League school or some other academically challenging institution.

T and I visited several schools together. I took my first airplane trip when we went to visit Duke University in North Carolina. When the coaches and deans learned T and I planned to be roommates, I got a big rush from jocks, scholars, and faculty. They told me repeatedly that I was just the kind of person who would do well at Duke and sincerely wanted me to come.

T and I decided on Duke. My family could not afford the tuition, so my father arranged for me to compete successfully for a new scholarship set up by one of his wealthy deacons. He reasoned that even though Duke was a Methodist school, it might still provide a good platform for my future ministry.

It was the summer of 1957. After I graduated from high school my father managed to get me another prearranged and totally mindless job. Accompanied by a bright man in his thirties with no ambition or curiosity, for eight hours a day, I walked from house to house with a tape measure documenting each building's footprint for the assessment of property taxes. My partner talked constantly about trivial nothings.

I was completely frustrated and decided to use my nights and weekends to read the entire *Encyclopedia Britannica* and made note cards to memorize during the day. By the end of summer I had read about one-fourth of volume *A*. The lessons buried in other volumes still awaited.

CHAPTER 4

To begin football camp, T arrived at Duke three weeks before I did. While my siblings stayed with Mama Blair, my parents drove me from Miami to Durham, North Carolina. My father insisted my mother sit alone in the backseat as the men took turns driving. He told me at least once an hour what a good driver I was. Otherwise, he filled the time with parables, advice, sappy stories with cornball lessons, reminiscences about his college days, and stories about his father and his classmates in the seminary. When we stopped at a motel, my father insisted that my mother and I sleep together in one of the twin beds and he staked out the other bed. My mother and I felt awkward but could not dissuade him. We slept poorly trying not to touch each other. My father smoked, paced, belched, and ate peanuts and crackers all night. Twice, he left the room for thirty or forty minutes.

When we found my dormitory room at Duke, my father left us so that he could walk the halls and pop into various rooms introducing himself to everyone, asking their hometown, and demonstrating that he knew someone from each place. After my mother and I unloaded the car, my father introduced me to my dormitory neighbors, saying very dumb and embarrassing things about me, his oldest living son. After shopping for things I didn't need and eating in a cheap cafeteria,

T Moorman and John Parrish matriculate at Duke University in August 1957.

my parents finally dropped me back at the dorm and drove away. I was very relieved to be free. For the first time in my memory, I thought I saw tears on my mother's cheeks.

T and I were roommates in the freshman dorm, and we both enjoyed our new world. Although I remained insecure and constantly afraid of failure, I loved Duke. Stimulated by the fact that there were so many students much brighter than I, I took as many courses as I was allowed and easily conformed to dormitory life.

T and I had no courses in common but saw each other at night unless he was out on a date or away at a game. After freshman year, though, I did not spend much time with T. We had different classes, and he ran around with the football players and the beautiful people and I did not. He became a nationally recognized football star, playing "lonesome end," a player who never came into the huddle. I would run into him occasionally on campus, and we would warmly greet each other, but we were no longer a part of each other's lives. Besides, all of Addie's plans had been fulfilled. I didn't need T's help anymore. I was on my own.

After my freshman year I lived with two classmates who could not have been more different. T. O., a handsome former high school full-back, was entirely committed to seduction of Duke coeds. He chose his wardrobe carefully, smoked long, thin "rat tail" cigars, and dated almost every night. On the back of his closet door he posted his coed "scorecard," listing the sex acts he had performed with various women. He often stated there was not a woman at Duke he couldn't get onto his chart if he really tried. He backed it up by taking bets on specific women. I was alternately titillated and appalled.

My other roommate, Bob, a juvenile delinquent and motorcycle hood, had grown up in Panama and was the son of an American civil servant and an alcoholic housewife. Completely unprepared for any college, he was admitted to Duke under a geographic and demographic quota system. Bob had an almost flawless photographic memory for the printed and spoken word. He even had to avoid radios because he was unable not to memorize advertisements, including phone numbers. To study he required an isolated place, a completely clear table, and absolute silence. Bob and I bonded and sought out empty rooms in the hospital or law school to study uninterrupted. At times, we would stay in our room using a noisy electric fan as white noise. Bob took many extra courses and set a Duke record for highest number of As.

My father had convinced the owner of a clothing store in Miami to offer him a "preacher's price" (a preacher's price, my father always explained, was somewhere between a brother-in-law price and a gift) for a full-length dark gray wool dress coat. I thought it was much too formal for college, but my father insisted that I have my first "real winter coat." T. O. borrowed it one night to go to a costume party as a wealthy pimp. The next day, he threw the coat and most of my clothes away. He forced me to go with him to an inexpensive collegiate men's clothing store and spend all my meager savings on new clothes of his choosing. Although it frightened me to use all of my spending cash on clothes, I interpreted T. O.'s concern as an act of kindness. T. O. and Bob agreed I had the "dumbest" clothes they had ever seen, insisting that Alfred E. Newman would be embarrassed to wear them. I did not have enough sophistication or taste to really understand what they meant. I remembered being teased mercilessly by my classmates for wearing short pants to junior high and not being able to explain to my mother why I wanted to wear long pants. T. O. called me "the blade" because I was so thin. For a while others also used that nickname.

I also took a large number of courses and studied constantly. I joined the Phi Delta Theta fraternity and, despite my social awkwardness, became president. The study of science, history, and religions of the world began to erode my ability to have fundamental faith in the all-powerful God and my personal partner, the Jesus of the Southern Baptist Church. Could it be that the Christian story was nothing more than helpful mythology, yet powerful enough to cause war? I was beginning to think about going to medical school and, privately at least, had given up on the notion of becoming a minister—becoming sort of a frightened agnostic who still wanted to be a believer. Even so, the Christian morality of my upbringing was still deeply embedded within me, and I tried to hinge my metaphysics more on faith than reason.

I was beginning to question everything I thought and believed, a position that my father inadvertently helped inspire. One day as I returned from an afternoon chemistry lab and walked into the common room of the fraternity house, I unexpectedly found my father talking with several of my fraternity brothers. Dressed in a shiny cheap suit and dangling clip-on tie, he pretended he didn't notice my arrival. He was quizzing my fraternity brothers about their hometowns and demonstrating that no matter where anyone was from, he knew someone from the area. I didn't know if he was bluffing, but some of my classmates knew of the people my father mentioned.

At a time like this I later realized that my father looked and behaved like Lyndon Johnson, with the same accent and pliable face, almost a caricature, initially charming but at the same time inauthentic, as if he were wearing a mask to disguise his true intentions. For the first time I openly recognized his phoniness and was embarrassed by it. I no longer respected him, yet I realized I still feared him and gave him power over me.

I couldn't tell if my fraternity brothers were engaged by his charm or making fun of him, entertained by the country manner. After more than an hour I finally extracted him from the growing crowd filling the room. When I asked him where he had placed his bags, he said he didn't have any luggage. I realized he had no extra clothing or toiletries of any kind.

In my room, my father explained to me and T. O. (Bob was taking a year in Spain) that he had flown in to go to Duke Medical Center the next day for some tests recommended by his physician. I was mildly concerned that he hadn't told me in advance and had no luggage, but my father seemed unconcerned with details. As I studied for a solid geometry test, T. O. kept my father engaged in empty conversation. T. O. insisted on giving up his bed and slept on the floor that night; he later told me he had passed up a guaranteed hand job (possibly a blow job) to help me through the evening.

When I went to class the next day my father was still asleep, but when I returned from my morning classes he was gone. Puzzled, I looked around the room for a note but didn't see any. Then I smelled him, a unique combination of tobacco, sweat, and dirty socks that I recognized as his. I called out and heard a voice respond from under my bed. I bent down and found my father lying on his back underneath my bed wearing only his underwear and socks.

Alarmed, I asked him what he was doing. In a calm and seemingly rational tone of voice he explained that he was trying to be as unobtrusive as possible. "Bubba," he said, "don't pay any attention to me. I don't want to disturb you."

I then realized he was crazy, something I should have already known. I told him to get out from under the bed and get dressed. He crawled out and sat on the bed, looking absolutely defeated. He was unshaven and thinner, sadder, and older than I remembered him. I left him and went to a hallway pay phone and called my mother. She had no idea where my father was and had been very worried. When I told her he was with me she was relieved, exasperated, and embarrassed.

My father had no medical appointment scheduled. It was all in his head. I reassured her that I was taking care of him. Then, as my father continued to sit calmly in my room, I called the Student Health Center and tried to explain what was going on. I kept getting referred from one person to another, repeating the whole embarrassing and confusing story of my father's visit, until I finally spoke with an intern at the Duke Medical Center. He agreed to arrange for an outpatient psychiatric evaluation.

For the next three days, except for daily visits to the medical center, my father stayed in my room. He did not want to talk. I shut down emotionally and buried myself in my studies. Under the guise of "campus tours," T. O. took my father for a long walk each day while I studied. I took him to the student cafeteria three times a day. Otherwise T. O. and I continued going to classes while my father insisted on sitting alone.

That Saturday, as suddenly as he appeared, my father decided to leave. He explained that he had three sermons, a wedding, and a funeral to preside over the next day. T. O. drove him to the airport, and I went to talk with the Duke psychiatrist, who told me that even though he found my father charming and likable he was very depressed and needed medication and aggressive psychotherapy. I asked him to send his recommendations to my father's doctor and to me so I could forward them to my mother. We never received anything from Duke.

My mother later assured me that she was fine and that my father was much better and seeing a local psychiatrist. I knew she was lying to protect me from knowing how miserable and hopeless she felt. Eventually, I learned he actually was being seen by a psychiatrist or a psychologist, someone in the church who would treat him for free. He and I never mentioned the visit again. Later, my mother told me that he did that kind of thing all the time. He'd just disappear. She once woke up in the middle of the night, and my father was missing. It was storming outside, and she found him lying on the lawn in the backyard, faceup in the heavy rain in his pajamas. She never asked him why he was there. Questioning him was completely unacceptable.

I tried to forget about the incident and focus on my studies.

Increasingly, my personal interactions and family issues were secondary to my ambition and curiosity. Although I had to work very hard to keep up, I had developed an intense love of learning. Even now, going into a library I get an adrenaline surge in anticipation of what I might learn. Still, the more I knew, the more I knew I did not know, so every academic achievement also inspired intense feelings of being overwhelmed by how much there was to learn and how far behind I believed myself to be. I regretted that I had wasted so much of my life with a lazy mind.

I rapidly became infatuated with biology and found that all of the sciences had a certain beauty, symmetry, and rhythm that I found seductive. I don't recall a pivotal "Aha!" moment when I decided to attend medical school. It happened gradually. I didn't have a burning desire to be an M.D. and treat the sick, but I grew to love science and evolution and human physiology and was fascinated by biology. At the times when I felt obligated to become a minister, I thought that becoming a physician might also be a way to combine my interest in science with the expectation that I would help others. I saw medical school more as a graduate school of biology and a medical degree as a pathway to further education.

I was good at being a student and felt I might never be any good at anything else. Late in my junior year I applied to medical school at Yale and was accepted, ensuring that my life as a student would continue.

I knew students who were members of ROTC, and I had wanted to join but felt I couldn't afford to take the time. I couldn't find a way to fit it into my self-imposed packed schedule. For now, my need to be a scholar trumped my need to be a soldier. I was so focused on my studies that I really had no idea what was taking place outside my cocoon at Duke, especially politically. I majored in political science but chose courses on the theory, philosophy, and sociology of politics and did not study the modern world. As a student I had a deferment from the draft, and while the Cold War hovered, I was all but oblivious to it. My childhood fantasies of becoming a soldier, waging war, and saving beautiful women from the clutches of danger had been replaced by fantasies involving my coed classmates and a desire to remain in the comforting arms of academia.

I doubt if I even knew where Vietnam was. I was completely apolitical and intimidated whenever the topic came up among my more politically savvy classmates. They would have long debates defending their allegiance to either the Democratic or Republican Party. I didn't even know the basic differences in the Vietnam policies of the Republicans and Democrats. I was much more interested in what Aristotle had to say about the state. Jack Kennedy had just been elected president, and the year before, in 1959, the first two American servicemen had died in Vietnam, but that event was as remote from my consciousness as the obscure contents of the encyclopedia I had tried to read a few years before. I don't remember ever discussing Vietnam at all. I was so distracted by the joy of learning and my fear of failure that I closed off much of the rest of the world. I paid more attention to a giant struggle going on just under the surface of my cortex—a growing dissidence between science and my Southern Baptist theology and morality. I did not yet know it, but the contradictions in my life would soon begin to surface.

CHAPTER 5

Even as I excelled academically at Duke, I remained socially awkward and bashful around girls, a completely inexperienced virgin. I had participated in a few mixed-group parties in high school and had even volunteered to be considered the steady boyfriend of my sister's best friend for chaperoned church-related social events. Otherwise, I was totally repressed.

Given my inexperience, the women at Duke presented an especially big challenge. Most of the Ivy League schools did not yet admit women, and the smartest and most accomplished girls attended places like Duke. As a result the women at Duke were not only more mature, sophisticated, self-confident, and socially aware than the men but much, much brighter. I was completely intimidated. Whenever I began to build up the courage to approach a girl to ask her out on a date, I always lost my confidence and backed off. I spent my first two years paralyzed around women, lonely and too frightened to have even a casual conversation. All my friendships were with men. I was especially close to Bob, and we studied together constantly. T. O. dated every night without fail and constantly keep us informed in detail about his exploits.

In my junior year at Duke I began to focus on Joan, a bright, red-headed classmate in one of my favorite political science classes. She had big breasts and a warm, smiling, attractive face, and her scores on exams were higher than mine. I lusted after her from a safe distance and sought out opportunities to converse with her about something with more content than the weather, parties, or sports. I planned chance encounters and memorized a list of interesting topics that would appear to be spontaneous.

Joan was surprisingly receptive to my "random" conversations, and I was delighted when she occasionally initiated encounters after class. I learned that she had grown up in Coral Gables, Florida, an affluent community about a mile from my Jewish middle-class neighborhood in Miami. Her father was a wealthy physician, and her mother was very active in Coral Gables's most elite social circle. Although we went to different schools, in one who-do-you-know conversation, I discovered that Joan knew more of the popular people in my high school than I did.

After six or eight brief encounters and three or four failed resolutions to ask her out, complete with predetermined, scripted dialogue on my part, I finally mustered the courage to blurt out an invitation to a fraternity party. She accepted, and to my relief when we got there she seemed unbothered by either my awkwardness or my inability and unwillingness to dance. We made small talk, and she had a couple of beers but did not comment on the fact that I was probably the only non-drinking student at the party. Despite my anxiety, I made it through the party and was able to add a brief good-night hug. I was emotionally exhausted afterward, and grateful to Joan for not humiliating me with either indifference or derision. I had survived.

A few weeks later I invited her to a football game and an after-game party at my fraternity. After that, I was still so bottled up that I didn't know how to proceed. I looked forward to seeing her in class and sometimes sat next to her, but I never asked her out again.

I returned to Florida for the summer, as did she. I planned to contact her but never built up the courage to do so. Once again, my father arranged a job for me. Again, I failed to rebel or to try to plan my own summer job. Although angry inside and knowing my father was partially insane, I quickly reverted to the quiet, pliable good boy. I worked ten hours a day with two black men in a landscaping business owned by my father's cousin. On a schedule that repeated itself every two weeks, we traveled from house to house in an old milk truck with two tall metal seats in the front. I rode in the back with the mowers, rakes, clippers, edgers, tillers, gasoline, hoes, and miscellaneous unidentified and seemingly useless parts. I often imagined that Joan's family would hire our services and fantasized that she would bring us lemonade as we toiled in the sun trimming the bushes. While I worked, Joan spent the summer water-skiing, partying, dating, and going to the pool at the country club. I assumed she had forgotten all about me.

Shortly after I returned to Duke for my senior year, though, a perky, full-bodied, attractive girl heard my name mentioned and introduced herself to me at a fraternity after-football-game open house. She was Joan's younger sister, visiting Duke for a weekend date. I was pleased that she had recognized my name and even more pleased when she told me that Joan enjoyed being with me and wanted to spend more time with me.

I knew what I had to do. I had to initiate another date without waiting for a chance encounter. Joan sounded happy to hear from me and accepted.

After several more dates Joan and I began to study together, and she introduced me to a side of social life on campus I had never experienced before. Joan taught me how to smoke cigarettes and drink alcohol, at first only with her but then publicly. I began to relax in her company. I became energized and more popular and confident. At times I felt like I belonged not only to Joan but also to the inner circles of Duke, to a group of students far more popular and socially successful than I had ever been before. I was in love with Joan and the new me.

I had never felt so alive. One day, while parked on a dirt road in the woods, I clumsily fondled Joan's breast. After a very quick reflexive downward shudder of her shoulders, she allowed me to look at and touch both fully exposed breasts. I had never seen or touched a woman's breast before. At age twenty-two, for me, this was a giant break-through. Over the next week, I was thrilled to discover that I could have access again and again. I loved the feeling of arousal and the inti-macy, emotions I had never allowed myself to experience before. We named her breasts Parmenides and Heraclitus and whispered about them in the library. I told T. O. and Bob, hoping to impress them, but they ridiculed me mercilessly about my virginity and bashfulness. I didn't care.

Joan and I spent a weekend together in New York. Despite the fact that I had already been accepted to Yale School of Medicine, I traveled to New York for interviews at Columbia and Cornell. Joan went with me, and we got a very cheap hotel room because I didn't have money.

That was the first night we slept together, but we didn't have inter-course. We were both somewhat reticent, and besides, despite my growing desire and shifting sense of morality, I still didn't think it was the right thing to do. I had been raised to believe that premarital or ex-tramarital sex was not only sinful but could ruin relationships and life itself, destroying any possibility for success and happiness. That seemed inconsistent with my observations at Duke and these new feelings I was having, but I was still a prisoner of my upbringing. I set limits because deep inside I was still afraid not to be a good boy.

By the time I was feeling bonded to Joan, I had already informed Duke and my parents that I was leaving school at the end of the fall semester of my senior year. I had managed to complete all my require-ments in three and a half years, and I was accepted to medical school. Although now all I wanted to do was spend a beautiful spring in North Carolina with a girlfriend, taking only courses that I wanted to take, my upbringing convinced me that doing so was both selfish and mor-ally wrong. First T and then Joan had introduced me to the concept of joy, but I could not quite grasp it. I could have stayed in school and en-joyed myself but instead, as a "good and obedient servant," left school, left Joan, and faithfully returned to the duty-filled prison I had allowed my father to create for me.

Despite my father's psychological issues, which were invisible to everyone outside the family, he had been appointed the executive vice president for public affairs and outreach of Stetson University, and now he and my mother lived almost on the campus. Through him I had access to all the library facilities. I planned to spend several months in an ambitious, self-directed program in philosophy and psychology, auditing classes and reading the world's great literature in my spare time before entering Yale University School of Medicine in the fall of 1961.

Yet when I arrived at Stetson, my father shamed me into taking a job as a stock boy in the campus bookstore. After a week I realized that the job had zero room for intellectual development, and I resigned in order to look for a job that included some intellectual challenges and growth. My father responded by getting me a job as a laborer on a highway construction gang. I yielded because I was obedient and thought it was the right, moral thing to do. Essentially, I gave up again. This time, I agreed to servitude with hard labor.

Six days a week for six months, my mother awakened me at 4:00 A.M. and served me a large hot breakfast. I then drove more than an hour to a work site in the middle of nowhere. Someone had decided to build a road across the flats and desolate pine woods of central Florida to connect two state highways that paralleled one another twenty miles apart.

The nearest structure of any kind was at least ten miles away. It was like working on a chain gang. Once again I did heavy manual labor, again being the only white laborer, for ten hours a day, before driving back home for a shower, a meal of leftovers, and a walk to the library. There I usually fell asleep after reading only a few pages.

I survived because Joan, to my amazement, did not abandon me in favor of someone else. We corresponded occasionally (phone calls were too expensive). Twice that spring she came to Florida for weekend visits, and we enjoyed our time together even though we slept in separate rooms in my parents' home.

One weekend that same summer Joan and I visited my mother while she was staying in Palm Beach in the luxurious home of one of her twin brothers. In the poolside dressing room, we had our first real sexual experience. I was overwhelmed, both enthralled and overridden with guilt and shame. I had sinned in the eyes of God and my father. I also knew making love with Joan was joyous and vitalizing. The next day we made love again. This time it was not an accident of passion. It was premeditated, deliberate, and consensual and already felt familiar, and the biochemistry bonded us. Sunday night, I returned to my home and job in DeLand, and Joan went to her home in Coral Gables. For me, the separation had a painful quality I had never known, including a physical discomfort in the center of my chest.

Later that week—I don't remember what words I used—I told my father I had special feelings for Joan. He reacted as if I had plugged him into an electric socket and turned the switch on. He had always wanted to be upwardly mobile and make friends with powerful people, so even though Joan was not a Southern Baptist but a Methodist, and had probably not been saved by Jesus, the fact that her family was prominent and well connected compensated for that. Besides, my love story was his, and all about him. He saw a chance for drama, control—and a trip to Miami. Later in my life I found out why he longed for trips to Miami.

"Oh, you're in love," he said, speaking the words as if his mouth were filled with syrup, and he then began to orate as if I were the congregation and he the preacher delivering a sermon. He spoke eloquently and at length about the sanctity of marriage and the blessedness and resilience of my mother, whom he kept referring to as the "Rock of Gibraltar." While his words bore little resemblance to the life and relationship I had witnessed in our household growing up, I dutifully listened in silence as he repeatedly told me how pleased he was that I had first shared my feelings with him.

He called his siblings in Georgia to rejoice in his good news. "Bubba's in love, isn't this wonderful?" he said to them. He decided that I was getting married and it would be exciting and it would be his show. He decided—not me—that we would go down to Miami by train and that I would propose to Joan.

I was not consulted, yet I did not resist. My sexuality had been so delayed and suppressed, at once titillated by Madison Avenue and the Playboy philosophy yet driven underground by Jesus, a well-intended stoic mother, a moralistic and hypercritical father, and my own shy introversion, that my first sexual experience led me to accept marriage to "make it right." It was simple to resolve all my conflicts. Just get married. It was the right thing to do. I could be both a good person and a sexual person. I took the honorable path and sold my old car to buy a ring for Joan.

When we got to Miami, my father borrowed a car and dropped me at Joan's house in Coral Gables. When I got to the house late in the afternoon and asked for her, she wasn't home. She was on a date. She clearly didn't think we were a monogamous couple. I sat in the family room with her mother and made small talk and watched television for a while, then excused myself and went into the backyard to wait alone. It was dark before Joan returned. I clumsily told her that I had come down to ask her to marry me.

Joan was surprised and seemed temporarily confused, yet pleased, and after a few moments stammered out the word "yes." Then, as if she had forgotten something, she said she had to talk to her mother and father. I stayed outside.

When Joan told her mother, who had been drinking, she was dismissive and said, "Oh Joan, we'll talk about that tomorrow." Then Joan told her father, "Dad, I've decided to marry John." Despite the fact that he and I had chatted earlier that evening and I had been over to dinner several times, he said, "John who?" He didn't know who I was.

I don't think her father particularly liked me, but he didn't like anybody. At home he was terminally grumpy and negative, a functioning alcoholic. A gastroenterologist with a very successful private practice, he would stop at a bar for a couple of drinks on the way home, and by the time dinner was served he was already in his cups. The fact that I was going to medical school made me acceptable, but I don't think he was impressed. I was just this skinny guy with glasses who was socially awkward, a nice man but not a scholar, socialite, business major, or football star. Joan's dad confided in her that in the elite social circles, my father was considered a phony and possibly a philanderer. Her parents finally accepted me because that's what Joan wanted. Her mother took over and planned the wedding, setting a date six months in the future. It was my father's proposal and Joan's mother's wedding.

That fall, when I moved to New Haven to begin medical school, Joan moved to New York City to live with two of her Duke classmates and began a six-month executive training program at a bank. Only a short train ride from New Haven, Joan visited me almost every other weekend. Against the rules, she stayed with me in my tiny room in the men's dormitory. We spent our time in various campus locations where Joan read while I studied. Often she would sit on a high stool next to my cadaver, reading, while I carefully dissected various organs.

The arrangements for the wedding and even the wedding itself are something of a blur; it just seemed to happen. At the rehearsal dinner Joan's parents' friends were intoxicated and overdressed and clumsily gushing over Joan and me. I looked around and suddenly felt trapped. I knew nothing about their world, the country club set, but when I was up close and personal it felt very empty. I felt that I was escaping one counterfeit world, that of my father, for another.

I said to myself, "Who are these people? I don't want to be a part of this." These people had been playing tennis or having drinks on the patio while I was cutting their grass. I also realized that I didn't know what being in love was or what marriage really meant. I should have already had four or five relationships, and this was beginning to feel like a moral and emotional shotgun wedding. I had been so constricted by religious goodness that now I allowed myself to trade one kind of prison for another—but it was too late to turn back. Besides, I was caught up in a wonderful romantic bubble and anticipated a passionate, caring, fun sex life with someone I wanted and loved.

We had a big church wedding in Coral Gables with a couple of hundred people in attendance, everyone in fancy dress, and then a reception at Joan's house. Her parents wanted to have a champagne fountain, but they agreed not to because my father wouldn't allow drinking. Instead Joan's father set up a bar in the kitchen with a case of his favorite beverage, Wild Turkey, so everybody could drink as much as they wanted. The duplicity started right away.

For our honeymoon, my father convinced a former parishioner to arrange a complimentary night at the luxurious Fontainebleau Hotel on Miami Beach. When we arrived there after the wedding and reception, I was sunburned, exhausted, and depressed, and Joan had trouble putting in her new diaphragm.

Just as we climbed into bed the phone rang. It was my mother. Gil, who was now fourteen and had been sent away to military school, had run away. She wanted me to go find him. Joan and I interrupted our honeymoon, picked up my mother, and spent the next three days driving all over the South, calling the police every few hours as they passed along tips and leads.

We finally surprised my brother with an older girl in a motel in South Carolina. I gave the very sexy but somewhat common woman money for bus fare and drove Joan, my mother, and my brother one hundred miles to another city where my father was conducting a one-week revival meeting. Every few minutes my brother would threaten to jump out of the car, so I would speed up and run stop signs to make him choose between staying with us and dying. When we arrived at my father's motel, I left Joan and my mother in the car while I delivered my brother, then stayed in the room to make sure the loud and emotional encounter would not escalate into physical fighting.

After the insane honeymoon, Joan and I drove to New Haven. Gil went back to military school. I lost myself in medical school, and Joan gave up her place in the bank's executive training program, something made easier by the fact that all the women in the training program were subsequently offered secretarial or administrative assistant positions while the men became managers within the banking system. To pay our living expenses, Joan studied for a teaching certificate and then drove an hour each way to teach sixth grade. We secretly shared my room in the single men's dormitory, but once we were discovered we were expelled and moved into the married dorm, then expelled again when Joan became pregnant.

We moved to a cheap third-floor walk-up apartment; it was quite obvious that a kitchen and a bathroom had been carved out of an attic so the landlord could rent that floor. After our daughter, Susan, was born, Joan's mother lived with us for several weeks. Launching myself into the absent-father role, I studied nonstop and spent most of my time at the medical school or hospital. In what was known as the "Yale system," there were no tests at all until after the first two years, and then again at the very end, so one never knew how well he or she (six women in a class of one hundred) was doing. It created a lot of anxiety for me; I was anxious and I never felt I was working hard enough. Unless Joan insisted that we spend time with other married couples, I spent every waking moment studying or hanging out as an observer at Yale–New Haven Hospital. We stayed in New Haven during the summer and holidays while I worked as a lab technician to make money or to do the research required by the medical curriculum. Essentially, without going anywhere I had left home.

After I completed Yale in 1965, Joan, Susan, and I moved to Ann Arbor, Michigan, for my internship and residency in internal medicine. For the next two years I worked at least eighty hours a week and totally immersed myself in being a trainee, often not coming home at all two or three nights a week.

Since the time that Addie Moorman decided that I belonged with the achievers, I had been anxious, driven in equal parts by competition, love of learning, and fear of failure, always surrounded by students and trainees who I believed were more capable intellectually, socially, and psychologically. By the time I was a house officer at University Hospital in Ann Arbor, my fear of failure had become my dominant emotion. I responded with an exaggerated feeling of responsibility for my patients, certain that my failure to know everything could lead to serious harm. I could only keep my patients safe if I read and reread their entire medical record and compulsively consulted textbooks. There was time and room for nothing else.

We had our second daughter, Lynn, there. I was so focused on my hospital responsibilities that when she was born I brought an intern to the delivery room with me, so I could use the birth of my own daughter as a teaching moment.

I saw my marriage as about me. After Lynn was born, Joan's mother moved into our tiny apartment again. Otherwise, Joan spent two years basically alone with two babies. Her generosity, kindness, love, and eroding self-image made her an enabler to my selfishness. Meanwhile she created a community of wives and mothers and formed a warm communal neighborhood spirit.

While I was in training at University of Michigan Medical Center, my father asked me to arrange a second opinion before his local doctor performed a relatively simple transurethral surgical procedure to treat a recently discovered prostate cancer. I arranged for him to see the most senior internist and urologist at University Medical Center. He was hospitalized and underwent radical surgery and bilateral orchiectomy before he was started on high doses of estrogen.

What had I done by intervening? Did he have unnecessary surgery? If he had been my patient, would I have automatically trusted the old and old-school senior professor surgeon? He had not only had major surgery but also had his balls cut off and was told he would develop breasts!

My father went back home, and I went back to work.

I was married, twenty-six years old, still in training, and the father of two young girls, yet because I was a physician, I was eligible to be drafted. At the time all medical doctors were eligible for the draft until age thirty-five. I received a letter from the U.S. government that strongly suggested that I volunteer for an officer's commission as a doctor in the U.S. Navy. Because all my student deferments had expired, if I did not volunteer I would be reclassified as 1-A and ordered to report for induction as an enlisted man at entry rank. I volunteered for a commission, which automatically allowed me to spend another year in residency before reporting for duty.

Neither Joan nor I was particularly upset about my impending military obligation. In fact, in many ways we were looking forward to it. I was earning $3,600 a year as a resident, not the kind of money that permitted luxuries. We hoped that a military salary would give us a start on a down payment for a house. We also hoped that during my time in the service I would have much more time to be with Joan and our children. We would start again.

For the prior six years, as I focused on medical school and my residency training, I had paid little attention to Vietnam or anywhere else. Military action in Vietnam was something in the news, but I never thought about it. I remember seeing helicopters and wounded soldiers on television, but I had never met anyone who had been there or had been drafted, and I was only vaguely aware that our presence there was beginning to inspire protests.

I simply assumed that either the war would end or I would be allowed to fulfill my military obligation by spending two years in the Public Health Service or the National Institutes of Health, career-building options open to many of my colleagues. The worst outcome I imagined was that I would have to serve stateside and then return to my training in internal medicine.

When I received orders to report to Camp Pendleton in California, I wasn't sure what that meant. I made several phone calls to Washington and then drove there from Ann Arbor to meet with people to try to find out. My orders meant I was going to Vietnam.

I learned, though, that I still had another option. I could accept an assignment aboard a ship for a year, possibly docked in the States. After that, I might be given a stateside billet, or, depending on how the war was going, I might still be sent to Vietnam for the second year of my two-year obligation.

Joan and I talked about it, and I told her that if I went to sea I might be away for two years, including perhaps a year in Vietnam, but if I went to Vietnam I would just be away for one year because in my second year I would be quarantined in a stateside assignment. Joan was mostly just a listener, though. I could sway her in any direction. I was in charge of the decision. I did not know at the time that being assigned to a ship often meant working 9:00 to 4:30 five days a week and living on land in the States with one's family.

I chose Vietnam. Although one part of me felt like a victim drafted against my will, in another sense I felt like a volunteer. I was pulled to go to war because it still appealed to my childhood fantasies about being a soldier.

There was another factor, too. My assignment in Ann Arbor at the time was on the adolescent leukemia service. It was awful. Someone was always dying. At that time most patients with leukemia did, sooner rather than later. For reasons unclear to me, the teenagers were all hospitalized on the same ward. The therapeutic approach used at University of Michigan Medical Center was to give toxic drugs to the point of near death and then hope the disease would go into remission. The side effects were horrendous: nausea, vomiting, extreme fatigue, weight loss, diarrhea, nosebleeds, and infections. We were constantly moving patients around so long-term roommates wouldn't have to watch each other die. It was a horrible experience, knowing all these young kids would die, and knowing there was nothing I could do about it. That was part of the reason I was relieved to go to Vietnam, and it shows how clueless I was about what I would be facing; I went to Vietnam so I wouldn't have to watch teenagers die.

My departure loomed over our marriage, and by the time it drew near I had been saying good-bye to Joan for months. Ever since getting my military orders I had thought about it every time I looked at her. Happy times made me sad, and sad times made me angry. As we realized the full meaning of my orders, a strange distance grew between us. We were bracing ourselves. No social or intellectual encounter with any group could lessen the thought of impending separation. Our personal interactions and sexual intimacy could not relieve the anxiety of loss. Waiting to leave was a futile contest. There was never enough time together—but, in an odd way, there was too much. We got sick of saying good-bye. For emotional and financial support, Joan decided to spend the year of our separation with her parents in Miami.

When I fully realized I was going to war, a toxic wanderlust began to take charge of the quiet, good boy. I had a chance to die or to start my life again. I had a chance to be a soldier.

Because of the routine of my life, I spent a lot more time with a nurse, Elaine, than I did with Joan. I was at the hospital all the time, and so was she, often volunteering for extra night shifts. She was beautiful and sexy, quick-witted, and highly energetic, and loved by patients and staff. I was infatuated with her. Elaine thought I was bright and funny, sexy, sophisticated, and cool. It was such a pleasant feeling to be an object of admiration and lust. This was the first time I felt I was not actively earning someone's affection; I was being me, and she sought me out. Because I was still so insecure, the adoration was intoxicating. We were strongly attracted to each other, and at times in passing on the ward we secretly touched, but we never had any form of sex. I was preserving my marriage, and she planned to save herself for a shining knight. As the date of my departure approached, I kept it a secret that I was sad about leaving Elaine.

A few days before Joan and the girls and I were to leave Ann Arbor for Florida, several of my fellow residents (all male) organized a send-off party. No wives attended, and Joan stayed home with our baby girls. We went to a beer hall called Bimbo's, a roadhouse with a country band. They served only beer, pitchers and pitchers of beer, and buckets of peanuts. Everyone was expected to throw the peanut shells onto the floor.

We got drunk. I had actually never been intoxicated before. Because more than two drinks gave me a severe hangover, I believed I had ineffective liver enzymes. I remember marching around singing "The Marines' Hymn," wailing about the halls of Montezuma and the shores of Tripoli, both places as real to me as any place in Vietnam. There were other people from the hospital there, some I knew and some I just recognized. They joined us as we marched around the room and sang, crushing peanut shells underfoot. An inebriated and seductive dietitian joined our group and sparked poorly disguised alpha male competition for her attention. At the end of the night, emboldened by the beer and the swagger of a soldier going off to war, I took her back to her apartment, had clumsy sex with her, and passed out. When I woke up in the middle of the night, I slunk back home.

My hangover was severe, but I made it though my last day of work at University Hospital. Only one teenager died. Remembering most, but not all, of my one-night stand, I felt elevated and released. With a still cloudy head, I looked at it as an accomplishment, a real achievement given my shyness, and with my blunted affect, bass voice, and beer breath, I bragged about it to the other residents and received very supportive feedback.

I also felt very guilty and evil and ashamed, both of breaking my wedding vow and, paradoxically, of not having my first drunk and one-night stand until age twenty-six. I was on my way to war and was already splitting apart, and over the next year the war would make that split even clearer and deeper. I could have a good side and a bad side, and the bad side was a secret I found both exhilarating and shameful. I hadn't even gotten to Vietnam, but the change in my psyche and values had already started. I had already broken that glass.

Joan and I put our two girls, ages one and three, into our ten-year-old Chevrolet station wagon and drove to Florida for still more good-byes to my family near Orlando and Joan's in Miami. Our marriage hadn't gotten off to a very good start. As we drove, mostly in silence, I kept looking over at Joan in the passenger seat, searching for the happy, social, bright, popular redhead who had been my college sweetheart. Her fine features were coarsened by giving birth to two babies and by the purpose of our trip. She had left a potentially exciting New York City life to follow me to New Haven. She gave up a chance for an interesting job to take my name. She slept with me on all the nights I was at home, worked as a teacher to put me through Yale Medical School, and gave me my children. She spent two years in freezing Ann Arbor with two babies and a husband who was never home and who now had cheated on her. She had been alone days and late nights, with meals, bottles, diapers, bedtimes. Now she was going back home to live with her parents.

During our long silences I realized for the first time that I was afraid. For weeks my usual professional anxieties had been charged with vague fears of bodily harm and thoughts of my own violent death. I no longer wanted to go to war. I was being forced down a path my inner little boy desperately wanted, and I did not want to go. I didn't share with Joan or any one that I was afraid.

When we left my parents' home in Winter Park, my mother tried to be brave, but her lips were trembling and she was tearing up as I hugged her. My father stayed inside the house. When I went back in the house to find him he was in his bed, lying in the fetal position, crying and almost unresponsive. During the drive from Winter Park to Miami, the girls were unusually fussy and agitated.

My flight from Miami to California for military training left in the afternoon. Joan's mother kept the kids outside so that we could be alone. It became difficult to find words to interrupt the thickening quiet. When it was finally time to leave, Joan drove me to the airport and stood next to the car while I got my luggage from the trunk. "Take care of yourself, baby" was all that I could manage to say.

I kissed her and turned away. *We'll start again in a year,* I thought.

In late July 1967, I reported to Camp Pendleton in California. Along with thirty other civilian doctors in military fatigues and heavy black leather boots, I spent twelve days learning to be a soldier. We jogged and did calisthenics in unison in the hot sun. I won a mile run that many of my colleagues wouldn't or couldn't finish. We learned to salute (palm down) and recognize military insignias. We listened to lectures on the history and fortitude of the U.S. Marines, the despicable, cowardly, and dishonest habits of the enemy, and comparisons of the M-16 and AK-47. Although we did have one lecture on the treatment of malaria, there was no information or training given on other tropical diseases, medical evacuation, triage, or trauma care.

Three days before I was supposed to leave for Vietnam, I was given twelve hours' notice that I had a two-day leave before my departure. I asked Joan to fly out for a two-day stay in San Francisco for yet another good-bye. I chose to meet her at the airport in my military dress khakis and tried to act like a brave and stoic warrior. Deep within, I wanted to return to Florida with Joan or just get on with it—enough with the good-byes. My one-year tour of duty in Vietnam had to start before it could end. Our separation had nothing to do with causes or campaigns. It had to do with the calendar.

On the night before I left for Vietnam, I lay in a California hotel bed with Joan and felt my marriage beginning to crack as I began to protect myself from emotional intimacy. I was separating from wife and lover and friend and mother of my girls, and, it seemed, from any last hope of unconditional love. We spent most of the night awake lying in bed in silence, occasionally sharing an L&M cigarette.

Joan could not face another good-bye, either. On the morning of my departure, she called a cab and quickly left the room without speaking.

I spent the rest of the day with a local friend from medical school. He grimly drove me around the Bay Area all day, then delivered me to Travis Air Force Base, where I met the other doctors from my Camp Pendleton group. Two of our group were either too drunk or too sober to show up and missed our scheduled departure. One was rumored to have fled to Canada and the other to have received a last-minute reprieve from his Vietnam assignment. I never learned what really happened to them.

The flight from Travis to Okinawa was scheduled to leave at 10:00 P.M. but was delayed ten hours, stringing out the departure for accompanying wives, sweethearts, and families. One doctor and his wife stood all night in silence leaning against a wall holding hands. A little girl kept striking her father's chest with closed fists and sobbing. Mom scolded the child while Dad made no attempt to protect himself or conceal the tears running down his cheeks. A dental officer stared at his beer bottle as if he were trying to divine his future in the reflection in the brown glass. One man spent the night already writing letters home. Another kept reviewing photos of his family in his wallet. Still another man at the same table read. Each wore the same tight frown.

As dawn and the time of our departure approached, four notes of Sibelius began to cycle in my brain. I watched the second hand circle, click by click, around the black face of my watch. I finally understood:

I would not be returning for one year, 365 days. Maybe I wouldn't be back at all.

By sunrise when the flight was finally announced we shuffled like zombies toward the aircraft. Paralyzed by some strange venom, I submitted myself to war without hesitation.

BOOK TWO

THE GOOD SOLDIER

CHAPTER 6

Wearing khaki casual, I flew to Vietnam in a commercial airline full of other soldiers, complete with stewardesses serving drinks and smiling as if we were businessmen on our way to a convention. We stopped in Okinawa, where I received three injections in each arm, and with headache, fever, and chills, I boarded another commercial flight to Da Nang. In my shirt pocket I carried my orders, which said to report to A Medical Battalion, 3rd Marine Division in Phu Bai, but I had no idea about how I was supposed to get there.

When the plane door opened and I walked out and took my first look at Vietnam, the change was abrupt and dramatic. Inside the plane, even though it was full of soldiers, you could still imagine you were somewhere in the United States, but once the door opened, that fantasy evaporated. The landscape was wholly unfamiliar—a military air base extended as far as one could see: miles of runways, hundreds of helicopters, fighter jets, and military transport planes. The intense August sunlight was almost blinding, and the air was heavy and thick and shimmered with heat waves. There were soldiers everywhere and in an instant I knew I was in the middle of a war I knew nothing about. I had left the United States as a husband, a father, and a trainee in internal medicine at an academic hospital, and now the familiar smells of babies and hospital wards had been replaced by the odors of diesel fuel, exhaust, and sweat. I suddenly realized that I was a military officer with a combat unit of the U.S. Marines. There were no reminders or evidence of my past.

Amid the chaos of the base, no one seemed to care about my arrival. I spent hours in various lines, often with no idea what the line was for or where it led, showing my orders to enlisted men with clipboards and then standing around. No one seemed to expect me. I felt as if I could have stayed on the airbase for weeks without anyone noticing.

Finally, after thirty-six hours, I caught a military transport plane to another large military base next to the village of Phu Bai. I walked toward a big red cross on the side of a small one-story wooden building. There, I reported to a naval NCO who sat at a plywood desk shuffling papers. I gave him my name, and for the first time my presence seemed expected. Along with six other doctors I was sent to the quarters of the division surgeon. He was a large man in his midforties, prematurely gray, slightly obese, and soft. We introduced ourselves, mentioning our home states and places of training. Any specialty training beyond internship was listed next to our names on a blackboard. There were four doctors straight from internship training, one anesthesiologist, one general surgeon, and me, a partially trained internist. The four doctors without specialty training were immediately assigned to infantry battalions in the field, a sign, perhaps, that things were not going well. Four separate jeeps took them away immediately. The remaining three of us were assigned to the hospital company, "A Med," in Phu Bai.

The division surgeon gave us a tour of the medical compound. He was in no hurry. Within a few moments he let us know he was going home in eighty days, and it became clear that anything that would kill some time was welcome.

To make it easy to receive casualties, A Med was next to the airstrip, a prime target for any kind of enemy attack. We passed a wooden hut with a tin roof adjacent to a large mobile refrigeration unit. A five-foot-high wall of sandbags, stacked in two rows, surrounded the structure except for a narrow entryway that made a slight jog so that in the event it was shelled, no shrapnel could enter. A sign read GRAVES REGISTRATION.

Our guide didn't slow down as we passed the hut. "This is Graves," he said, "completely staffed by marines, not navy. From the field, the dead go directly here, where they are washed down, identified, and put in the freezer until the next flight south. They're embalmed in Da Nang or Saigon before shipment back to the States. Some of the grunts working here volunteer for this duty. Some are assigned. Others may be mental cases or want to be embalmers someday. On a busy day, especially if it is hot, this place smells terrible." He didn't seem to like either the marines who worked in Graves or soldiers who were so thoughtless as to get killed on a hot, busy day. He had never been inside or met any of the marines.

"We are referred to as a clearing station, the first stop for the wounded and dead, brought by helicopter, fixed-wing aircraft, truck, jeep, litter, or in the arms of fellow soldiers. The casualties go directly to Triage." The *whump-whump* rattle of a landing helicopter made it difficult to hear. Several marines, one of whom had a stretcher, ran out to meet the craft. They pulled a man off the helicopter, and it was gone.

The young man on the stretcher was so black that the mud on his skin looked pale. He was completely naked, and his boots were between his legs. There were no weapons, uniform, or personal belongings. He was long and muscular, and his spidery fingers curled around the sides of the bouncing litter. His body glistened as sweat reflected the morning sun; the sweat on his forehead did not drip but remained like tiny drops of oil fastened tightly to his skin. He stared straight ahead at the sky. Suddenly, as he passed by, he arched his back, threw back his head, and his perfect white teeth parted as if he were trying to speak. A spasm wrenched his face into a grotesque mask, and his chest heaved rapidly. The muscles of his steel arms bulged as he gripped the muddy stretcher, and his belly was as rigid and flat as a washboard. From a small hole in his abdomen, a snake of red and brown slithered onto the litter, staining it red-black and brown-purple.

His left knee was flexed, and his long, uncircumcised penis flopped over on his right upper thigh.

As he passed me, he raised his head involuntarily as if to prevent the contracting straps of his neck muscles from tearing off his jaw. His neck veins swelled in protest. His mouth opened again, at first for air, but then in a silent plea. Because he extended one muddy hand toward me and looked directly into my eyes, I turned to follow him. All my training as a physician and instincts as a human being screamed for me to help. Adrenaline coursed through my body, and I was, for a moment, almost paralyzed with fear. I could not imagine caring for a patient so badly wounded. We kept walking.

The division surgeon, who seemed not to notice him go by, was still talking about the compound—something about the marines putting the protective sandbag blast wall in the wrong place. He was ready to show us Triage, the main casualty sorting area, a large, open room measuring fifteen by twenty meters. Reinforced on the outside by sandbags, the wooden walls contained floor-to-ceiling shelves filled with bandages, first aid gear, and bottles of intravenous fluids. Square wooden posts supported a bare tin roof.

In this area, six naked men lay on a row of canvas stretchers supported by metal sawhorses. Doctors and corpsmen were working quickly and calmly over the wounded with very little conversation. The division surgeon continued talking without acknowledging the casualties or the medical personnel.

On the first stretcher lay a very large, muscular boy. Earlier that day, any football coach in America would have wanted him as a tackle or a defensive end. Now, his left thigh pointed skyward, ending in a red-brown meaty mass of jellied muscle, twisted ligaments, clots, and long bony splinters. There was no knee, and the lower leg parts hung loosely by skin strips and tendons. A tourniquet had been placed around his thigh, and a corpsman was cutting through the strips of tissue with shears to remove the dangling segments of calf muscle. Lying separately on the stretcher was an intact boot containing the lower leg and foot.

In the second position, a sweating doctor was administering closed cardiac massage on a flaccid, pale, thin boy with multiple open wounds. A second doctor was bag-breathing the boy—using a trach tube to force air into his lungs. The vigorous chest compression produced only the audible cracking of ribs. Next, a light brown soldier lay on his stomach. A baseball-sized chunk of his right buttock was missing, yet there was very little bleeding. He seemed in no distress and raised his head to watch the action around him.

The same soldier who had beckoned to me minutes earlier lay in the fourth position. He now had intravenous fluids running into one arm and a loose bandage over his abdomen. Next to him a corpsman was starting an IV on a boy racked with shaking chills.

At a distance from the others a young man lay with the top half of his head wrapped in huge blood-soaked bandages. No part of his body was moving except for a slow, unsteady rise and fall of his chest. A tube stuck out of his nose. Each breath made a grunting snort as he lay there, awaiting death.

The center of all activity was Triage, the first stop for all wounded and sick who were still alive upon arrival. The dead went directly to Graves. Beyond Triage, a covered concrete walkway joined several wooden one-story structures called "hooches." Each small hooch had screen walls, a wooden floor, and a tin roof. Some contained rows of simple collapsible metal beds; some were set up with tables and equipment for debriding and dressing minor wounds; others were used as treatment rooms or housed X-ray equipment. Behind the hooches were two pressurized rubber buildings that looked like giant inflated tubes, called MUSTs (Medical Unit, Self-contained, Transportable). One was used for sick soldiers, while the other was for wounded soldiers recovering from surgery. About fifty meters away from this tightly grouped complex of buildings were quarters for doctors and other officers. Five men lived in each of ten small hooches, evenly spaced in two rows of five. One hooch standing alone was used as the Officers' Club (O-Club), complete with card tables, several upholstered chairs, and a polished wooden bar.

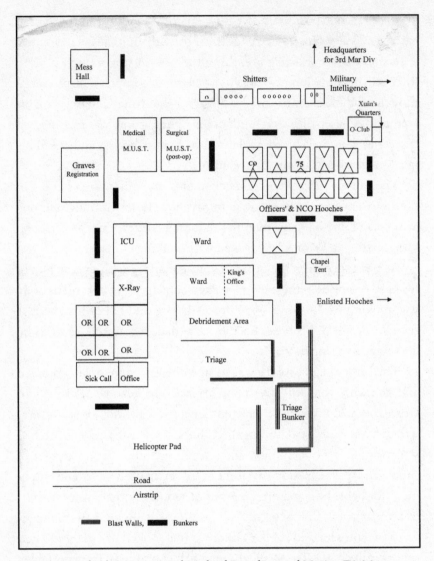

A Med: A Medical Company, 3rd Medical Battalion, 3rd Marine Division.

I was issued a .45 caliber pistol, bullets, a flak jacket, a steel helmet, two canteens, green jungle fatigues, and jungle boots. My casual khakis went into storage—a costume worn only for one transition: USA to Vietnam. Because I believed physicians were not supposed to carry weapons, I kept my pistol under my bed covered by my flak gear.

I shared quarters with four other officers: a surgeon, an internist, a psychiatrist, and a marine officer. I would encounter two of them every day as part of my work. Parker Powell, the chief surgeon, was a handsome, well-built, and self-assured professional. In his midthirties, he had sandy brown hair, nearly perfect facial features, and a warm, accepting smile. The wife and children pictured on his desk were as wholesome and attractive as Parker himself. He always was either in the OR or in the hooch reading—it seemed not to matter to him which. He seldom went to the O Club to drink. Although his comments were interesting, insightful, and succinct, he only spoke when directly addressed. He was always balanced, steady, and calm. He was in Vietnam to do a job. He would do it well and go back to his private practice in Fresno, California.

John Parrish in his hooch.

Commander Parker Powell, M.D., in hooch 75.

Stan Myers, the division internist, was a pasty-pale, slightly pudgy redhead. When we first met he was pleased to find out I was trained in internal medicine and said he might make me his assistant. When I made rounds for the first time with Stan, we went over each of his sick patients in slow, methodical fashion as he taught me about malaria, dysentery, skin ulcers, and other illnesses related to the tropics and war. I was very interested and hoped I could serve as an internist, but I soon learned that as a general medical officer (GMO), my real job was to take care of the wounded.

My first morning treating casualties seemed endless. Although I didn't realize it at the time, it was a slow morning, and I spent much of the morning chatting with the corpsmen. I allowed myself to think that perhaps this was not going to be such a bad job.

At about noon, five badly wounded marines were rushed into Triage. Two other doctors also appeared out of nowhere. It was obvious that two of the wounded men would live until we had more time, so each doctor began to care for one of the more critically injured marines.

My patient had a head injury. His skull was broken and bleeding. My hands were shaking as I put a pressure dressing over the top of his head, started an IV, drew blood for type and cross match, and examined him from head to foot as I had been taught in medical school.

Lt. Commander Stanley Myers, M.D., finishing medical rounds. Alex Roland is behind his right shoulder.

As we worked, Parker came by to check on each patient to see who might need to go to the OR immediately. He was the final judge regarding the priorities of treatment. He approached my station last.

I began to report on my patient's condition, just as I had been trained at the hospital in Ann Arbor. "Head injury," I began. "Blood pressure still good, pulse is regular at sixty. Pupils are dilated and respond very little and sluggishly to light. He has decerebrate posturing at times [an involuntary flexion of his arms and legs, often a sign of severe brain injury.]"

Parker was not even listening to me. He pulled my crooked bandage off the patient's head as I kept speaking. "Lungs are clear, abdomen is soft," I went on.

He grabbed a handful of scalp hair and raised the head up off the litter. Mashed brains slid like jelly out of the broken skull and onto the litter.

"No other evidence of injury," I continued. "His . . ."

He let the head flop back down, dropping it like a dead animal.

"Are you shitting me?" He gave me a brief look as if I were crazy and then turned away to help the other patients.

I continued my report. "His corneal reflex is absent and . . ."

A corpsman who had been watching the whole time spoke up. "We usually just leave these, sir. Not much we can do." There followed an empty and helpless silence. These? The soldier would be left to die and then taken to Graves.

"We don't have time, sir. You'll get used to it."

I stumbled out of Triage, my hands covered in blood and brains, feeling stupid and lost and useless.

I quickly learned that the sound of incoming helicopters heralded the arrival of casualties, many of them American boys only a few months removed from their senior prom and not yet eligible to vote. We had capacity to house up to fifty marines whom we could treat and then return to duty in a few days. We stabilized the more severely wounded, performing surgery only if it was urgent, then transferred the living and dead to the rear by fixed wing aircraft to military hospitals or by helicopter to hospital ships.

I was wholly unprepared for the carnage I witnessed, which I would soon learn was not anything unusual but the norm in a very abnormal place. At Yale, the medical students on surgery rotations were basically observers. Trainees could then choose internships that were "straight medical," "straight surgical," or "mixed." Because I chose a straight medical internship and immediately entered internal medicine residency, I had essentially no training in either the principles or practice of the acute care of minor or major trauma. I was preparing for civilian internal medicine and had been placed in a war zone to take care of casualties—unprepared and untrained.

Assigned to the marines during one of the war's most violent periods, I saw war in its most hideous form, in death and in the blood and pain of wounded marines sacrificed for a cause neither they nor I nor perhaps anyone understood. I was informed that the role of medical personnel in a war zone is not to save lives for the sake of saving lives, or for any moral reason, but to conserve military manpower. Our primary goal was to prevent illness and take care of sick and wounded casualties to keep them from having adverse effects on combat efficiency. We were supposed to keep soldiers in the field, keep the sick from getting sicker, and send the wounded back to the war as fast as possible. I quickly discovered that although this reasonable sounding goal was only rarely in conflict with my training, my ethics, and my instincts, what I thought did not matter. In a very short period of time I became adept at ignoring and burying my own reactions, and somewhere deep in my soul I began warehousing my feelings. While I was in Triage there would be no room for political, moral, spiritual, or intellectual concerns.

Young men's lives passed through my hands as I treated as many as thirty patients a day, with wounds more destructive and life-altering than anything I had ever encountered, a situation for which it was impossible to prepare and for which I was woefully unqualified. I did my best but not once felt like it was enough. There were times I treated wounded soldiers continually for more than twenty-four hours. Dismembered limbs and other body parts flowed through my hands like some hallucinatory human disassembly line.

Most mornings, Stan and I made medical rounds, ran sick call, and read all the chest X-rays. During the rest of the day I would function as a general medical officer (GMO) giving first aid to casualties in Triage and assisting in the operating room. Since my medical skills were far superior to my surgical skills, which were almost nonexistent, I liked being the assistant division internist better than being a GMO. I was determined to take excellent care of sick soldiers, please Stan, and make myself very useful. I hoped I could prove to be so useful that he would request I stay in Phu Bai beyond the usual three-month tour and not ever be sent to the front lines.

I studied Stan carefully. He was hard to read through his syrupy good-old-boy style yet seemed to be a genuinely good person. He never drank, never used profane language or told dirty jokes, never criticized or spoke harshly to anyone, and was never mean to any-body. He read his Bible, hung out with the chaplain, went to Sunday church services, and smoked two packs of Salems every day. As a fully trained internist, he rarely went to Triage to treat casualties. I was most impressed by the fact that he was a high school friend of Elvis Presley.

Stan said he was "tickled pink" to learn that, as the son of a South-ern Baptist minister, I was practically raised in the church. As he got to know me, he worried about my soul and tried to return me to the fold. He wanted me to attend the informal Sunday worship services and join him playing cards with the chaplain. More importantly, he seemed to like working with me.

Stan assigned me the responsibility of being the 3rd Marine Divi-sion snake expert. Any soldiers or civilians in I Corps bitten by a snake would be brought to me. To prepare myself I read a box of books about snakes and wrote a very detailed treatment protocol that Stan distributed to all the doctors and corpsmen in I Corps. From pictures, I learned to identify many kinds of snakes. I had to learn to identify snakes by their body color and scales because marines almost always shot off the head or smashed it with a rock or the butt of a gun. Over the following months, I treated three poisonous and four nonpoison-ous snake bites. One marine was killed by a land mine while chasing a harmless snake that had bitten his buddy and a Vietnamese man bitten by a snake was already dead when he arrived.

In Phu Bai I began each day in Graves by examining the bodies of the dead that had accumulated after sundown the night before. No new bodies arrived after dark, because it was simply not worth the risk to evacuate the dead during the darkness. In Phu Bai and in the field I saw many dead and dying marines. They were nothing like the waxy cadavers I had worked with in medical school, or the bodies laid out in the funeral homes that I had seen as a boy with my father. In these men you could conclude the instant life had come to an end. I grew familiar with the soldiers who died instantly in the field, en route to Triage, quickly before our eyes, or agonizingly slowly despite our most exhausting efforts.

At the moment of death and for a brief time thereafter I would look into the faces of the dead. I touched and straightened their hair. I closed their eyes. I wiped blood, mud, mucus, and vomit from their cheeks with my hands. After a while, the hemoglobin faded from the superficial vessels of the skin, making white boys whiter and black boys blacker.

I noticed that marines seldom looked directly into the faces of the dead. Marines in the field and helicopter crews somehow knew when it was time to cover the face. I never covered the faces unless they were mutilated or frozen in grief or pain. Somehow it seemed wrong for the dead to become faceless.

Not all were killed by the enemy. Some were killed by other marines, both by accident and on purpose. On one occasion one of our own assault helicopters wiped out a marine reconnaissance squad mistakenly thought to be enemy. On another occasion a marker flare drifted away from its intended site marking enemy positions and settled directly over twenty wounded marines waiting medevac, and American artillery killed three marines and most of the wounded. Some soldiers were killed by Vietnamese civilians. Some were killed by a well meaning, frightened corpsman who accidentally gave too much morphine. Some were killed by vehicles, snakes, plane crashes, overdoses of hard drugs, mud, water, bacteria, bunker cave-ins, or even tigers. Malaria, hepatitis, cellulitis, and encephalitis all took a toll. Some fell from watchtowers or bridges. Some drowned crossing rivers with ninety-pound packs.

Death was not subtle or romantic. Death was very definitive, complete, final, and ugly—sometimes vulgar. It is not possible to be much deader than a headless body swollen from lying in the mud for three days, getting hosed down, tagged, zipped in a green bag, and flipped into a freezer. A marine is just as dead when he cradles his head in the hands of some poor navy doctor, barfs blood in his lap, and then, as fingers start to relax their grip on his shirt, just stops breathing. One is never more dead than when he's completely blown away.

However they died, in Phu Bai the dead were our temporary guests during their journey home. I described the wounds, determined the cause of death, pronounced them dead, and signed forms. I struggled to believe that each marine must not have died in vain. I wanted their deaths and the death of millions of civilians to represent noble sacrifice on behalf of eternal principles, but I was tempted to think these deaths could be rendered significant only by acknowledging that they were tragic sacrifices in a futile war.

After a few weeks of treating casualties, I began to feel more comfortable working alone in Triage, but I still wanted to have more experienced doctors available. I learned a great deal from Parker, who was excellent at Triage and first aid and was a phenomenal surgeon. He made it pleasant, even for an inexperienced internist, to assist him in surgery. He encouraged me, complimented me, and tried to convince me to become a surgeon.

During my early days in Triage, I tried to maintain the discipline of my academic medical training and carefully studied each wound to determine the exact extent of nerve, vessel, and muscle damage. I tried to estimate the viability of tissue, the salvageability of extremities, and the physiological changes induced by trauma, reducing each wound to a few neat descriptive phrases that pointed the way toward treatment. However, these wounds were not the clean, neatly arranged pictures found in textbooks. There were often multiple wounds, each worse than the other. The soft tissues could be smashed, torn, burned, or jellified and mixed with dirt, debris, and pieces of clothing or gear, making fine anatomic distinctions impossible. Defining the exact extent of damage often made little difference in the emergency treatment.

Most decisions were obvious. Any seriously injured man needed IV fluids, and those with low blood pressure were given blood. The decision to remove dead, damaged, or infected tissue under local anesthetic or surgery in the operating room was usually immediately obvious. A period of observation was seldom necessary or practical. A penetrating wound and a rigid abdomen required a laparotomy (an exploratory surgical incision through the abdominal wall to assess damage). An upperbody wound with fluid in the chest cavity often needed a tube for drainage. A blown-off leg was a blown-off leg.

Metal fragments from explosive devices could be hidden deep within the body. Their size and exact location were not always apparent by examining the entrance wounds alone. We tried to find the "frags" using X-ray or palpation, or just sticking our fingers or a hemostat into the entrance wounds and searching for the track from skin to frag. At times I couldn't find a frag even when it was evident on X-ray. I worried both about exploring wounds too vigorously and not being aggressive enough.

Eventually all the wounds began to look similar. I couldn't process all of the sights and sounds. I could only incorporate certain fragments. A total embrace of all I witnessed was not necessary, practical, or, for me, even possible. I was overloaded, yet my job required me to remain focused and efficient. The mangled flesh, the stench, the sounds of pain, the faces, the individuality and sacredness of each boy were blurred and partially buried as I let in only enough information to do my work and provide first aid and comfort to the wounded soldiers.

I became closest to the two men in the hooch who did not treat sick or wounded marines. If there was a father figure in our hooch, it was King Price, the division psychiatrist, a forty-year-old bright and opinionated bachelor who spoke with a sophisticated vocabulary, precise enunciation, and slightly effeminate gestures. A large man, at least six foot three, he was thick and flabby without really being fat. Only a psychiatrist could get away with being as nonmilitary as King. After work hours he wore Bermuda shorts, sandals, and a sport shirt or dress slacks and a white dress shirt—or nothing except bikini briefs. Every outfit, including his jungle fatigues, was accompanied by an ascot of loud and shocking color. When the commanding general of the 3rd Marine Division decided King's hair was too long, King shaved his head completely and grew a thick mustache. He could go for days

Lt. Commander King Price, M.D., relaxing in the O-Club.

without going to the chow hall because his locker was always full of delicious goodies sent by his mother.

Each day King spent five or six hours interviewing psychiatric casualties, determining whether they would be returned to their units, sent to the rear, or sent back to the States. The few patients he thought most interesting and treatable within days he would keep in Phu Bai for intensive short-term psychotherapy. King had trained a group of older corpsmen so well that they could handle almost any psychiatric emergency without him. He was, therefore, seldom busy after 1600 hours (4:00 P.M.).

Only the more seriously disturbed marines got to see him. Most were treated in the field or in battalion aid stations by corpsmen or GMOs. Besides acute "battle fatigue" or anxiety reactions, King saw boys accused of homosexuality or drug use, young men caught with hard-core pornography by a righteous superior, and victims of acute and chronic alcoholism. Many of his patients were discipline problems, borderline sociopaths who had had trouble relating to authority figures long before entering the service. King commanded respect because a statement from him could make you crazy by definition. For soldiers, depending on their intended career path, that could be very bad if it marred your service record—or very good if it sent you home.

King had an impressive breadth of liberal arts knowledge and an insightful and interesting opinion on every topic. He opined about men, stress, war, and prevention and management of psychiatric symptoms in the military culture. He was troubled philosophically about the role of a psychiatrist in the military because he helped men prepare for and adjust to what he considered murder and atrocities. He was always suspended in ambivalence because, strategically, he had been told that psychiatric support best served the military (and secondarily the patient) when soldiers were treated immediately after showing incapacitating signs or symptoms. They needed to be kept as close to their comrades as possible, and it had to be made clear to the soldier from the very beginning that he was expected to recover and return to duty. Quickly.

King had been drafted and was against American military presence in Vietnam. Although he was careful about public statements or disagreeing with the two or three men in our battalion who outranked him, in our hooch, he often led discussions about the stupidity and bumbling execution of the war. He was sympathetic to soldiers who wanted out. He felt that although marines were all volunteers, many were essentially drafted because they had so few other options in the United States, or they were unduly influenced by a gung-ho father or a skilled recruiter. He knew that his military mission was to keep as many marines as possible between him and the demilitarized zone (DMZ).

My hoochmates and I all assumed King was homosexual, but we never talked about it or acknowledged it in any way. No jokes, innuendos, or direct or indirect messages of prejudice or acceptance. I assumed we all believed we were protecting King from the military culture he served so well. By unspoken contract, we kept King's sexual preference locked in a private box that we never opened even when King was not present.

King and I bonded immediately. He was twelve or thirteen years older than I, and to him, I became a strange mix of adopted son, friend, patient, and professional colleague. I always felt he was studying me and knew my inner self. I found myself telling him everything about my family and my life story. During private conversations I began to realize that everything I ever thought or believed or felt was cracking into pieces I held together behind a facade. It was a very successful facade. King shared with me that my colleagues saw me as a strong person among the doctors, good-natured, great sense of humor, easygoing, and at peace. I hardly recognized who he was talking about.

One day when we were alone in the hooch, King approached my desk and interrupted me as I sat writing a letter. Standing over me, he put both his hands firmly on my shoulders and looked straight into my eyes, his face only inches from mine.

"John, you make yourself out to be a victim"—he held me there for a few seconds—"and position yourself here as a bystander." I pulled out

Lieutenant John Parrish and Lt. Commander King Price in hooch 75.

of his grip and stared down at my desk. Price shrugged, took a step back, and twirled his mustache as he watched me. "You are already playing reluctant warrior," he said. "Next, you may even try to become a hero." After a long pause, he added, "Be very careful." Finally he looked away.

By invading my space, King had shaken my story line. I tried to pretend it hadn't happened, alternately doodling and staring into space. He could see what I thought no one could. Somehow he knew that I was already breaking apart, that my exposure to war was causing fractures only he could see. Just as I could tell when a soldier was going to die from his physical wounds, King could already sense my psychic damage.

Then he made his proposition. He offered to send me home. If I ever had more than I could take or if I felt the stress was going to break me, I was to tell him. He would fill out a few papers, and I would be on my way home within hours. He cautioned me not to go to the trouble of demonstrating or acting out the fact that I was losing it.

King went on to tell me about one physician who was medevaced home abruptly when he suffered a severe compound fracture of his leg falling down the two wooden steps at the door of his hooch on his first night in Phu Bai. It was rumored that he had wedged his leg between two steps and broken it on purpose. In any case, his Vietnam tour lasted just two days.

With great confidence King told me he would arrange for me to be stationed in the United States. It could be done within any twenty-four-hour period. Completely confidential. No questions. No repercussions. Offer was good until King finished his tour in eight months.

"I'll try it for a while" was all I could manage to say. King returned to his lawn chair. Immediately I made a list of all the things I would do to make myself a better military doctor. I would convince an intelligence officer to teach me to speak Vietnamese. I would volunteer more often to assist in surgery. I would read more and train to be physically, mentally, and spiritually fit.

King never mentioned the conversation again but I knew it was a standing offer.

About a week later, a doctor appeared in Triage. Covered with red dust, he was still wearing his flak jacket and helmet and had a clip in his .45. During a constant barrage of shells from mortars and artillery, he had remained in the same bunker for five days without sleep. Badly injured marines were constantly being brought to him, and he couldn't get enough choppers to take them all out. He had no blood, no fluids, and no sterile gear and couldn't do anything but try to stop bleeding and give morphine. When a chopper did make it in, the unit often lost more soldiers trying to get the wounded from the bunker to the craft, leaving him with even more soldiers to treat. Finally, on the sixth day as he helped load casualties into the helicopter, he jumped on the chopper himself. Now he was in Triage.

Afraid he would be considered AWOL, I hustled to our hooch to ask King what to do. He scribbled something on a piece of paper and told me to have his corpsman put the doctor to bed for the night. He would see him the next day and decide what to do. Then King laughed and said the doctor from the field might be the only sane person he would see that day. During the night, the doctor disappeared. I assumed he somehow got back to his unit.

Alex Roland was the only nondoctor in our hooch. Twenty-three years old, five feet nine inches, tight, muscular, and bald, Alex was the typical lean-and-mean marine. Even when he was off duty he wore his dog tags outside a very clean high-neck T-shirt with pressed jungle fatigue pants, starched hat, and shiny boots. His immediate goal was to survive a tour in Vietnam while keeping two relationships going by mail so that if he survived his year in Vietnam he would have the option of either—or neither—woman. A disciplined extrovert, always cautiously assertive, Alex loved only one thing more than his own opinions: the thrill of debate. If he was winning an argument too easily he would switch to his opponent's position to embarrass him with a more convincing statement of the position or to trick him into defending Alex's original stance.

Marine Lieutenant Alex Roland in hooch 75.

Bright, ambitious, and relentlessly competitive, Alex found living with four physicians interesting and was determined to fit in. When we were busy, Alex would come to Triage to help the litter bearers or just watch. Once, as Alex stood near the entrance of Triage, a dead body fell from a passing litter. Two nearby marines jumped to pick it up. One marine lifted the body by the armpits. The other started to grab the legs, but he didn't know where to place his hands because the entire pelvis and legs were torn to shreds. Alex just grabbed the body by the belt buckle and jerked it back onto the litter, as if he were putting a box back on a conveyor belt. He didn't sleep much and often coaxed me into late-night conversation. He drank heroically but was never drunk and never seemed to have a hangover.

When we first met, Alex gave me insect repellent, a can opener, and a couple of marine handbooks about guerrilla warfare as a welcome present. "If you ever need a jeep, just let me know," he said with a grin. "I'm in charge of Motor Transport." Then he brought his face closer to mine. "And if you ever need your ass kicked, I'm a damn good wrestler." He laughed. "Tension mounts up here at times."

Alex marveled at how he came to be the highest ranking marine officer in the medical battalion and ended up living with the head surgeon, internist, and psychiatrist of the Third Marine Division. He told me that I, a lowly GMO, had been selected as hoochmate by King and him because on my first night in Phu Bai after only a few minutes in the O-Club, I threw a beer can to crash down a giant beer can castle they had meticulously constructed on a coffee table.

Alex wanted to know about my twelve-day training at Camp Pendleton, comparing it to his six years of military education, including three at the U.S. Naval Academy.

"What can you learn in twelve days?" he asked, puzzled.

I started down the brief checklist of topics that had been discussed superficially. "Field sterilization of water, conduct when captured, salt pill requirements, malaria prophylaxis."

"Were all of you doctors?" he asked. "How about the instructors?"

"All thirty of my classmates at Pendleton were physicians," I told him, "but none of them had a military background. Some bored officers and enlisted men gave lectures. None of them were doctors or corpsmen."

Alex stared at me; he didn't seem to blink much. Slightly unnerved, I kept going. "There was no time spent teaching history or theory of war. No one felt obligated to justify the war, discuss morality or freedom, or argue democracy versus Communism. The only human abstractions even mentioned at Pendleton were the stubbornness of the enemy and the camaraderie of the marines."

"No talk of honor and country?" he asked.

"No," I said, "just facts. There was a war going on, and Americans were getting wounded. Doctors were needed, and we were those doctors. We were given no lessons on how to take care of the wounded, no tips on survival."

Alex shrugged and gave me his condensed rules for survival. "The rules are simple and logical, but responses have to become automatic because the stresses of the moment could preclude logical thinking. Never stand in groups or gather too close together in open country. A single incoming round can get too many people."

He shifted to lecture mode. "On maneuvers, don't give or return salutes, and don't wear any rank insignia, because snipers can use these cues to pick officers for assassination. Immediately hit the deck at any loud noise. Don't run for a bunker till there's a pause in the incoming. An upright, running body is more likely to be struck by flying shrapnel than a prone body. Shrapnel goes up and out. Sleep as near the ground as possible. Sleep under the ground if possible."

I lit a cigarette and offered Alex one. I told him about our being taught to break down and reassemble a .45 pistol—and then being instructed not to carry a weapon. He muttered something about survival tactics taught by marines who had never seen combat.

"At Pendleton, they taught us we were part of a giant machine made for the business of war. The collective attitude evolved from being individuals to the herd mentality of a Boy Scout camp, then football training camp. Comradeship and competition—we became gladiators. Boys who had watched war movies, read war comics, and played games were now taught to play the game with real weapons. It seemed like a game. Each drill sergeant was completely invested in it, and we were invested in it, too." It was hypnotic.

"You really went for that shit?" Alex's face was unreadable.

I nodded.

Alex shook his head. "What's the very least you can do to make a doctor into a soldier—a member of a new order? Even after six years of military education, I'm not sure what's decoration and ritual and what's real."

Until that moment I hadn't realized how much I had changed in only a few short weeks in Vietnam. The cracks in my psyche that I had first perceived in the days just before I left for Vietnam had grown wider. A different person was emerging.

I had no sense of a greater purpose. My mission now was personal, my war a short-term pursuit of survival. Don't fall. Don't get hurt. Don't draw attention to myself.

"Make it through the day," Alex said. "Do whatever it takes to make it through three hundred and sixty-five days."

CHAPTER 7

In Triage, all the GMOs and surgeons were quick to help one another. If a colleague stabilized his patient while I was still working on mine, he would immediately come to assist me. Since there was no way to train for the kinds of war wounds and trauma we were seeing, the experience of other doctors was invaluable. In my first few days in Triage I learned more about trauma management than I had learned in my previous six years of medical training, the kind of hands-on training that could never be duplicated in an academic, clinical setting, but also the kind of training I hoped I would never need.

Parker Powell was my favorite instructor. He stayed calm and focused, and I tried to adopt both his attitude and his methods. He taught me according to an old adage used in surgical training that I had heard in medical school, "See one, do one, teach one." In one of my first days in Triage Parker was treating a marine with an obvious chest wound and other upper-body trauma. Without hesitation, almost without thinking, his practiced hands inserted a drainage tube in the chest wall of his patient. As he did, he gave me a brief lecture.

"With an injury like this," he explained, "blood or air can accumulate inside the chest wall. With no route of escape, the pressure can compress one or both lungs, leading to asphyxiation and death, even if the initial wound is not life-threatening in and of itself."

The next time a soldier needed a chest tube, it was my turn, and over the next few weeks all the doctors let me put in the chest tubes. I got very good at it, learning to make entry just above a rib to avoid the blood vessels and nerves that run along the bottom of the rib, and feel the sudden change in resistance when the tube would pop through the chest wall. I even learned to do a little sidestep at the moment when I thrust the tube into the chest to avoid getting blood on my pants as it shot through the tube. I was soon teaching others how to insert chest tubes and avoid the stream of blood.

Lessons like these helped me, to a degree, keep the war at a distance as I mentally tried to view what I was doing as an extension of my medical training. In fact, I tried to fill as much time as possible mimicking my life in the States and doing what I could to continue my studies in internal medicine. I had brought a thick textbook with me, which I studied almost constantly, poring over the pages at my plywood desk in the hooch, pushing away the images of war with the clinical descriptions and specialized vocabulary of medical texts. I also read books left behind by other soldiers, usually about war, and each time I came across a word that was unfamiliar, I would turn to a large dictionary that had been left in our hooch and look up the definition and etymology of the word, tracing it back, moving from one word to another, following a path that took me away from Triage and away from the visceral reality of the war into the quiet, manageable library of my mind, where wounds and injuries had no face, no sounds, and no smell.

Alex gave me a jeep and a driver, and I sometimes went into the city of Hue, only a few miles from Phu Bai on the main highway. Most often I was accompanied by Xuân, an attractive young Vietnamese woman who tended bar at the O-Club and brought drinks to the early arrivals lucky enough to sit on an old couch or in one of the two upholstered armchairs. Only five or six men could sit at the bar at a time, and there was only room for another ten or twenty to stand around talking in small groups. From 6:00 to 10:00 P.M. Xuân was extremely busy.

Vietnamese women were brought by truck from Phu Bai and Hue to wash clothes, polish boots, iron, and clean. They spoke very little English, and we rarely saw them because we were working. Those "house mice" were always off the base by 2:00 P.M. Xuân and her room-mate, who worked in the Enlisted Men's Club, were the only women on base at night.

Xuân was very grateful for the opportunity to visit her family in Hue. In return, she acted as my guide and interpreter and helped me learn enough rudimentary Vietnamese to make basic conversation with civilians. These lessons complemented the private lessons given me by a friendly intelligence officer, who focused his teachings primarily on terms needed to take a medical history.

Even though Hue was allegedly "secure," there were VC—Viet Cong—mixed in the population throughout the South, and as an American, despite the presence of a driver and his M-16, I knew I was never truly safe. Being with Xuân, who knew the city, the language, and the culture, provided some insurance and kept me from inadvertently wandering into dangerous situations.

I told myself that there were plenty of practical reasons for my friendship with Xuân, but that wasn't all there was to it. Very soon we began to grow closer, moving toward a relationship that could violate both my marriage vows and military rules. I knew that physical intimacy was truly dangerous. If we were discovered she would lose her job, and if the wrong person in Hue knew she was having a relationship with an American soldier, it might cost her her life; if I was discovered, my stay at Phu Bai could end in an instant and I could be sent to the field, where my life could be in danger every day.

Xuân was young, pretty, and very energetic. Her breasts were full and set slightly low, and her hips were wide for her small size. At work in the O-Club, she always wore an inviting smile and a silk *ao dai*, the traditional Vietnamese dress with long silk pants and a bright-colored tunic split from the floor to the thigh. She spoke English well enough to parry back when teased. Before 4:00 P.M. I began to carve out twenty to thirty minutes from sick call, medical rounds, or work in Triage to sit in the shade with Xuân to practice my halting Vietnamese. After 10:00 P.M. we would sometimes sit and talk in the moonlight.

She was a fun and patient teacher, mixing vocabulary lessons with the story of her life and asking me questions about the United States; in turn I asked her about Vietnam. She had grown up on the streets of Hue, raised by her mother and brothers after her father never returned from a military maneuver against the French occupiers. When the Americans had come, most of her family had fled to the North. She married a soldier in the Army of the Republic of Vietnam (ARVN) who had reportedly been killed by the VC in an ambush, but she also heard rumors that he had defected to the North.

On occasion there were "movie nights" on base; a movie would be projected outdoors onto the side of a storage bin that had been painted white. One night when Stan was visiting with the chaplain, Alex, Parker, and King were at movie night and I sat alone at my desk, medical book open, simultaneously trying to understand the war and keep it away, neatly contained within some medical definition, I heard the door to my hooch open. It was Xuân. Without speaking she began to rub my neck. I responded and placed my arm around her, then reached under her *ao dai* and felt the soft skin beneath her silk pants. Silently, she motioned me to follow her.

We crept to her quarters behind the O-Club and within minutes had furtive, forbidden, desperate sex. In the nearly dark room, alone with each other, for a few moments there was no time or space for war. The pattern was set. Although everything in my upbringing told me that extramartial sex was wrong, that I was a good boy, now that I was a soldier it was different; the rules were different, and so was I. I had already crossed the boundary once before, on the night of my going-away party in Ann Arbor, and I now found it ever easier to cross again. Working kept the war away. Fatigue kept the war away. Possibly, risky behavior and sex could keep the war away.

Xuân and I met very infrequently, sometimes in her quarters during movie night, once in mine, twice in a small bunker. She usually sought me out, and she insisted on a set of strict rules. We spoke very little during these meetings, and then only in Vietnamese. There was virtually no foreplay, and our sex was brief, frantic, and almost ritualistic. When we would meet later, during the day, to practice Vietnamese or go to Hue, we would not acknowledge the physical part of our relationship.

Sometimes when I went into Hue I would visit the Vietnamese Provincial Hospital. Although nominally operated by the government of South Vietnam, it was completely staffed by volunteer civilian doctors from Germany, France, and the United States, all of whom spoke English. On occasion I would help out, appreciative of both the company and the chance to care for patients who were ill with disease and not wounds of war, at least not directly.

Two or more patients shared each of the dozens of beds that were crowded into large but otherwise bare rooms. Family members lived and prepared meals for the patients on the floor between the beds. Most of the children wore no clothes. Some of the oldest patients urinated and spat on the floor. In the oppressive heat and humidity, the smell of the unwashed patients and bodily wastes saturated the air. Hoards of flies buzzed about the room, their flights sometimes interrupted by the pathetic fanning of a family member. Small groups of men and women squatted wordlessly in every corner, taking turns drinking watery rice soup from rusty tin bowls and feeding wasted children. An ancient, black-toothed woman ground leaves and herbs in a wooden bowl with the bottom of a Coke bottle.

To these people, illness, like war, was just another aspect of life to be suffered, another reason to wail out in grief, a transient and common display that did not materially affect the misfortunes of life. It seemed to me as if the Vietnamese were befuddled by the presence of the foreign doctors. Our time-conscious and businesslike approach to sickness seemed completely out of place to them. Day after day these white doctors, although repelled by the scenes they witnessed, returned, believing they could alter sickness and change the fate of their patients. The Vietnamese seemed less certain. Although it was rumored that the doctors had medicines that were very powerful and could be effective in the short term, long after the doctors were gone the old Vietnamese woman would still be grinding her concoctions.

In another part of Hue in a two-story concrete building was a hundred-bed tuberculosis hospital run by a small group of dedicated Vietnamese Catholic nuns. Unlike the provincial hospital, their wards were spotless. Stone floors were waxed, and the walls shone from near-constant scrubbing. The air smelled of creosote, pine, phenol, and eucalyptus. Beds in the large, open wards were clean and neat, and each contained only a single patient dressed in spotless robes. Family visitors stood quietly at the foot of the beds. The nuns acted as nurse, doctor, orderly, maid, and technician, exchanging roles silently in a fluid and seamless manner. Although a nearby building with beds for ten or twelve wealthy Vietnamese patients was visited regularly by a Vietnamese doctor, no physicians directed patient care in this big hospital.

With permission from my CO, I offered my services to the nuns. I was the first physician to offer help, and they were very pleased. They had been taking care of more than a hundred inpatients by themselves using what knowledge they could gather from textbooks and French and Vietnamese medicines supplied by the Catholic Church. I felt like a missionary.

When I could, I would spend as many as two or three mornings a week in Hue at the TB hospital. One of the nuns, Maria, was a very well trained nurse and spoke English. She was pleasant and extremely bright, and she became my head nurse, first assistant, interpreter, and friend. She spent hours organizing and preparing for my visits, selecting those patients who most needed my attention. She kept me extremely busy. I usually examined twelve to fifteen patients—those who were new admissions, were not improving, were very sick, or were ready for discharge. I would look at X-rays she selected and then walk through all of the wards to discuss problem patients. I never discovered where the X-rays came from and assumed all the patients did, indeed, have tuberculosis. Maria assured me that the Vietnamese doctors who sent the patients confirmed the diagnosis in advance.

I saw mild, moderate, and severe TB of lungs, skin, brain, bones, and kidneys. On most of my visits, several patients needed to have fluid drawn out of their lungs by the insertion of a needle into their chests. Although I had done thoracentesis a few times under supervision during my training on the TB ward at the University of Michigan, I was always apprehensive being the only person responsible for execution of the procedure. When I realized the sisters were repeatedly giving me the same needle to use on each new patient, I began to smuggle equipment from A Med to the TB hospital.

Ever eager students, the sisters questioned my every decision and learned quickly. Their baseline knowledge was impressive. Their eagerness to learn and work hard would put most American medical students to shame. Most of the patients were poor and had been sick for some time before seeking help. Maria told me that some of the patients were VC. I didn't care.

Unfortunately, patient cooperation was sometimes minimal. Patients regularly just walked away from the hospital or refused to take their medicines, either unconvinced of their effectiveness or afraid of side effects. What discipline there was stemmed more from respect for the sisters—or fear of them—than from understanding or concern about their disease or respect for me.

Work in the TB hospital helped time pass and got me away from the constant influx of war casualties. Three mornings at the hospital in Hue returned some structure to the typical week. For the first time in months, I was aware of what day of the week it was. At least the misery in the TB hospital was a different kind of misery for different kinds of people.

My jeep driver would drop Xuân off at her house and pick her up on our return trip. Some drivers were reluctant to drive down the side streets of Hue or to break the rule against carrying civilian passengers, but since Alex was in charge of Motor Transport, I didn't worry about those rules. I got to know every mile of Highway 1 between Phu Bai and Hue. Sometimes the only way I could accomplish all of my jobs was to work twelve or more hours a day. Stan was understanding and tolerant and did more than his share of internal medicine work at A

Med. He did not, however, want to visit Hue or see the civilian hospitals himself. For a while this schedule helped preserve my mental health by crowding out a growing number of painful and unwanted images of severely wounded men and imagined horrors to come in the future.

My motives were not entirely altruistic, though. At some point, I knew, I was supposed to be transferred from Phu Bai and sent into the field to serve with the infantry. Working at the TB hospital, helping out at the provincial hospital, learning Vietnamese, serving as Stan's assistant, and becoming a snakebite expert and a chest film radiologist were all part of my conscious plan to become essential to A Med at Phu Bai. In my fantasy I hoped I might still be able to stay in Phu Bai even if my relationship with Xuân was discovered, due to the irreplaceable nature of my work. I was still trapped in the heroic daydreams I had as a child.

All of these self-created responsibilities and missions were a shield for my mind, a dodge, and a way to keep from fully engaging with everything that was happening around me. I didn't realize it then, but I was already far along in the process of developing strategies to keep the trauma of the war from taking over my psyche completely. Overwork, hypervigilance, exercise, and placing myself and Xuân in risky situations left no time to look inward.

Like my more seasoned colleagues, I learned to protect myself from the horror and sadness of Triage yet remain effective and efficient by consciously experiencing people as "casualties," by viewing them as their injuries or illnesses. This was not a marine private who carried a packet of love letters in his helmet but an amputation and a collapsed lung. This was not an officer with a name and a family and a past but a fractured arm and broken jaw. This wasn't a flag-draped casket but a charred cadaver in a body bag.

I tried to distance myself from psychic impact by focusing on the tasks of diagnosis and treatment. I processed my daily life as if it were a documentary, objectifying horror and describing wounded soldiers as vivid, shocking art forms. By experiencing wounded people as their gross anatomy and physiology, I avoided intimacy. I used professional challenges and simple denial to hide an enlarging hole in my soul. I tried to contain horror by medically codifying it. In turn I was a detective, a reporter, and a scientist. Every day, I was less of myself than before.

I could usually predict when a soldier was going to die in my hands. For those with severe head injuries, multiple torn solid organs, and extensive burns, it was immediately obvious. Seeing brains was a sentence of death, and brains under my fingernails became a dreadful fear. I sometimes scrubbed my fingernails as a ritual. In others, the inflection point was more subtle, but I could sense a definitive change in status from "salvageable" to "no real chance." It was like being able to look into the future, irrevocable and sure. I came to recognize when a conscious soldier first knew he was going to die.

Yet even as I became hardened to the horror and waste, accustomed to seeing severe trauma, and more comfortable in making decisions, I began to wonder just who these wounded kids were. I tried to tolerate allowing the wounded soldiers to become specific people. I began to see them as individuals. I sought to know them, even if only briefly.

I started to ask them their names and hometowns. I encouraged them to tell me about themselves. Disciplined to the end, or else in shock, wounded marines usually remained quiet and patiently waited their turn to be treated. When time allowed, I would attempt to initiate a conversation as I worked over them. I might be with a seriously wounded man for a few minutes several times during a one-hour period. Often I might spend from twenty minutes to an hour or more debriding wounds and probing for shrapnel in wide-awake boys who were not gravely wounded.

Most of the wounded I cared for were low-ranking enlisted men who looked like the kid down the block, and many had only been in Vietnam a few months. They weren't particularly angry or bitter— yet. That would most likely come later back in the States, when they saw guys walking around and laughing with two arms and two legs.

Right now, they were just glad to be alive and relatively safe. They might have just seen a buddy on the left and a stranger on the right get killed, yet they were still alive. Their pain tolerance and stoicism were very impressive.

Often, without any expression of emotion, some of them stated that they had killed a certain number of the enemy. Some asked me questions. "Am I going to lose that arm? . . . Hey, Doc, will this get me home? . . . Is my pecker okay? Can I use it again? . . . How can my foot hurt so bad when it's still out in the field somewhere?"

The only time they showed emotion was when they asked about their fellow soldiers or told stories. "Sully was point. We lost contact, heard no shots. We found a hand in the middle of the trail. Then a foot, then another foot. Then a pecker and balls all in one piece. Not till we found his head did we know it was Sully. They cut him up and left him for us to find on the trail. We never found his body. Then I had fuckin' point for the rest of the day—you're wondering why I shot first—blew her fucking head off? Turns out she was alone . . . crazy fuckin' war—could give you nightmares."

I asked for war stories partly because I felt that fate had assigned me the role of witness, but I was also intensely curious. Whether they are told once or a thousand times, most war stories are probably never recorded. I began to feel an obligation to remember and report. Because I was more educated and older than most of my soldier patients, I thought that maybe someday I could be their voice.

I discovered that soldiers might tell different versions of the same firefight, that the truth was disassembled and cumulative. If eight soldiers on a patrol were ambushed and two were killed, two wounded, I might treat the wounded and examine the dead. I could then recreate the war story in its most primal state, participate in its evolution, and watch each character enter and then exit the stage. Nine accounts of being pinned down all night in a mined rice paddy, listening to the wounded screaming, pleading for help, or begging to be shot until one at a time they fell quiet in death. Ten accounts of an ambush. Dozens of accounts of the siege at Khe Sanh. One hundred accounts of the fall and recapture of Hue during the Tet Offensive.

At these moments of my interaction with the soldiers, it seemed that I was closing in on the "truth." I was not just ten years older and a doctor, I was also their savior, their safe place. I might save their lives. They had no reason to magnify, minimize, or distort their story—it might never be told again. The stories in Triage were, possibly, the only uncensored versions of the battle, created before guilt, shame, justification, and anger distorted reality. Before heroism or glory laid claim to memory. Before the narrator imagined he had some control over events. Before interpretation. Before revision. In the zone between physiological stress and psychological disassociation and protection, lies to help protect and preserve their self-image had not yet been told.

I tried to give the soldiers permission to emote. Pain and fear sometimes eroded their discipline. Panic exhausted them. Pheromones of power, endorphins of trauma, fight-flight hormones, and physical exertion depleted the receptors in their brains. Blood loss weakened their defenses. The euphoria and primary surges of survival had peaked. In this moment of nakedness, hundreds poured out their stories. We both knew we would never meet again.

I knew more about the nature of the injuries than did the wounded narrator-soldier himself. I looked very closely. I put my hand inside them. I measured, analyzed, examined, dissected, palpated, smelled, and manipulated the invasions into their bodies.

Then they were gone. I didn't know how their war stories ended. I didn't know how their war stories changed over time nor how their bodies healed nor how their lives were affected.

I was immersed in the side of the war equation that records the costs in body, mind, and spirit. I myself did not have the perspective of the warrior's mind—I was not trained to kill, fight, survive, and endure. I had no line responsibility and no obligation or skills to enhance the war effort. In the decisions to kill or be killed, I could be a neutral observer ready to care for the wounded, including the enemy.

After weeks of "who," I then began to wonder "how." What were the circumstances of the tearing of the flesh? I tried to picture each battle scene and to reconstruct the moment of impact. I would estimate the nearness of the enemy, the angle of fire, the posture of the soldier.

When metal and flesh intersect, flesh is destroyed. The owner of the flesh has no control, and the flesh itself has no thoughts. It is alive but at the moment of impact inanimate. Small metal objects moving very fast slash through flesh, cut, explode, rip, and tear, causing shock waves. A boy absorbs all the force or else the fragment blows out a gaping hole in his body as it exits. The soldier can be physically repositioned. The exit hole is often much bigger than the entry hole. Within a few seconds blood may seep, flow, or even pump out of either or both openings. After an instinctual attempt to relate the impact to something familiar or imaginable (a giant cross-body block, the kick of a horse, a sudden pressure wave, a blow from a baseball bat, or being hit by a truck), the soldier experiences a few moments of disconnection, confusion, anesthesia, disbelief, and disorientation. Pain may be delayed so that a soldier may see his wound, notice his bones or viscera, in an unreal, disassociated state of shock and disbelief. Then he knows he's hit and begins to wonder horrible things. Then he feels pain and pleads for help.

It can come from anywhere. I treated one soldier who was knocked out when a flying arm hit him in the back of the head. Another soldier lost an eye when he was struck by a human tooth blown explosively through the air.

As more time passed I became concerned with a different, more basic question. Continuing to talk with the troopers, I constantly asked myself, "Why?" I had never questioned that part of war before. Since I had been a boy it had simply been a given, and the expectation that I would someday go to war as a soldier had been a presence as real as Jesus. Now it was here, and I was holding on as the war and I finally intersected and careened through a year.

As days and weeks changed to months, individual soldiers again began to look similar and the stories blended one into the other. I woke each day in Phu Bai feeling more and more exhausted, but by this time I could do my work almost automatically. Every day—all day. Brief encounters with men I would never see again.

Even as I sought escape, I simultaneously began to develop a lurid fascination with the visceral details of war, as if familiarity could somehow strip those details of their power and impact. I developed an increasingly pornographic attraction to the absurd beauty and awe of war. Instead of looking away, I looked closer, seeking an intimate view of brutality and raw power, ultimate control and complete victimization, the visceral rush. By looking into the eyes of death, destruction, and mutilation, and seeing, feeling, and touching, I wanted to overload my circuits. I wanted the total impersonality of death to merge with the intimacy and individuality of life.

Approach and avoidance. I wanted to accept responsibility for everything I saw, yet wanted to hide from it at the same time. I was the ultimate voyeur, the vicarious warrior. The controlled and prolonged terror of being responsible for the salvage and repair of torn and exploded bodies made me long for the exciting terror of battle, a place where there is little control, responsibility only for self-preservation, and permission to briefly go berserk.

I was surrounded by battlefields and close to the grunts in the field. A part of me wanted to be them. In Triage I was focused entirely on their survival, and if I were them, that meant I would also be focusing entirely on my survival. Instead, I was absorbed by their survival.

I had no other battle.

CHAPTER 8

February 29, 1968. It was the beginning of the Tet holidays, the Vietnamese New Year. Casualties had slowed to a trickle, and everyone on base assumed that because of the holidays, things would remain slow. I decided to go into Hue, and this time Alex volunteered to drive me himself. We dropped Xuân off near her neighborhood so that she could spend a few days with family and friends. Proceeding toward the TB hospital, we got caught in unusually dense and slow traffic immediately behind a bus. On the back bumper of the bus, standing and holding on to a rail was a young man, perhaps twenty years old.

As we were stuck behind the bus I noticed that the young Vietnamese man was looking at me, really staring, far longer than was socially appropriate. He was only ten or fifteen feet away. It made me uncomfortable, and I looked away, but each time I looked back he was still staring at me. As our eyes locked I suddenly realized that he was looking at me with true hate. Without breaking his gaze he reached very deliberately inside his jacket. It suddenly struck me that he could pull out a gun and shoot me right between the eyes. I froze.

Then it was over. His hand reappeared holding a pack of cigarettes. He must have seen me suddenly exhale and relax. His eyes now flickered with contempt and utter disdain. Then he slowly smiled as if to say, "You were lucky this time. I'll have a chance to kill you later." It was extremely unnerving.

That was the beginning of a very strange day. Usually, when I arrived at the TB hospital the nuns were all business because they wanted me to see as many patients as possible; they met me as soon as my jeep pulled up and hustled me inside to see the first patient and the next patient and the next while my driver waited with the vehicle. They knew I could not stay long. Sometimes it took me half an hour or forty-five minutes to make my rounds, and sometimes it took a few hours. Sometimes I simply didn't have enough time and would have to leave before I had seen everyone, so they usually rushed me right to the patients.

This day, though, they said that because it was Tet they were having a little party, not for me, just a little get-together for the staff, and they asked Alex and me to join them. I took off my belt with my gun, as I always did when I entered the hospital, and we sat with the nuns in their habits drinking tea, eating little cakes and pastries, and making small talk.

Suddenly another sister rushed into the room and started speaking Vietnamese very quickly and excitedly, so fast that I had no idea what she was saying. In an instant the other nuns set down their teacups and started scurrying about.

The head nurse, Maria, turned to us and said, "I think you better go now." I didn't understand and started to protest, but she was insistent. She even went over and took my gun belt out of the drawers and handed it to me. Then she ushered Alex and me out of the door, almost frantic, telling me over and over again, "I think you better go," then adding very quickly, "Pray for us."

We had no idea what was happening but started driving back to the base. There was suddenly much more civilian traffic than usual, much of it moving out of town, and people walking rapidly or running down the streets with worried looks on their faces. We were also being met by jeeps and other military vehicles full of marines moving fast toward the center of town.

This was very strange. Although there was a war going on, Hue, the old provincial capital and a religious center, was believed to be quite safe and had never come under mass attack. The base at Phu Bai was only a few miles away, and Hue was considered heavily defended.

I started hearing small-arms fire, first in the distance and then closer, coming from almost every direction. We stayed low in the jeep, and as our anxiety increased Alex drove faster. As we crossed a bridge I could see marines with their weapons out and clips in their machine guns running along the riverbank as if they were chasing somebody, looking into the water and then taking cover.

When I got back to A Med in Phu Bai, it was disconcertingly quiet. There were no casualties, no sick calls taking place, and very few soldiers milling about. Then we started to hear that Hue was under attack.

It was the beginning of what came to be known as the Tet Offensive: a surprise attack by the Viet Cong on several key cities of the South, an attempt to show their might and demonstrate that they could attack anywhere, anytime, and that no place was safe or free from the war anywhere in South Vietnam. In Hue and elsewhere, in fact, Viet Cong had infiltrated many of the cities, blending in with the population and waiting for a signal to begin the offensive.

I now remembered the young man on the back of the bus and the way he looked at me. He was probably VC and, knowing what was about to happen, had looked at me with such contempt because even though I was only a few meters away, it was not yet time for him to take out his gun and open fire. He knew that time was coming, though, and resented the fact that it had not yet arrived and that he could not make me, an officer—he could tell by the insignia on my collar—his first target.

A few hours later trucks began to pour into the base, full of casualties. For the next three weeks, they came in to us nonstop. Every position in Triage was always full. The staff at Graves was kept constantly busy, making arrangements for the dead.

It would prove to be one of the most violent periods in the entire war. Even though American troops eventually won a military victory, turning back the onslaught and recapturing Hue in a battle nearly a month long, historians would later see the Tet Offensive as one of the war's turning points—the point at which the end of the war and the reason for fighting it seemed so far off as to be impossible to see.

I would later learn that the nurses in the hospital had managed to evacuate some patients but had stayed behind to care for those who had been too sick to move. The patients had then been executed in their beds by the Viet Cong for the crime of being treated by an American doctor. Many of the nuns were also killed for the crime of working with me.

Almost everyone the VC thought was working with Americans was killed, sometimes after being brutally tortured. There was a Vietnamese man who worked on the base as a barber but lived in Hue. He was sent to A Med as a sort of message, both to us and to any other Vietnamese working on the base. He was alive, but his hands had been cut off.

Xuân had been in Hue visiting her family when the battle began, and she did not make it back to our base. As the days passed I heard nothing from her, and it was impossible to get into Hue and discover what might have happened. I assumed she had been killed. There were so many casualties the O-Club was closed, and we were kept so busy there was no time to mourn.

For the first few days the bodies lay on litters on the runway and fields like a scene from *War and Peace*. For the first forty-eight hours we worked nonstop sorting out the wounded from the dead. At one point I passed out from exhaustion and was found slumped over the body of a soldier. Whether he was alive or dead I do not remember. Our CO finally set up a compulsory sleep schedule. For six out of every twenty-four hours we were ordered to leave Triage and rest.

The battle for Hue went on for weeks. When the VC were repelled and casualties finally slowed, everything was different. I was transferred to Dong Ha, the northernmost medical post in South Vietnam.

The expanded war now took away my civilian work. A fully trained internist was going to replace me as assistant division internist.

In Dong Ha I was assigned to a medical facility even closer to the battlefield, a forward clearing station within range of fixed enemy artillery in the DMZ, and I spent the rest of my war in a rotation. About once a month I was sent wherever there was a need for a doctor, whether it was in the field or in the rear, replacing doctors who, for one reason or another, had to leave: R&R, the need for a specialized service, illness, psychiatric breakdown, or simply because the division surgeon felt like making some changes. Then I'd be sent back to Dong Ha. Had I been an embedded reporter assigned to cover the full scale of the American military experience in Vietnam, I would not have had a better opportunity as I hopscotched from one hot spot to another, witnessing the war from many sites and perspectives.

Shortly after I began to work in Dong Ha, there were two doctors among those I treated. One of my classmates from Camp Pendleton was in coma. I examined him quickly and tried to arouse him. Some withdrawal from deep pain was the only response I could elicit. The medevac tag was written in ballpoint pen: *Barbiturates overdose?* The tag was from one of the infantry outfits that had been taking heavy casualties for several weeks.

Was this a suicide gesture to get off the battlefield? A suicide attempt because he was through with life? Temporary psychosis? Acute depression? I didn't know. Probably he didn't know. All the possibilities were equally sane in this insane world, and the difference between them was very thin. Pump his stomach. Diurese him. Send him back to see King Price in Phu Bai. Possibly then back home to his family.

One day a large helicopter landed with twelve wounded and four dead. Two of the wounded were North Vietnamese Army (NVA) officers, a valuable treasure. One of them talked to me as I bandaged a shrapnel wound in his leg. He was a doctor who had walked from Hanoi to the DMZ to work in an underground hospital. Moving from one hospital area to another that morning, he was wounded and captured. He was not afraid, and his wound was not serious. I left him to work

Alex visits John at Dong Ha in March 1968.

on another wounded man, and when things quieted, I returned again to talk. He was dead. How could that be? His wound was superficial, and his blood loss had been minimal. A marine on a nearby litter had seen him take a pill. He must have committed suicide. His Vietnamese colleague on the next litter, who had heard me talk to the doctor in Vietnamese, spoke to me in that language, slowly and simply to make sure I understood him. "The doctor of North Vietnam walks a hundred miles to serve. The soldier of South Vietnam will not defend his own village."

It was steamy hot in Dong Ha. I sweated profusely and had trouble staying hydrated. On one occasion after several days of cough, malaise, and headache, I developed severe pain in the left side of my chest. With my hand on my side, I could feel the inflamed surface of my lung drag along my chest wall. With my own stethoscope I found that I had lost all breath sounds over my lower left posterior chest. Knowing a chest X-ray would show pneumonia, causing my CO to relieve me of duty, I secretly started taking antibiotics and kept working. For several days I was dizzy and short of breath and every cough felt like an ice pick stab in my side. Yet I kept on.

On my first excursion from a military base to a new assignment in the field, I went by jeep over miles of flat country to the Wash Out, just beyond the Cam Lo River. As we passed the outer perimeter of the Dong Ha base, the driver and the marine in the backseat put clips into their M-16s. The other passenger in the backseat, a corpsman who had just arrived in country, slipped a clip into his rifle, too. His hands were shaking so badly that I was afraid he was going to shoot one of us.

Previously I had only carried a gun on my trips into Hue, but in the field I carried one with me nearly all the time. Trying to act like I knew what I was doing and trying to hide my own fear, I slid a clip of shells into my .45.

As we bumped along, I studied every bush and tree on the side of the road. I turned my collar insignia into my shirt so my rank wouldn't flash in the sun and aid a sniper's selection of candidates for death.

What the hell was I going to do if the enemy did start firing? What good would a .45 be against a sniper or, worse, a surprise attack? I

John Parrish in the field July 1968.

hardly knew how to use it anyway. My thighs ached from the tension and from trying to keep my balance in the bouncing jeep. I expected to be shot at any minute or to hit a land mine and be blown away. I wanted to ask the driver about our chances of being fired at or getting blown up, but I knew his answers would not have helped. I also felt obligated not to express anxiety. Nothing happened on the trip, but I felt no safer when I left the jeep to enter my newly assigned tent. My body was on full adrenaline alert.

Eventually I grew accustomed to the fear. Sometimes I found it boring.

In the field I began to identify with "the wisdom of the grunts," the philosophy of teenaged American kids, the foot soldiers who were actually fighting this war and carried it with them every minute of every day. They reminded me of the random nature of the war's killing machine, where soldiers died each day not for a great cause but primarily because someone failed to observe some small detail he had either forgotten or could no longer be bothered with. Too exhausted in spirit to snap a flak jacket closed; a shard from a grenade penetrated the heart. Too depressed to clean a weapon; it jammed and left the soldier defenseless. Too spaced out to care and too tired to give a fuck; chronic anxiety and dull routine existed side by side in the marine's mechanical, systematic search for the Vietnamese, an enemy who was everywhere and nowhere, one whose presence was announced in explosive bursts of brutality, killing and violence coming at any time and at any place, then retreating just as quickly. The end of a skirmish or battle brought little relief, just the knowledge that the next fight was out there, a second, an hour, a day, or a week away, as certain as the sunrise.

The grunts saw the war up close, in its most stark and basic terms: To most of them, missions to "search and destroy" seemed much more authentic than "pacification." They were in Vietnam to kill gooks, period, not make friends with the Vietnamese. Some did it well, and some enjoyed it—often making up the rules as they went. Target practice from helicopters. Close contact and killing by hand. Shoot. Explode.

Burn. Blow the fuckers up. Kill by day, come back for a movie at night. Stay alive. Do what you have to do. Trust nobody. Go home.

"It don't mean nuthin'" was their mantra. The grunts who did the fighting and those who supported them in the rear were not concerned with abstract morality, politics, opinion polls, or military strategy. Once they were in the field their goal was simple survival, to do what they were told to do, to make war, to protect their buddies, to wear down "the enemy," and to kick ass. They did not see themselves as either liberators, bullies, or imperialists. However, after being in Vietnam a very short time many came to feel the country could not be saved, only destroyed. In that mission there was clarity.

Brought into their units one at a time, made to fight for thirteen months and sent home alone, the grunts had difficulty connecting their personal tours of duty with the aims of America's war effort. Some soldiers began to see themselves as victims not only of a guerrilla enemy but also of American foreign policy, and for the first time by talking to recent arrivals I began to sense the degree to which the war had become unpopular back home.

I never heard talk of fighting Communism or saving or protecting the Vietnamese unless it was said in derision, as a sick joke, graveyard humor. Most marines could not state a coherent political position, nor debate or defend their personal philosophy, but their attitudes were clear. I saw UUUU written on helmets and carved on wooden tables and trees and 4U as a tattoo on battle-scarred arms. I soon learned that the acronym meant "The Unwilling, led by the Unqualified, doing the Unnecessary, for the Ungrateful." That was the logic of their war. I, the educated university man, was a student, and they were the teachers.

When I was with the infantrymen I could feel their intense anticipation of battle, of contact with the "enemy." Even among supposedly friendly local villagers the marines knew there were bands of people who wanted to kill us, and it was difficult to know the difference between a friend and an enemy. There was constant anxiety as every marine knew that at every instant someone was scheming and dreaming of ways to kill us.

"Charlie" was out there to be hunted, or at least defended against. He had to be killed, or tricked. He was everywhere and nowhere. The marines feared, respected, and hated him. Yet they wanted and needed to kill him. That was their job. It was a deadly game, a high-stakes hunt. In the early part of each new play, we were bait and he was predator. Then, when the time was right, we called in airpower to reverse the roles.

In the bush anything not essential was forbidden. They lived as primitives. Yet the way the environment could switch from the deprivation of the field to the beer, hot dogs, and ice cream available at a base was jarring. A brief helicopter jump into a safe landing zone or a jeep ride farther to the rear could change a primitive jungle to an American mall, or a war zone to an all-male picnic. A VC rocket could change it back to hell again. Kill by day, come back for a beer and a movie at night—and any day could be your last.

My respect for the grunts continued to grow. "It don't mean nuthin'" was an admission of the absence of a clear mission but also a surrender to reality, to all the forces outside one's control: chance, chaos, and evil. Absurdities outweighed conventional expectations. Things just didn't add up. "It" actually meant everything, but there was no better way to express or explain it. The soldier focused his energies on staying alive and gave up on the larger issues. There was no other language that could articulate "it."

I hated what the soldiers in the bush were doing, but I admired their willingness to do it and felt very connected to them. Part of me wanted to get even closer, loved what they were doing and longed to go with them on every mission. I didn't just want to hear their war stories. I wanted to participate in them. Yet, at the same time, I hated the war and I was very fearful. I wanted to strike out and strike back, fight and fight back, but I was confined by my role as doctor.

Paradoxically, when I was assigned to infantry units in the field I often had very little to do. The severely wounded or very sick were usually medevaced to medical support facilities before I even saw them, and marines in the battlefield do not often complain of minor illnesses, aches, or pains.

At times when I was in the field, separated from direct care of the wounded, I came to love being a soldier. I kept my .45 on my hip at all times. I had an M-16 acquired from a dead marine. Compared to giving first aid, the war of a soldier was a more dramatic, exciting, and dangerous occupation.

The grunts taught me to pray to a new god, DEROS, which stood for Date Eligible for Return from Overseas. The fact of the fixed, 365-day (thirteen months for some grunts) rotation influenced *everything*, including to whom one related, and how, and whom one trusted. DEROS slipped into all conversations with new acquaintances as an aside, a sotto voce statement of faith—"I've got ninety-six days left."

The concepts of bravery, honor, heroism, justice, war, and even peace were overwhelmed by a personal plan to survive for one year. Any concept of winning was secondary. All thoughts, feelings, commitments, loyalties, goals, and values served DEROS. This was especially true for the army draftees—less so for the marine volunteers.

The grunts accepted constant fear and worshipped DEROS. Everything that kept one alive mattered, and everything mattered only because it kept one alive. Calendars became sacred writings with their own metrics. DEROS was a cult. It controlled body and mind absolutely and was much more important than capturing hills or fields or villages. Body counts were to please the CO and pass time. Stay away from FNGs (fucking new guys), whose mistakes could get you killed, and "short-timers" because they were jinxed and often got blown away with only few days left to go.

The faith of DEROS was this simple: Enter—stay alive—exit. Don't get too involved. Kill every yellow person you see if you have to. Women and children could do you in. Trust not. Be afraid. Kick ass. It's no sin to kill or steal. Frag your fucking officer if you need to. The only sin is not to make it through your tour. The calendar was God, and DEROS was the Jesus who led the way to salvation.

Preserving one's life, maintaining one's personal honor, and executing our country's policy were not only exceedingly difficult but also sometimes contradictory. Temporary dangers began to feel arbitrary, a feeling heightened by that fact that warriors were shuttled back and forth from war zones to "rest and relaxation" centers in exotic foreign ports. In between deadly assaults on villages or hills with numbers and no names, eighteen-year-old boys were treated to a sexual, alcoholic Disneyland. Military objectives became less impelling, classic war stories became less romantic, and military scorekeeping became less interesting and relevant.

I tried to integrate my two worlds, incorporating the shock of a single seriously wounded man and the personal devastation of a single untimely death, remembering and embracing the full impact of the death of my own brother. I got lost in ideas of proportionality, legalisms, national will, and acceptance of war as a legitimate tool for politics. Why did I not protest with all my might?

During one assignment, each morning at dawn, a large group of expressionless marines with full packs, extra ammunition, heavy gear, radios, and mortars walked, half awake, single file, past my tent and out into the trees in the distance. Each night they returned tired and dirty, the salt of dried sweat on their fatigues and faraway, blank stares frozen on their faces. At times fewer returned than left. It was always the marine carrying two M-16s that looked most hurt, confused, and bitter. The sick, wounded, and dead were taken by helicopters directly from the place they fell. I rarely noticed anything but their absence.

When marines are surprised in jungle terrain they first dive for cover, but rather than stay in place to be picked off one man at a time, they are trained to advance toward the enemy and respond with a frontal assault. Fewer will die if the enemy guns are extinguished quickly. The individual is prepared to take on risk for the good of the group. This tactic makes sense to the company commander, the gunny sergeant, the drill sergeant, and the marine unit as a whole. What is so unbelievable about the marines is that it also makes sense to the kids up front—the boys who charge the machine guns. Such training makes the marines an efficient killing machine. Such rearrangement of young men's thinking wins battles.

The same group identity, carried to its extreme, makes each individual in the unit important. Rather than leave a dead or wounded marine behind, the entire group may take heavy additional casualties to retrieve him. The group may even risk being sacrificed for the individual. Loyalty to fellow soldiers prevails over everything. By comparison, patriotism, captured land, spoils, treasure, or any concept of winning the war means little.

Most of the action happened while the marines were on patrol. The patrols, which took place nearly every day, seemed unconnected from any larger battle plans. Some were lonely missions to update military intelligence. Others were intended only to maintain a "presence" for local farmers and villages, and others were designed to disrupt the communication and supply lines of the enemy.

The major reason for patrols was "search and destroy," or to "find, fix, and destroy" the enemy. The object for the infantry was to lure the enemy into contact, often at great risk of casualties. Marines often felt they were used as bait. Then, once the enemy was located, airpower and artillery did most of the destroying. In the places I served, once they made contact the soldiers themselves were rarely involved in prolonged firefights. When they did, there were usually horrendous losses and casualties on both sides.

The VC and the NVA, in contrast, had a much different strategy. Unless they felt they had the advantage of superior numbers or position, meaning a great ambush site or protection from air strikes by the weather, forest canopy, or proximity to friendly troops or villes, they did not permit their patrols to make contact. They felt they could win the war simply by remaining out of reach, by outlasting us. They did not worship DEROS, but they used it to their advantage, knowing that many of our soldiers wanted nothing more than to serve their year and then leave. Enemy warriors were more willing to sacrifice themselves for nationalism. They believed that they were fighting for a cause and that we were fighting to keep from getting killed.

The grunts described their days according to levels of "bad." On a simple "bad" day, the grunts' only real enemy was the country itself:

hills, mountains, humidity, rain, insects, jungles, and rivers. They each carried sixty to one hundred pounds of gear through thick growth and treacherous footing with heat, mud, snakes, leeches, and razor-sharp elephant grass as hazards.

On a "badder" day, they lost a few men to booby traps, killed when they took a step without looking, walking into some kind of barbed punji trap or setting off a trip wire attached to a grenade or stepping on a mine. On the "baddest" days, the soldier on point was killed, picked off by a sniper, a few more died in the initial firefight, and others were killed or wounded as they waited for the firepower to arrive by air and kill or chase away the enemy.

There were no "good" days.

These patrols' exits and returns were without conversation, drama, or question. Those who died, died. Those who lived, lived. They filed back past me, ate, cleaned their weapons, and went to sleep. At dawn, like factory workers, they sullenly went back to the rice paddies, the woods, the jungle, and the hills. They would walk and sweat through another day, and most would end up again back at camp. They spoke of their task in euphemisms. Patrol was "a walk in the sun," "dangling the bait," "baiting the bush," and "humpin' the boonies."

Each phrase meant the same thing: Find the enemy, make contact, kill or be killed, and return. Trap, block, and hold. Air support and artillery support. Movement, forward observers, reports and intelligence. A game played from the colonel's tent or by a senior officer in a helicopter, moves communicated by telephone, radio, and courier and then executed by the grunts.

In my first three weeks in the field, we lost two corpsmen—one killed, one wounded. I lost count of how many marines were killed. The helicopters took the dead and the wounded directly from the place they fell to my friends in Phu Bai or back to Dong Ha.

Whenever a grunt was killed, his buddies said he had been "wasted," a word that was not a euphemism at all but unusually specific and accurate. It was also used for all forms of killing by both sides and sometimes applied to the needless destruction of homes as well. Patrols, sweeps, missions, and search and destroy operations continued every day as if part of life itself. Absolute boredom was shattered by brief episodes of intense terror. Killing time between killing times was a problem.

For one three-week period my tent was only ten to twenty meters from a giant artillery gun. At random times during the night marines fired shells to harass and cause fear, aimed at no fixed target but the blackness. Each night I was among those who fell victim to their goals. There would first be a sharp crack that seemed to lift me off the ground, stop my heart, and fire every synapse in my brain all at once. Then there was a quick mental convulsion followed by a psychic weakness as I felt the shock wave pass through my body. At times I felt pain in my ears and throat or chest that lasted for hours. I did not hear well for days at a time.

On one occasion I accompanied a corpsman and his driver on a trip to the ville to run errands, which usually included a visit with a Vietnamese family the corpsman had adopted and was supporting with food and money. As we drove slowly down one crowded street, a very young boy threw a crude wooden box with metal casing, wires, and a flashlight battery taped to its side. It landed in the jeep right next to my feet. I froze. The driver quickly but carefully picked up the device and flung it into an opening between two huts. It did not explode. The driver stepped out of the jeep and aimed his M-16 at the boy running away, but the corpsman grabbed the barrel of the gun and pointed it toward the ground. Amid simultaneous profane exclamations, they struggled with one another until I told them to let the boy go. Days later on the same street, another driver was fatally wounded by a simple bomb thrown into his jeep.

On one assignment, I attended the colonel's daily briefings. He explained how effectively we were keeping the enemy off balance, not allowing them to move closer to us. He didn't seem to hate them. They were simply insects that had to be kept away by antiseptic vigilance.

The colonel did not consider dead marines as "wasted." Death was a part of war. He spoke of them as KIAs (killed in action), WIAs (wounded in action), and body counts (dead Vietnamese of any age or sex). His scorekeeping was so unemotionally methodical, I was tempted to think he sometimes saw his own men as replaceable units.

A thin man in his late forties, with piercing eyes, a sardonic smile, a big cigar, and a nasty disposition, the colonel was unable to speak to anyone, even the chaplain, without using abusive and profane language. This lack of tact was so obviously practiced it insulted no one. The officers tolerated him and did everything he said without question and, usually, without much resentment. The enlisted men did not seem to hate him, but his rank made them avoid eye contact. He called me "Doc," as did everyone, for even though I wanted to be seen as just another soldier, I was not.

One day the colonel sent for me to meet him on the bank of a river just south of the bridge. He wanted to show me four Vietnamese bodies that had washed ashore during the night. The colonel was standing over the bodies, and he started asking me questions as I approached.

"Okay, Doc, how long have these NVA been dead? How old are they? Were they dead before they hit the water or did they drown?"

"How do you know they're NVA?" I asked.

"Too fucking fat and healthy looking to be VC. Short-ass haircuts. One of them had on fucking heavy cloth fatigue pants. Villagers said they never saw the cocksuckers before. Four young men found all at once, and nobody's missing from the ville. Shit! Do these guys stink. Fuck. Peasants probably caught the bastards stealing rice and killed their ass and threw 'em in the goddamn river. Or maybe . . ." He paused. "Hell, I'm the one s'posed to be asking the goddamn questions. Just examine the fuckers, Doc. Come to my tent when you finish." He walked back to his jeep and was gone.

Four naked, swollen, and waterlogged bodies lay side by side on their backs. Each had a massively swollen face. Eyes big as apples bulged out of their sockets. Lips were three times normal size. Each mouth was open and round like that of a fish, with a huge splitting tongue sticking out. Thin bloody fluid trickled from their nostrils.

Massive edema and rigor mortis held their arms up and out in front of them with fat fingers reaching toward the clouds. Their scrota were the size of softballs, and their swollen penises stood erect. Their knees were bent in identical frog-leg positions. The smell was overwhelming as hundreds of flies circled around them busily inspecting the mouths and nostrils. There was not a mark on the front of their bodies. I tried to turn one of them over, but he must have weighed several hundred pounds. My driver helped me flip one body over. Even facedown in the sand, the arms and legs did not change position. There were no signs of trauma on the body. I didn't bother to flip the others. I had to stand back because the smell was making me sick. I rinsed my hands in the river, walked back to the road, and leaned against the jeep. Several small children approached and began to throw rocks at the bodies and strike the bodies with sticks. The older ones yelled profanities in broken English for our benefit.

"Fuckin' NVA."

"VC, number ten."

"Fuckin' bastards."

The younger kids began to sing and chant as they skipped and danced in circles around the bodies, laughing and screaming as they struck at them. The villagers across the river ignored us all, living and dead. The bored marines standing watch on the nearby bridge paced back and forth. Several jeeps and troop transport trucks vibrated across the wooden bridge. A Vietnamese family passed by in a small boat, allowing the current to carry them toward the bridge. The kids continued their happy dance.

"How did they die?" asked my driver.

"I don't know," I said, "but I will invent a story that will make the CO's day."

Sometimes the patrols stayed out in the bush for days at a time. I only went with them when the colonel went. When he asked me to go, I was never sure if it was a request or an order. In any case, I always went, eager for the action but afraid for my life. Luckily or unluckily, nothing much happened. Once when I was helping to medevac a wounded marine, a bullet went through the aircraft immediately above my head. I was surprised how little noise it made—like a small wooden stick hitting an empty tin can.

Most of my understanding of life in the most dangerous situations came from talking to grunts. What I didn't learn in Triage, I learned just being in their presence in base camps, mostly listening to them talking to each other. When healthy, the grunts might ignore the "doc." Because I had no real authority over them, I tried to keep the lowest possible profile.

I began to sense that their willingness to kill grew over time. They were worn down and worked up because the enemy was everywhere, and gooks, dinks, and VC gradually came to seem less human. The chain of command became diluted and fuzzy, and as fatigue increased, the rules of engagement became less clear. The teenaged boys were trained to kill and had awesome firepower in their hands at all times. As tensions built, so did a vague pressure to act, if only to fight boredom or relieve anxiety. Sleep debt, fear, grime, hunger and thirst, sore feet, self-preservation, instinct, and covering your brother's ass dominated poorly stated missions. Killing sometimes followed for mixed reasons.

On another of my assignments the western perimeter of the camp bordered on a "free-fire zone." Anyone or anything that moved in that area could be shot, mortared, or bombed. The military maps had it marked as such, and supposedly all civilians in the nearby villes had been warned to stay clear of the area. Each morning at the same time, a large military truck lumbered fifty meters into the free-fire zone to dump garbage from the camp—food, broken equipment, tattered clothes, photos of girlfriends who had written Dear John letters, tin cans, cardboard containers, wrappers, and bottles.

The dump was a temptation the Vietnamese from the villes found impossible to resist. They hovered in the jungle nearby, watching, waiting for the truck to arrive. As soon as the truck left the site the Vietnamese would nervously scamper into the dump, picking through our garbage, collecting cans and leftover food items that to them were treasures and necessities.

At the edge of the base just inside the wire, there was a watchtower overlooking the dump. The platform, surrounded by two layers of sandbags, was about five meters aboveground. The marines assigned to the tower had free rein to shoot the looters in the dump. Over time they turned their assignment into a sick game. They used the villagers as target practice, competing with one another to see whose rifle shots could cause a villager to jump in fear, or who could shoot the closest to a villager's feet without hitting him or her. The loser sometimes shot off a foot or a leg by accident, or a ricochet maimed an accidental victim. Others, out of meanness, hatred, anger, desire to add a notch on their rifle, or just plain boredom, shot to kill.

I was restless and took every opportunity I had to roam around the base, and one day I went up onto the watchtower. I had never been there before and was having a cold coffee and a cigarette with three marines as the villagers scurried around below, nervously looking up at the tower.

One of the marines looked at me. He must have noticed the insignia on my collar that identified me as a physician. "Hey, Doc," he asked blankly, "you want to shoot someone? You ought to know what it's like to kill someone." Then, to justify the killing, he provided the logic behind the offer. "If we don't keep the gooks away from the dump, one of them could shoot a mortar round at the tower or onto the base, or plant a land mine and blow up the garbage truck. The only way to keep them away is to shoot 'em."

This particular marine had invented his own twisted stratagem to keep the dump safe. He figured out that no single approach worked for more than two to three days. If he used the same tactics every day, the peasants would figure it out and become accustomed to it.

So he worked randomly. No matter how many villagers were looting through the garbage, for a few days he would only fire warning shots. A few days of warning shots would be followed by a day of shooting extremities, then a day of kills, then maybe two days of extremities, one day of warning, and another two days of kills, a day of warnings and a day of kills and then another two days of extremities, and on and on. The Vietnamese never knew what day it was. It was like a lottery, only he controlled which ball came up, and when.

The marine saw my reluctance and bargained with me. "I tell you what, Doc. If you shoot a dink I promise that we'll make a special trip, go out and get him, and bring him back to you so you can fix him up."

I refused, and after finishing my cigarette and staring down into my coffee cup for a minute, I left the watchtower. Later, I learned that the marine had shot and killed a peasant. My refusal to wound a villager had resulted in a death sentence.

Another person wasted.

CHAPTER 9

I was assigned to the relative safety and comfort of several posts in the rear. For the first time in months, I was not living with grunts and I had free time. I learned that King Price had left Vietnam, and with him, so had my opportunity to take advantage of his offer to send me back early.

By this time I actually longed for a return to Triage. "Home" was not back in the United States with Joan and my children. "Home" was in Triage. There, lost in the embrace of blood and gore, I could convince myself I had a purpose and become too exhausted to contemplate my larger role in war. Now the absence of wounded and dead warriors gave me the mental space to examine my military mission. This became my most difficult time in the war. With no other purpose, in the rear I felt a duty to find meaning in the war so I could convince myself the dead had not died in vain. I looked for their sacrifice to give some authority to their death. I began to think their deaths had meaning only in the service of exposure of the truths of war. I wanted to go to a place where I could bear witness. That provided another reason to return to my USA home.

In the bush I was more aware of grunts humping in and out every day to kill or be killed, and I was afraid of Vietnamese I couldn't see. In the rear I was less afraid of the Vietnamese people but was constantly reminded of the magnitude of our war machine. I was safe, but only physically safe. It was great to be away from the incoming artillery at Dong Ha or mortars in the field. Occasionally enemy mortar teams managed to slip in close enough to shell my posts in the rear. That was unusual but still disconcerting. To discourage enemy artillery, some of the large military bases had been purposely positioned next to small villes. The marines, who were sure they would know if NVA regulars were in their immediate vicinity, were convinced that incoming mortar shells came from the local Vietnamese peasants, rice farmers, our own Vietnamese labor force, or ARVN-by-day-VC-by-night warriors. Regardless, my multiple assignments in the rear were much safer than my previous posts.

Everybody got up early and seemed busy doing something. Everyone had a job, a fixed assignment. Messengers walked around carrying messages. Drivers were always waiting for somebody or driving them somewhere. Helicopters flew in from somewhere and left again. Soldiers were concerned about polished boots, salutes, rank, regular work hours, and clean bodies. There were more jokes, laughs, free time, alcohol, hot showers, paperback books, clean T-shirts, and clean socks. Mealtime was longer, with more conversation and better food. The PX was like a mall; a warrior could buy toiletries, super sudsy detergents, movie magazines, scented stationery, condoms, cigarettes, cheap cameras, collar insignias, coconut-scented sunscreens, and souvenirs.

In the rear there was definitely more use of drugs, especially marijuana, by the enlisted men. At the front a marine caught smoking grass on watch was likely to get the shit kicked out of him by his own colleagues. No such reaction occurred in the rear. In fact, there seemed to be peer pressure to use drugs. Nevertheless, I saw only a few men stoned beyond the ability to function while on duty.

My official job with some of these rear elements was boring and uninspiring. Sick call was sometimes my only job, an ever-present line of penile drip, snotty noses, fevers, and skin infections. Patients were logged in and seen only at certain times, some by appointment. They even read old magazines and bitched about how long they had to wait. The population was older. Headaches, chest pain, and back pain were the most common maladies among a variety of other nonspecific complaints. Sometimes I even saw the same patient more than once. I actually knew if they got better or worse. I even had my share of problem patients who didn't get better—or didn't want to—but kept making appointments anyway. Like the general practitioner back home, I had repeating "pain-in-the-ass" patients.

While the kill-or-be-killed mentality saturated the minds of many soldiers in the field, for many of the noncombatants in the rear, the war could have been on TV or a movie screen. They bartered, smoked, and talked through a routine each day and tried not to confront the war directly. Still their war exacted a price. They suffered from a kind of smothering boredom and loss of purpose. Unlike the grunts in the boonies, their lives were not made more meaningful by being inserted between orgies of complete animal fear, human violence, and powerful camaraderie with other warriors. In the rear some felt that the price of survival was the lack of real affection, nobility, and the opportunity for heroism. There were no emotional peaks of fear, anger, and hate, just a daily accounting of the passage of time.

In addition to military rank, there was another unspoken pecking order, and everyone knew it. Even FNGs in the rear quickly became expert at figuring out who among their peers had been in combat and who had permanent support roles in the rear. Subtle body decorations, ways of moving and behaving, and displays of dominance and toughness all carried powerful messages. Those recently immersed in battle had a rapidly evolving slang used as a secret language.

The soldiers in the field referred to those with permanent noncombat support positions, especially those who were a decade or more older and of higher rank than the grunts, as REMFs, which stood for rear-echelon motherfuckers. REMFs and combat soldiers were occasionally openly hostile to one another, but at some deeper level they respected their mutual dependence. Despite the increased danger in the field, or because of it, neither really wanted to be the other, and in that they were both alike.

Sometimes the contrast between the minimalist existence of grunts in the field and the comparatively luxurious life of soldiers a few miles back seemed absurd, but soldiers accepted it. It was as if they had been born into a caste system they could complain about but were powerless to change. Some of the professional REMFs believed the grunts in the field deserved to suffer because they were not smart enough or clever enough to work the system and maneuver themselves into a permanent noncombat support position in the war machine. At the same time, they felt a subtle, unspoken jealousy of every grunt who had killed or barely survived. The REMFs would return home with no authentic war stories to tell.

In the rear, my runs were long and hard. I kept an uncomfortably fast pace and ran well beyond pain, nausea, and dizziness. Depending on my assessment of the "dress code" of the post, my garb ranged from boots, socks, and shorts only to the addition of jungle fatigue pants, a belt, and a green T-shirt. I never carried a canteen or salt pills. I ran until my knees, lower back, and heels throbbed and cramps crippled me. Occasional tears and moans were hidden by sweat and grunts. I wanted my physical pain to exceed, expel, or justify my psychic pain, existential depression, and loneliness. I tried to time my runs so that when I did surrender to pain and exhaustion, I would be forced to walk a long way back to my hooch. Sunburn, overexertion, high body temperature, and solar-heat load triggered chills and disequilibrium as I tried not to stumble, stagger, or fall on my way back.

Travel was more easily available to me during some assignments in the rear. I jumped at almost any reason to go almost anywhere, to do anything, to check on something, to deliver something, to pick up some supplies, to instruct corpsmen about snakebites, to talk to troops about malaria pills. I knew that I could die any second, even in the most "protected" places in Vietnam, and it occurred to me that moving about I Corps was more dangerous than staying in one place. I managed to make several trips to Da Nang to visit the navy hospital. At least that was the excuse I used.

One day when I was back in Dong Ha working in Triage a friend of mine, a helicopter pilot, came in to help carry a wounded person. As he was leaving to run back to his helicopter he said, "Oh, by the way, Xuân says hello." I ran after him and found out she had survived the Tet Offensive and was in Da Nang. He had run into her at one of the Enlisted Men's Clubs working as a bar girl.

During my next assignment in the rear, I gave myself permission to go to Da Nang, telling the CO I needed to pick up something or check on something. In some posts I had the freedom to "hitchhike" anywhere. At any time I could just hop on a helicopter and leave. To me, it didn't matter what kind of craft. I rode in all sorts of choppers, from tiny observation bubbles to attack helicopters and flying cranes known as Jolly Green Giants, but most of my trips were in old, rattling Hueys. Flying at a hundred to a thousand feet, it was unnerving to see how abruptly and often the scenery changed from typical U.S. military "property" to open country, jungles, rice paddies, and villages and then back to a military base. There were numerous wasted, defoliated strips of land hundreds of meters wide filled with craters.

While riding in helicopters, I was always afraid of being sniped at from the ground. In most places, we had the air, and the enemy had the underground via an extensive network of tunnels. Exact ownership of the land was always uncertain. In open country, we had the day, and the enemy had the night. That was part of the attraction. Being on the helicopter, vulnerable to the enemy, put all my synapses on high alert.

I found Xuân. She had managed to stay hidden during the peak of the battle for Hue, then had fled to Da Nang. I stayed overnight in her small house with her two young children and an old woman housekeeper. In the middle of the night an angry group of Vietnamese men came to her door and had a loud argument with Xuân as I hid inside. She never told me why they were so angry or what they wanted, but I felt I had put her in danger. Another time we stayed in a hotel, but that night Da Nang came under a rare mortar attack and I spent much of the night hiding under the bed—not because it offered protection from shrapnel but because people were running up and down the halls and knocking on doors. For the second time during my tour, I put a clip in my .45. Nothing happened.

I visited Xuân several times over two or three months and then chose to say good-bye. It was too dangerous for me to walk the streets of Da Nang alone, and my ability to travel was always unpredictable. Besides, DEROS was only a few months away, and I was starting to believe I had another life and another home in America. Whenever I visited Xuân, we always knew it might be the last time we saw one another. In the unpredictable time of war nothing was certain but, paradoxically, all things seemed possible. It was always easier to assume we would meet again. It was a very painful experience for both us when I told her I chose not to find her ever again. She was very hurt and sad but did not ask me to change my mind. For weeks I dealt with my own sorrow by fantasizing about going to find her one more time. I never did. I later learned that Xuân (I pronounced it "Soon") was a nom de guerre for her work with Americans. I never knew her real name. As much as possible, I decided to spend the rest of my time in Vietnam in "America," staying on U.S. military bases surrounded by Cokes, beers, mess halls, and marines. White men and black men. No women. No Vietnamese people unless they were wounded by American weapons. Xuân made things easy and bravely let me go.

When I was assigned to Headquarters Battalion, I lived in a hooch with two lawyers, bright young career military officers, educated at government expense. They were kept busy with cases of marine killing marine, marine killing civilian, marine raping civilian, and a variety of military legal issues. The marines in the rear had more time to get VD, use drugs, and have fistfights and racial brawls. Sometimes, when a nineteen-year-old bundle of frustration happened to be carrying his weapon and got angry after too many beers, he shot somebody.

At my insistence the lawyers discussed the technical, social, and

legal distinctions between murder and war. They dazzled me with ter-
minology and legal justification of waging war. The complex but specific categorization, protocol, documentation, and careful scholarship
of murder contrasted with the ambiguity and vagueness of decisions to
go to war for abstract economic, political, or intellectual reasons. The
pathways and precision of accountability, blame, and punishment were
very different.

For my lawyer hoochmates, it was clear and simple. By social contract, the state is given the right to kill its own citizens through capital
punishment and to kill soldiers and citizens of other nations by declaration of war or "police action." Even in peacetime, the right to kill can
be granted to guards if a "lethal force authorized" sign is posted on U.S.
soil in sites of high importance for national security. Conscription can
be used to press citizens into serving in the national killing machine.
Individuals cannot kidnap others, but the state can imprison criminals
and crazy people and draft soldiers into service.

I learned that in civilian law all deaths are neatly classified as natural, accidental, and homicide or suicide. For "natural" deaths a physician
can determine cause. For others a coroner must decide the appropriate category and cause of death. The lawyers had differing ethical
opinions but agreed that, legally, murder and war were different because the state had the right to kill outsiders or its own citizens. Unless
wearing a uniform, citizens did not.

The lawyers divided the moral reality of war into two parts. War is
judged twice: First with reference to the reasons states have for fighting, the "justice of war" (*jus ad bellum*), and second with reference to
the means adopted to fight the war, "justice in war" (*jus in bello*). However, they added, war lies beyond (or beneath) moral judgment. Categories of right and wrong do not apply when life itself is at stake and
human nature is reduced to its most primitive form. Self-interest
and necessity lead people to do what they must to save themselves and
their communities. "In time of war, the law is silent," they said in
English and Latin. "All's fair in love and war" is a dictum that has generated centuries of arguments about moral behavior and human nature.

They claimed it was too early to apply theories of just warfare to Vietnam. I wanted to suggest they talk to a few grunts, but I didn't say it.

We had long, abstract discussions about "rules of engagement," "laws of war," and "limited war." The lawyers explained that setting limits to armed conflict reinforced the principle that the aim of warfare is to incapacitate the armed forces of the enemy and not to cause severe, indiscriminate suffering among combatants and civilians alike. They were not sure how that applied to Vietnam either.

The lawyers were curious about the legal aspects of the role of the physician in war. I reminded them that Hippocrates' second most famous saying was "He who wishes to be a surgeon should go to war."

While assigned to HQ I was ordered to be an "expert witness" in a murder trial. A sergeant had killed one of his unarmed men by shooting him in the chest at close range. He claimed self-defense because of the threatening words and gestures used by the boy. I was asked a few questions about how the size of entry wounds normally compare to size of exit wounds. To me, these questions and my answers had no real bearing or influence on the case. After many accounts from witnesses, diagrams, angle of fire studies, and descriptions of wounds, the sergeant was found not guilty of first-degree murder but was to face possible court-martial on other charges.

My easiest assignment was with the rear elements of the Reconnaissance Unit, the Special Forces of the Marine Corps. These men were the toughest of the tough, the leanest and meanest, and were highly trained in the skills of survival and the art of killing. When I was with them they were waiting between missions. Few of these men ever came to sick call. Those who did had usually been treated (or mistreated) by a corpsman because they had made it a point of honor not to seek my help.

Listening to their abusive banter or stories of their most dangerous missions, coupled with the stern and stoic quietness that some projected, made me realize once again real life was out in the jungle, the rice paddies, the rivers, and the mountains. The important things were behind enemy lines and in forbidden places in the field. The enemy—"Charlie"—was there to be spied upon, avoided, fooled, killed if necessary, but he was only a part of the picture. "Out there" the Special Forces were against the whole world. They had to conquer the elements, the enemy, and their own fears and come back alive.

The more severe the test, the better they liked it. Barely making it back was a victory. Barely making it back and being ready to go again was a greater victory. Making it back and *wanting* to go back again, greater still. I saw two men fight over who was to be the last member of a behind-the-line helicopter drop. As punishment for fighting, neither was allowed to go. They left for the chow line with arms around each other's shoulders, consoling one another for their poor judgment and bad fortune, pissed off that on that day neither would have another chance to cheat death.

Many of these men were in their second or third tour in Vietnam. Some said they would stay until the war was over. Driven to test their physical and emotional discipline, addicted to the hunt and kill and intense focus on survival, they wanted no other life. This special sauce was seasoned with varying amounts of patriotism or an overall sense of American war goals.

The most powerful war stories I heard in Vietnam came from these soldiers in their second or third tour. They used their stories to track their own changing values and attitudes. They could poke fun at the disintegration of their idealism. They could give examples of the loss of their framework of social order. They could speak with authority about alienation from former friends, families, neighbors, and classmates at home. They could speak with shame of the breakdown in their own character and demonstrate with pride the correlating loss of all sensibilities and sensitivities, except for their overwhelming will to survive and acquire the skills they needed to do so.

Many of these men had not signed up for repeat tours until after they had been back in the States for a time. One marine in his second tour told me that after his first tour, nothing seemed important. "I mean like *nothing*," he said. "My job, my paycheck, school, my friends. Nothing. Here, in Nam, *everything* is important. I mean it's important as hell if you wear your helmet or not. An untied bootlace can kill you. It's important where you sleep, when you sleep, who's next to you, and who's awake while you sleep. It's important how and where I walk, when I eat and how much. My job here is important. And my buddies really need me." Another marine told me, "Back home nothing I did was important. I was seen as a piece of shit doing shit jobs. Here in the bush every little fucking thing is important as hell."

In the rear I began to realize that people in the United States knew more about the war than I did. I might have known more about individual inside glimpses of the war, but they saw the bigger picture. For instance, every day I had treated marines who had been in Khe Sanh just minutes before. I knew of their wounds and causes of death. I knew details about the atrocious conditions of their underground lives. I knew that large black rats would gnaw at any exposed flesh, making a stinking mess of the dead and producing nasty sores on the living. I knew that at night the marines could hear the enemy digging trenches closer and closer to their perimeter. I knew that the chronic fear of the impending "final assault" that never came alternated with the extreme boredom of an entirely underground life, coupled with burning panic when it was time to go aboveground to gather supplies from an airdrop or carry wounded and dead to a helicopter.

Of the larger plan, the "why" of the battle, I knew nothing. From newly arriving American troops I discovered that the average citizen in America actually knew much more about the siege of Khe Sanh than I did. Back home, Joan could see diagrams of the base and TV footage of supply airplanes landing and taking off. In her mother's living room in Florida, she could hear expert opinions and keep track of the exact number of dead and wounded, the tonnage of bombs, and the positions of the enemy. She knew that the firepower unleashed on the NVA in Khe Sanh in the spring of 1968 was five times greater than the explosive power of the atomic bomb dropped on Hiroshima. Joan knew that by late March the artillery and napalm had eliminated all the jungle growth and life from the hills, leaving only a barren, ugly landscape and nowhere for the NVA to hide. After horrendous losses, estimated at ten to fifteen thousand dead, the NVA retreated. My parents knew that by leapfrogging airmobile operations and carefully placed artillery, on April 6, 1968, the air cavalry met up with relief marines moving along the road to Khe Sanh. Then the remaining NVA disappeared, and the battle for Khe Sanh was over.

Three months after this protracted and horrific battle, Khe Sanh was abandoned. Without fanfare the marines destroyed, bulldozed, blew up, burned, and leveled the base. In a few hours the marines did to Khe Sanh what the NVA could not do in seventy-seven days. The only thing the marines left at Khe Sanh was an abandoned airstrip that was too difficult to dismantle. Six hundred marines had died. Only 1,600 NVA bodies were found because most were carried away into the jungle or completely blown away. Then Khe Sanh was officially declared worthless, not worth defending, of no military significance, strategically unimportant.

I didn't know any of that at the time. I was caring for the wounded. Later I would wonder who decided Khe Sanh was not of military value and why the analysis could not have been made about six hundred marines earlier, or one hundred marines earlier. Or even one marine earlier.

Toward the end of my tour, one of the engineers learned how to get network news from British and U.S. television and an English-language radio station in Tokyo. Now I could sit in the middle of a war, have a beer, and chow down on facts, figures, diagrams, and political commentary. Immersed in a war machine, I had access to stateside information: reports, essays, editorials, and speeches by opinion leaders. At one point, as I sat in an intelligence officer's air-conditioned trailer, we watched live television coverage of a helicopter assault on an "unfriendly" village only a few hundred meters away.

One day in a desk drawer I found a handwritten statement:

FINISHED WITH THE WAR:
A SOLDIER'S DECLARATION

I am making this statement as an act of willful defiance of military authority, because I believe the war is being deliberately prolonged by those who have the power to end it.

I am a soldier, convinced that I am acting on behalf of soldiers. I believe that this war, upon which I entered as a war of defense and liberation, has now become a war of aggression and conquest. I believe that the purposes for which I and my fellow soldiers entered upon this war should have been so clearly stated as to have made it impossible to change them, and that, had this been done, the objects which actuated us would now be attainable by negotiation.

I have seen and endured the suffering of the troops, and I can no longer be a party to prolong these sufferings for ends which I believe to be evil and unjust.

I am not protesting against the conduct of the war, but against the political errors and insincerities for which the fighting men are being sacrificed.

On behalf of those who are suffering now I make this protest against the deception which is being practiced on them; also I believe that I may help to destroy the callous complacence with which the majority of those at home regard the continuance of agonies which they do not share, and which they have not sufficient imagination to realize.

My first thought was that this declaration had been written by the doctor I was replacing or found by him on the body of a marine. But I noticed the date and author also handwritten on the bottom of the page, "S. Sassoon, July 1917." This handwritten declaration was well worn, but it was not fifty years old. Someone had copied it and placed it in the collection of literature in the desk drawer. I copied it into my notebook and learned later that Siegfried Sassoon was a British soldier and poet during World War I.

I thought a great deal about King's offer to send me home after my first few weeks in Vietnam. Had he made me that offer because I seemed excessively vulnerable, or because he knew I would refuse? Was the proposition King's way of being extremely intimate by penetrating the very core of my manhood?

I began to wonder how many more days I had left before I became a psychiatric casualty. Could I be so cushioned with R&R, trips to Hue, beer, and dreams of DEROS, as well as my precious sense of righteous mission, that I would deter or, at least, defer my own form of combat fatigue? Would emotional collapse come before or after I was taken home? Maybe it would be better for me to collapse in situ and be removed from this place. Was I propping myself up for too long—long enough to be scarred deeply, perhaps forever? Should I have taken King up on his offer of a no-questions-asked psychiatric medevac?

Being in new groups every fifteen to twenty days, I had little chance to build the trust and confidence it took for me to participate in deep sharing with men. I had never felt as lonely as I did in the middle of a large military compound in Vietnam surrounded by the marines I was supposed to keep healthy enough to stay at war.

Once on my return to Dong Ha, I discovered my desk overturned and my books and gear all over the room. I picked up my chair, sat at my desk, and looked around at the mess. Just in front of me, directly opposite my desk chair in the wall of the hooch, were two large shrapnel holes—one chest high, the other head high. Two or three days later while I was assisting in surgery, a shell hit just outside the OR and sent shrapnel ripping through the walls and ceiling. We pulled the unconscious marine onto the floor and, as the surgeon, the anesthesiologist, and I lay on the ground, continued the operation. The shelling continued, shaking the ground, and shrapnel passed through the OR several more times.

Despite the danger, I was both unsettled and relieved each time I went back to my triage duties in Dong Ha. I needed my smaller righteous mission in Dong Ha to save me from thinking of my personal responsibilities. I needed to fight the war by saving people who were killing people. Yet each time I returned to Dong Ha, I was overwhelmed by how all things seemed to be the same. The stream of casualties was a never-ending river of waste and destruction. Nothing was different. There was no sign of progress and no evidence of winning. Nothing had changed since I began this war a lifetime ago. The wounded soldiers were there whether I was there or not.

The marines in Graves Registration worked on. Washing, tagging, and bagging. In Dong Ha they did not seem to require any doctor's signature for their activities. Why, then, in Phu Bai, did I go by Graves each morning to sign forms? Had all my morning trips to Graves in Phu Bai been a ritual made up by me? By the marines in Graves? One advantage of Dong Ha was that there was less time to think such morbid or transcendental thoughts. There is nothing like an endless supply of casualties arriving singly or in groups to keep one focused on the specific needs of others. I buried myself in work.

In Dong Ha, each day I was not overwhelmed caring for wounded, I went for a run. I wore a rotten pair of shorts, sweat socks, jungle boots, sunglasses, and dog tags, but no flak jacket, uniform, or hat. For those few moments I needed to sweat and hurt and leave myself vulnerable to attack. Although I could always hear a helicopter approaching, for those few moments I was not available to the dead and wounded. In the midst of risk I was safe from horror and responsibility. Yet as soon as I heard a helicopter I would turn and run straight for Triage, hoping that by the time I arrived, I was not needed.

During one very early morning run I heard a helicopter approach. Although it took me several minutes to get to Triage, I was surprised to find it empty. The doctors who had automatically stumbled out of their hooches when they heard the chopper had all returned to bed when they found that there was no one to treat.

I saw a Vietnamese woman standing alone in the center of the helicopter pad. She was holding a baby in her arms. The naked baby had a small hole in his abdomen and was dead. I approached the woman and tried to explain to her that we could not help. The woman pleaded with me and tried to hand me her baby. She seemed to expect me to restore life to the child. Surely the Americans with their jets, magic operating rooms, and scientific weapons of destruction could fix one small baby. She was very insistent.

We moved to the edge of the helicopter pad. Should I pretend to try to help the baby? I wondered if a few hours of food and safety would help the woman. She could not stay on the base. Should I send her baby to Graves? I told her repeatedly in Vietnamese that I was sorry. She did not understand me—or understood but did not believe me. She did not know where she was and had no way of getting back to her own ville. She stood stranded with her dead baby in the middle of America, probably miles from her ville, without food, money, transportation, family, friends, or sympathy.

Why had she been brought to us by helicopter? Who killed her baby? Should we add the baby to our body count? Had brave American soldiers risked their lives to save the woman and her village from the hands of the enemy? Or had tired, frightened, confused, and hate-filled American boys burned her village, raped her daughters, and killed her child? In this war the baby might have been wounded while the ville was being liberated by the VC or from the VC, or while the allied forces were shelling it. This woman could not begin to understand these things. Neither could I.

I wanted to go home, but I also wanted to stay in Vietnam forever and work all day, every day in Triage. If I could not stop the process, maybe I could do damage control. Still, I realized I could not make a difference. I could be replaced. Someday I would be replaced. Nothing I did could stop the flow of casualties and destruction. I could do nothing to stop the war, but each time I returned to the rear, I felt I was abandoning wounded soldiers, and new demons came to get me. I began to realize that a part of me would remain in Vietnam forever, and another part would die there. Outside the war zone I no longer knew who I was.

As DEROS approached, I gradually recognized just how much I was using emotional distancing and psychic numbing to survive, how much I had integrated the notion "Protect yourself at all times." I had come to Vietnam as a soft man, sensitive, insecure, and uncertain. Now I was becoming very hard. I was no longer crushed when we put soldiers to sleep in the operating rooms and they did not wake up. Now, when I was awakened in the middle of the night to see a casualty, I was relieved to discover that he was already dead; I could go back to sleep.

My departure from war was as sudden as my entry. DEROS arrived. One day in Dong Ha after the wounded were unloaded from a helicopter, I became the doctor that got on the helicopter and was flown to Da Nang Airport. Once there I boarded a commercial airline for the United States, not knowing a single person on the plane. I was a stranger.

BOOK THREE

THE GOOD DOCTOR

CHAPTER 10

As soon as the plane left the runway in Da Nang, a spontaneous cheer went up among the passengers, uniformed soldiers like myself who had finally found their salvation in DEROS. Perfect American round-eyed stewardesses began to serve drinks; they still had to check IDs to make sure each soldier was old enough to have alcohol. No matter what one had done in Vietnam, if one was underage on the airplane, no drinks.

I don't remember much about the flight or the return trip to America. It was too jarring and disconnecting, and I was still thinking about the casualties that had been left behind. I could still see the injured soldiers being carried into Triage. Five minutes earlier I was the one responsible for stopping the bleeding, for stanching the war, if only in the body of one soldier. Now it was someone else's job. As I had been, the new doctors would be inexperienced. By this time I had treated over a thousand wounded warriors, and my skill and self-confidence had grown significantly.

Although happy to be leaving, I was abandoning my responsibilities. I was escaping and felt guilty. It didn't help that I was alone. In earlier wars, such as World War II and Korea, soldiers went to war as a group and returned as a group, often by boat. They spent time with each other and had a chance to talk each other down and adjust. In

Vietnam we were sent to war as individuals and came back as individuals, traveling by jet, with no transition time. I received no debriefing of any kind and was given no opportunity to decompress. No one else on the plane knew what I had done during the war, and I had no idea what anyone else on the plane had done. People stayed in their own heads.

This time my stay in Okinawa was very brief, with barely enough time to get my dress khakis out of storage, where they had been for a year. I threw away my jungle fatigues but kept my jungle boots, planning never to part with them. I caught another commercial flight to Travis Air Force Base outside San Francisco. No one acknowledged our arrival. We individually found our ways off the base to join or contact family members. My orders told me to report to Oak Knoll Naval Hospital in Oakland, California, in fifteen days. Suddenly a free man, I got a ride with another solider into San Francisco.

While I had been in Vietnam, Joan sent me a letter several times a week. Because mail delivery was inconsistent, I sometimes got two or three letters at once. Depending on how busy I was, I would write once or twice a week. I usually had nothing much to say. Our plans were for me to get a hotel in San Francisco and for Joan to leave the girls behind and come spend a few days with me before we went back to Florida to see the girls and my parents and the rest of our families.

In dress khakis, my seabag over my shoulder, I went to one hotel after another, asking for a room. I planned to call Joan and tell her to fly out as soon as I found one, but no matter where I went the clerk always had some excuse—"I'm sorry, but we're all full . . . Sorry, we just booked our last room . . . Sorry, no vacancy." No one was really impolite, but I thought it was strange that there didn't seem to be a vacant hotel room in all of San Francisco.

Finally, about the third or fourth time I was turned away, a doorman took me aside. "Listen, buddy," he said, "let me give you a hint. As long as you're wearing that uniform in this city, you're not gonna get a room." It was my military uniform and Vietnam medals that made me an unwelcome guest. The doorman was not defending that stance, or telling me that was how he felt. He was just telling me what was happening.

I was shocked. Before that moment the Chicago riots, the antiwar protests of the flower children and the students, the civil rights marches, and the hardening of American attitudes about the war had all been little more than puzzling newspaper clippings to me. I was completely unprepared for what that meant in reality: the indifference, the fear, and the outright hostility toward men in uniform that many Americans now felt. Of course I had noticed the hippies who were seemingly everywhere, but only now did it strike me just how much things had changed.

I realized I was returning to a much different country than the one I had left only one year before. In Vietnam my military uniform was commonplace, and as an officer and doctor I was respected and valued. In my head I had played out Hollywood movie scenes of the brave, war-torn returning hero. Now that I was really back my uniform was the object of scorn and repulsion. In actual fact, I was treated like a contaminated being—Vietnam veterans were beginning to be seen as baby killers, people who had been complicit in a war that was not only unpopular but was seen as something evil. I also knew I was broken in ways I could not yet understand.

Without putting down my seabag, I went to the San Francisco airport to fly to Miami. All the flights were booked, so I had to fly standby, and each time a civilian was added to the list, my name was dropped farther down. It took more than twenty-four hours to get a flight. When I finally arrived in Miami and Joan met me at the airport, I had a massive headache and major jet lag, and I was angry and exhausted, unable to show emotion or affect. I sensed soft relief, vague comfort, a fragile sense of safety, and a quiet joy, and nothing else. The demonstrative celebratory thrill I had imagined was lost forever, and I no longer cared.

Nothing seemed real. My girls, one and three years old when I left, two and four when I returned, didn't recognize me and hid behind their mother. "That's not my dad," Susan insisted. Lynn clung to Joan, looking at the floor, refusing to make eye contact.

I took a long hot shower, clumsily made love to Joan, and slept for more than eighteen hours. When I woke, the girls had gone to bed. Unshaven and groggy, I joined Joan and her parents at the dinner table. Joan's father was intoxicated, and her mother could not stop talking about every random and trivial thought that came into her head. Joan's parents and later my parents tried to bridge my lost year by talking about recent events and offering color commentary on family news. The topics seemed arbitrary and meaningless to me. Now that I was completely surrounded by the civilian world, I felt socially ill at ease. I volunteered nothing about the war, and everyone was careful not to ask. We all talked around it, as if I had never been there.

After a week of being treated as a guest by family, I drove Joan and the girls cross-country in our ten-year-old Chevy station wagon and reported to my stateside assignment at Oak Knoll Naval Hospital. I had another year left to serve.

In a military setting, living in a small apartment, serving with military doctors and still taking care of troops and their families, I had time to think and rebuild my social skills. The process of reintegration was slow and laborious. I had returned to a country that had profoundly changed, to a wife I no longer knew, and to children who did not recognize me.

At the navy hospital I was somewhat shielded from how much American attitudes toward the war had changed. Except on the weekends, I wasn't a part of the greater society, but I was curious. Dressed in civilian clothes I occasionally took Joan and the girls into San Francisco. We walked the streets in Haight-Ashbury or picnicked in Golden Gate Park, where I was shocked to see antiwar demonstrations, topless women, drugs and sex and rock 'n' roll. The air smelled like marijuana, and amateur musicians in carefully tattered clothes were everywhere. I thought it was interesting and titillating, but I didn't feel involved.

I was older than the joyous dancers and still hadn't processed my experience enough to be overtly sympathetic with the antiwar movement and the flower people. As much as I hated the war and knew how much damage it was doing, when I had first heard about the protests and marches while I was in Vietnam, I'd had mixed feelings. I was in survival mode. Instead of sending the troops home I wanted to keep as many healthy marines around me as possible. Now that I was back, part of me was still in Vietnam—and, unless disguised in civilian clothes, I was a target for the anger of the flower people. My short hair raised suspicion. Joan and I didn't talk about politics. I knew she was liberal and against the Vietnam War and militarism and what she considered the over-the-top nationalism and patriotic arrogance of our country. I really didn't know what I thought. Fortunately, Joan was tolerant of the inconsistency and confusion in my attitudes and thinking.

Besides, I was still a soldier. The demonstrators protested me. Watching the war on the news between commercials made me furious, and I would nearly go berserk thinking about the disproportionalities of killing. To throw a human into a fire is murder and the killer is held accountable. To rain down fire from scary fast-moving helicopters or from invisible giant bombers on thousands of civilians is foreign policy and the killers are called patriots or heroes.

For days the newspapers, radio, and TV covered the disappearance of a boy who was thought to have been kidnapped or murdered. There were all-night vigils. Hundreds of volunteers searching. Touching interviews. Angry protests. A cause to pause. A call to reexamine our values. Make our neighborhoods safe. Stop violence in the home. Everybody was involved and upset. At work people said how sad and awful it was. They were shocked, depressed, distracted from their duties.

I followed the drama around the scheduled execution of a man who kidnapped, raped, and shot a mother of two young children. In the media there were long debates about the wisdom, justice, effectiveness, morality, humaneness, and humanness of capital punishment. More vigils, placards, protests, and talk shows discussing a planned, organized killing by the government.

In Texas, a man on death row tried to commit suicide by hanging himself. He was not successful and remained near death for weeks in the intensive care unit of an academic health center. The state was determined to keep him alive to be transferred back to prison for his sanctioned execution, which took place only a few days behind schedule.

Each day I was at work in the navy hospital, our government sponsored the killing of fifty to seventy Vietnamese soldiers, used bombs to kill two or three hundred civilians, and positioned twenty to thirty American boys to die. Were the drafted boys kidnapped? Could the president declare a stay of execution for the thirty American boys who were to be killed tomorrow?

The killing in Vietnam was highly organized and sanctioned. It was far away and easy to ignore. If I could have found my voice I could have tried to explain the sadness and waste and horror surrounding the death of each soldier. Once the killing was classified as "war," it was removed from our common morality. It's not a part of us; it is less tragic and horrible. In fact, it may be brave, romantic, and patriotic.

I was still a part of the war machine. Every day I put on my uniform, and Joan and the girls drove me to work at the navy hospital. I was a REMF.

In California, mentally and spiritually, I was still motivated by trying to take care of wounded soldiers, but I had no responsibility for soldiers with physical wounds. During my time at Oak Knoll Naval Hospital I was assigned to several outpatient clinics, spending three or four months each in general practice, internal medicine, and dermatology. I rarely treated a soldier who had been in Vietnam or had been wounded. Even then, I never saw them for their war trauma. My primary responsibility was to take care of stateside sailors and their wives and children.

This was my first experience working in a free medical care environment. All military and civilian personnel and their families could be seen by a physician on the base any time of day or night. Compared to the busy, tense, hyperactive, high-pressure inpatient wards at University Hospital before the war, and my experiences in Triage, where

I had spent most of the past year trying to save lives, my work in the clinics was boring and completely unchallenging. I felt abused by bored housewives complaining about their vague back pains and headaches. I saw some of them as entitled, dependent, and lazy. In the internal medicine clinic, I would recommend a change of diet and prescribe blood pressure meds, monitor blood sugar, pass out Maalox, and diagnose morning sickness, fatigue, obesity, and a hundred other minor treatable real and unreal maladies. Serious or unusual problems were rare.

To get through each day I gave myself a cynical, self-directed challenge: "Today you will see forty to fifty patients in the morning and another forty to fifty in the afternoon. Several of them may be sick. Your assignment, should you choose to accept this mission, is to be nice to all of them and find the sick ones." When I finished a day at the hospital and returned to my tiny apartment, Joan would hand me a beer as I passed by on my way to our tiny six-by-twelve backyard to drink in silence. Then, after ten or fifteen minutes, I would be joined by Joan and the girls, and our California evening would begin. Despite the fact that for the first time in a year I was safe and working a normal 9:00-to-4:30 shift, surrounded by my family and the California sun, with all the benefits of living stateside, I felt out of place, distant, remote, and useless.

There was no crowd of vets that got together to rehash our experience or tell war stories. The doctors I encountered at Oak Knoll had not been to Vietnam. They were either drafted civilians who had been stationed stateside or assigned to a ship stationed in a U.S. port, or they were career military who were able to avoid going to Vietnam.

Although I had little direct contact with returning soldiers, I was still able to witness an endless line of casualties arrive from Vietnam, this time from the vantage point of serving close to the end of our well-organized medical evacuation system. The sick and the wounded I had treated in the field and then sent away had gone to hospitals in Da Nang and Saigon for further evaluations and then were flown to other facilities in Japan or the Philippines to be sorted out again.

Soldiers that could be repaired easily were kept in the hospital until they were healthy and rested. Then they were returned to active duty in the war zone. The severely damaged soldiers were disposable—their replacements were already on the way, draft cards in hand. When they were healthy enough to travel they were returned to the United States for further care, reassignment, or discharge from military service. The dead were bagged and shipped to their families.

Each day at Oak Knoll a large, specially rigged bus carrying casualties who had just flown in backed up to an outdoor loading platform. Corpsmen unloaded the litters bearing the wounded soldiers onto the cement floor like so much cargo. There was absolutely no hurry or urgency. The casualties were all awake, clean-shaven, dressed in clean blue pajamas, and relatively comfortable. They were clean and there was no blood.

A medical officer examined each casualty and decided which ward was most appropriate for continued care. No family or friends were present when they arrived. Families would be notified, but many could not travel to California to see their now armless or legless sons. As they were carried off the plane, loaded onto the buses, and then unloaded and sent off to the various wards, there was no fanfare. No band played a patriotic song; no color guard stood at attention; no military brass or CO shook their hand, thanked them for their service, or welcomed them back with a speech.

Nothing much was said at all. They slipped into the country almost unnoticed, as if they represented some embarrassing indiscretion. At the hospital loading and receiving dock, they were human freight to be sorted and sent on their way.

Even when the soldiers reached the ward, and their pain did not suddenly disappear and legs and arms did not regrow, they remained relatively quiet. Most were over the initial shock of being wounded, and most were well on their way to resignation. For many, though, whether they knew it or not, their war wasn't over. It continued and it was personal. It would not end in 365 days. It might never end.

It took me many months to let go of being constantly angry and sad that the line of wounded continued. Week by week I slowly shed the constant dread of impending overwhelming responsibilities. My rhythm of living changed, and I was free every day at 4:30 P.M. and all weekends. The air did not smell like a mixture of buffalo shit, body odor, diesel fuel, dirt, and grass. There were no helicopters, outgoing, incoming, snakes, mud, mangled bodies, and dead teenagers. I was not afraid of people who did not wear military uniforms. I never discovered brains under my fingernails.

I felt safe, and I committed my newly found energy to re-creating a relationship with Joan and my children. I deliberately tried not to think of (and certainly never spoke of) Triage, personal fear, Xuân, R&R, or my massive grief.

I loved my adorable girls, but when I was with them alone I felt more like a babysitter than a father. I did not exude self-renewing, joyous, unconditional love. Maybe I was not capable of such love. I loved playing with the girls in the pool but also made sure I simultaneously got my exercise. When I read to them or played games I was partly doing my duty. My capacity for connectedness had been severely eroded. I was walled in and kept others out.

I was always with Joan when I was not at work. She again became part of me, my friend, family, roommate, lover, and constant companion, but I had lost my ability for passion or romance. Joan was totally committed to me and the girls, but I felt her physical and emotional responses to me were always a two-step process. She always had to pass through a zone of disapproval, distrust, and resentment. At some level she no longer trusted me. She left Duke with great promise for a life with the beautiful and powerful people. She then spent three years teaching fifth-graders in Connecticut, two long winters alone in a tiny apartment in Ann Arbor mothering two infants, and a year with her parents, and now she was essentially living as a dependent on a military base. Somehow she sensed that I was not the same person she married. She did not, and probably could not, describe the difference.

Without speaking about it, with ease and confidence I returned to the vow of monogamy that I had assumed and maintained for five years before I was drafted into the military. I had a secret, though, which at the time I believed to be in a harmless, well-insulated place in my mind. I had occasionally corresponded with Nurse Elaine during my year in Vietnam, and once she had flown out to California to see me. We spent only one afternoon and evening together, remained in public places, and barely touched. She told me she was working in New York City. She also told me she was in love with me.

Even though I was not responsible for their care, the wounded soldiers in wheelchairs and on crutches from the rehabilitation wards were a common sight. One of them invited me to a party in a private room at Trader Vic's restaurant. Joan and I decided to make an appearance. When we arrived, thirty or forty young men wearing civilian clothes for the first time since their tours of duty were already inebriated. Amid brief introductions, awkward handshakes, and nods, we sat at one of the large tables and drank Trader Vic's sweet, potent drinks. We felt like intruders because no other hospital personnel or family members were present.

As we sat watching, I was gripped by a familiar, amorphous inner pain I had not felt since I had been in Vietnam. Joan was the only woman in attendance, and she and I were the only people in the room with functioning arms and legs. The soldiers paid little attention to us. These eighteen- and nineteen-year-old kids were far more focused on having their first social experience since being wounded.

Legless boys in wheelchairs were feeding those with no arms. An armless boy carried a legless boy piggyback to the head amid jokes about how they could help each other urinate. A one-armed boy struggled clumsily to strike a match and light his cigarette. They were all laughing. They were all drunk. Joan and I slipped away unnoticed.

CHAPTER 11

My last assignment at Oak Knoll Naval Hospital was in the dermatology clinic, and compared to my earlier assignments, I found it very enjoyable. I saw patients of all ages, they all had something noticeably wrong with them, and I seemed to have a good eye for identifying dermatological disorders. I quickly learned that in most cases I could make a diagnosis within seconds, recommend an appropriate treatment, and know that it was likely to help the patient considerably. I saw the same patient more than once, and it was usually very clear that the treatments were helpful. It was rewarding to solve real problems that quickly responded to treatment.

Before serving in Vietnam I had planned to go into private practice in internal medicine. After being in Vietnam and taking care of casualties, I was more certain than ever that I didn't want to be a surgeon or emergency room doctor, so I planned to resume my training in internal medicine after I left the navy. To be eligible for internal medicine boards, I needed two more years of residency, but because I had enjoyed the study of dermatology so much, I decided to train for a year in that field in order to make skin disease a sideline when I went into private practice.

Although I probably did not realize it at the time, that choice may have been a sign that I was retreating, in part, from the responsibility of making life-and-death decisions. As a doctor of internal medicine I would spend a great deal of time treating elderly patients with serious chronic illnesses, including arthritis, heart disease, lung disease, and strokes. Often it would be difficult to make a significant difference in the course of disease in a short time, and expectations for complete return to normalcy would be limited. I was ready for a chance to see patients who had something I could take care of and who got better in a hurry.

Just before I left the service I visited the dermatology programs at Yale and Duke and Harvard to explore the possibility of a one-year residency or fellowship. To my surprise, although it was only a week before the July 1 onset of the annual training cycle, all three programs were willing to create a special position and invited me to join them. I decided to attend Harvard. It was a prestigious program, and they agreed to pay me and arrange for me to get board accreditation in both dermatology and internal medicine. Also, I thought Boston would be an interesting place to live. I was in my dress khakis when I visited each medical center, and, in contrast to Duke and Yale, when I visited Massachusetts General Hospital (MGH) and Harvard Medical School (HMS) I felt respected and well received.

Shortly before I was discharged from active duty, I volunteered to be the scout and go to Boston for several days without Joan and the girls to find a place to live. I secretly flew to New York City to visit Elaine and convinced her to accompany me on my brief trip to Boston. We slept together during that trip, and she went back to her job in New York. I knew that this was a very selfish and inconsiderate lapse in judgment on my part. I did not fully incorporate how difficult it must have been for Elaine to help me find a home for me and my family. More importantly, I did not accept responsibility for the magnitude of my deception of Joan. The potential for emotional pain for everyone was enormous, but my soul was becoming callous and impenetrable. I had developed a strange lack of psychological awareness and a diminished ability to view the world from the perspective of others.

I had no justification for my sin. I was not a frightened exhausted

160

warrior passing through a foreign port between fierce battles. Neither was I a responsible husband and father in safe and comfortable American society. I did not know exactly who I was and I had an unmeetable need for a new attachment, a bold connectedness, risky behavior, and forbidden sex. I could not be contained, constrained, or comforted by Joan, my children, my profession, or my childhood Jesus. I needed an emotional bunker. I was also a macho male chauvinist pig and arrogant entitled male taker. To make matters worse, I may not have done the most thorough job of house-hunting. I ended up choosing a place that was convenient for my commute to MGH but less than ideal for Joan and the girls.

My new emotional shield worked in both directions. It not only diminished my availability for intimacy but also provided a hard, potentially destructive insensitivity to the needs of others, a defect in empathy. Outwardly a nice man, inwardly a hard-ass, I was willing to underemphasize or partially ignore the degree of pain my decisions could cause. I was not a good boy.

As Joan set up house in Boston, I disappeared again into my training, working long hours and spending very little time at home. Ironically, now that I was out of the military, my Vietnam experience, instead of receding into my past as a rarely used collection of stories, began to become more intrusive. While I worked and studied, I often found myself thinking about Vietnam. As much as I thought that part of my life had ended, it had not. It made me angry and sad and sometimes guilty that the American War in Vietnam continued.

Colleagues in liberal East Coast intellectual communities were occasionally distantly curious about my war experience. Many of my peers had spent their two years of national obligation in the Public Health Service or at the National Institutes of Health or other sites that advanced their education and enhanced their academic status. They were not only two years ahead of me in training but also formed an elite brotherhood from which I was excluded. With pride and a sense of self-congratulation for cleverness, they referred to themselves as the "Yellow Berets." Many of them had come from privileged family trees and attended private schools, and now they had learned new research and medical skills. I attended public schools and was tainted by war. I was out of my league academically and socially. I did not play tennis or golf and had never gone sailing or belonged to a social club. I did not speak French, and Parrish was not a name recognized by the Boston Brahmans.

When friends and colleagues did express any curiosity about the war, they wanted only short, crisp, controlled, and packaged information that fit their preconceived notion of what the war was like. In some circles, even mentioning that I had served in Vietnam was a conversation stopper. Although unstated, people would react as if I had said something socially inappropriate. I felt labeled as part of the cause and the execution of the war in a community that opposed it completely. I could tell people really didn't know how to deal with an actual witness of the war and, moreover, didn't want to deal with it—or me.

I did not have that luxury. The war was now part of who I was, and sometimes when interrogated, I could not help but give information about my military role. Those conversations could quickly become awkward if I became emotional, embarrassing myself and my audience with inappropriate expressions of feelings.

Joan and I might be out to dinner with another couple or at a cocktail party, just chatting and being sociable, telling the stories of our lives, how we came to be together and came to be in Boston, and the fact that I had been in Vietnam would come up in conversation. Someone might innocently ask, "Oh, what was that like being in Vietnam?" just as they would ask, "Oh, what was it like growing up in Miami?"

Usually, I'd just give quick, throwaway answers. "It was terrible," I'd say, or answer simply, "It was a long year," something brief and to the point because I really didn't want to talk about it. On occasion, though, people would keep asking questions, pressing me for more specific information: "Tell us, John, where were you stationed? Exactly what did you do?"

I could usually continue to deflect the conversation and respond obtusely, "Oh, you know, I just took care of casualties. It was the same thing day after day," hoping that the conversation would move on. Every once in a while the questions kept coming, particularly from a medical crowd that was accustomed to asking questions that in another social group might be considered invasive or inappropriate. "What kind of casualties did you treat, John? As an internist, what kinds of treatment could you provide and what resources and surgical backup were available to you? Were you in danger?"

Those specific, apparently innocuous questions might cause me to consider the actual answers, and my reply would become more descriptive and direct, setting off a chain reaction of personal responses that I was powerless to stop.

"I'd treat boys with their arms and legs blown off, with their stumps turned to jelly and their bodies opened up and their intestines spilling out on the floor. I would have to scrape their brains out from under my fingernails. I started each day examining recently killed teenagers." After a few moments I would realize that people didn't want the truth in detail and were already saturated.

By then, however, I didn't want to stop, I couldn't stop. To myself I thought, *Well, you really wanted to know, so now I'm really going to tell you,* and I would go on and on about the constant flow of casualties, the wasted lives, the gore, and the horror. I would eventually start to pick up on the cues that they had heard enough and realize that I had gone too far, or at least farther than they expected. The eyes of my audience would glaze over. Someone might say, "Could you pass the potato chips, please?" People would start to look away, focus elsewhere, check their watches, or excuse themselves.

They could walk away from the conversation, but by then I couldn't. Sometimes I would get so emotional I would start to choke up. I didn't want to take the psychic journey, at least not in front of other people. Joan would sometimes interrupt, take me by the arm and say, "I think we should go now, we promised our babysitter . . .," or else I would stammer out some excuse about some other engagement. Afterward I'd feel ashamed and embarrassed. I learned that such public displays of emotion were less acceptable in Boston than in the South. Also, this was a very competitive environment, and I had to be cautious about leaving the impression that I wasn't in control or was somehow damaged.

As I readjusted to the pressures and priorities of academic medicine and learned that my grief was unacceptable, I began to keep it secret. That was when I began to have occasional nightmares, vivid and intrusive daytime recollections, and a constant feeling of impending alienation, dread, uncertainty, and insecurity. When these feelings were most intense, I often imagined being in Triage.

On occasion, when I was at MGH and found myself rethinking my time in Vietnam, I would wander into the emergency room, half expecting the room to be filled with casualties and corpsmen and marines carrying soldiers on litters. When accident victims were being treated and the scene was somewhat frenetic, I would become anxious and hypervigilant and would have to suppress the urge to act. Suddenly feeling awkward and out of place, I would retreat back to the dermatology ward. The emergency room doctors appeared heroic and competent. In contrast I felt like a silly, wounded clown hiding in the quieter parts of the hospital.

Joan was the only person I could rely on to listen to my Vietnam stories. Although she tried very hard to be supportive, the content was very difficult for her. Sometimes I could only talk for a few minutes before I got too choked up to continue, but on occasion I could go on longer. She would try to listen until I was finished, but there were times I could tell she was tuning out. She might say, "John, I'm really tired; I have to go to bed. Let's talk tomorrow." Then Joan would go to bed and I would stay up, drinking beer and staring in the dark, replaying the same scenes over and over again.

Of course, there were some things that were very difficult for me to talk about. Joan knew nothing about my relationship with Xuân, but that was part of my war story. I think I told her gradually, first just telling her bluntly that I had broken our wedding vows and had a relationship with a Vietnamese woman while I was in Vietnam, and then slowly providing more details over the next week or so. Joan was hurt, and although she tried to be tolerant and forgiving, she could not help but add to the emotional distance that had been steadily increasing between us.

A few months after I told Joan about Xuân, I got sick with the flu. I had a high fever and was coughing and wheezing, and I stayed home for a week, which was very unusual for me. I was so focused on my work I generally ignored my own illnesses, but this time I was very sick and feeling really awful, inside and out.

As I lay on the couch, I gave Joan a full confession about my relationship with Xuân and subsequent infidelities with Elaine, who by this time had visited me twice in Boston. I even threw in a report on the one-night stand with the dietitian in Ann Arbor. I also told her what a wreck I was inside from my war experiences.

When I wasn't sleeping fitfully and immersed in fever dreams, I told Joan more than she wanted to know. Speaking in short installments, I tried to be very vulnerable and open and honest, and that was more than she could process. At times I would get exhausted or sleepy and stop talking, or Joan would walk off to be alone with her own thoughts as she took care of the girls. Then, after a few hours, she would express her hurt, and my trail of regret, guilt, and grief would continue.

This was the first time I let the dam really break. I wept with long noisy outcries. At times, Joan tried to hold me even though I had just hurt her deeply. I refused to be comforted. It was not possible. These protracted exorcisms went on for hours—long periods of silence followed by bursts of conversation, mostly just me talking and spewing out the unfiltered, unedited details of what I did and saw in Vietnam. My anguish and explosive range of emotional storms were much greater than any I felt while I was there.

As my illness retreated and I felt more in control, I tried to spin the infidelities in a way that I thought would hurt Joan the least. I framed the issue by claiming I was so wounded by war and left so vulnerable and frail that I became someone I didn't know, and that included having affairs with a Vietnamese woman and Elaine. I believed I was not totally responsible; my psyche had been terribly damaged, and I was temporarily crazy. This strategy was not very convincing to Joan—or myself.

Until my confessions and reexperience of psychic trauma, I don't think Joan had any idea just how psychologically unstable I was. I don't think I really knew either. That was a turning point. I allowed myself to have feelings, and to open up and express those feelings, rather than keep them buried inside. I had tried denial, and it wasn't working.

I pleaded guilty of infidelity of the most hurtful kind and sincerely pledged my faithfulness. I called Elaine to tell her I had confessed our sins and made a commitment to stop seeing her and to repair my relationship with Joan. I never saw her again. We stopped all communication. I heard that she was deeply unhappy. She never tried to contact me. My guilt and shame were compounded by the fact that I really cared for her.

Joan and I had so much work to do. With a great deal of crying, pain, awkwardness, and fear, Joan seemed to absorb it all. Despite her massive hurt, she told me that she would stay with me and be supportive. At the same time, she let me know that she felt like a war casualty herself, and that she couldn't be my psychological caregiver. She did not think she was the best partner for me to work through my grief and guilt. There were certain things, like my infidelity, she just didn't want to hear about, and other parts, like some of the more horrible events I witnessed, that she found too difficult to process—and I had so much to say.

Joan sensed that I had to emote and find some way to release. Afraid to do anything that might damage my professional reputation, I resisted suggestions to seek counseling. I did not trust any psychiatrist to keep my symptoms and therapy confidential. I assumed that if the leadership of MGH or HMS knew I was having severe psychological challenges, my career options would be compromised.

Joan suggested I write it all down, that perhaps if I did, I could make some sense of what had happened to me and that then I might not feel so damaged and evil.

I began almost immediately. When I wasn't working or studying, on nights and weekends, I spent nearly every waking moment writing down my war story on yellow legal pads. I had no notes or journals, but the memories were very clear, and I could remember many conversations word for word. I had never tried to write before, and at first it was difficult and awkward, but I was persistent and soon discovered that writing did help. Now that I had a place where I allowed expression of my feelings, they were no longer so intrusive during other parts of my day. For the writing to be useful I had to be honest, and I struggled to write honestly. It was painful, but it had to be done. Writing would take me back; the rest of the world would disappear. Sometimes it led me to episodes of painful grief, but the structure was helpful. I was able to work and study dermatology again without showing any signs of instability.

To avoid writing random, scrambled, repetitive scenes, and to give the narrative a sense of progression, I tried to add some structure and time lines to my wailing and emoting. I could not decide if it was more helpful to remain stuck in reexperiencing specific painful episodes or to work through the traumas by providing history, context, venue, and outcome, and then moving on. Should I examine the emotional explosion or the debris? Should I pull the most painful, horrible, and soul-damaging scenes and events into a story?

My written notes and descriptions evolved into a third-person, fictionalized story of a doctor in Vietnam. Although frequently shocked and horrified, the protagonist was a hero—a composite of John Parrish, Ben Casey, John Wayne, GI Joe, and the ancient mythic warrior. While I wrote, I created and preserved a comfortable distance from my protagonist, granting him an alluring role as physician, soldier, officer, and gentleman, making him attractive and sensitive, endowed with a remarkable reservoir of empathy and stoic, macho resolve. He was the picture of resilience. He had impressive surgical skills. He was a slightly more grown-up version of the soldier I had fantasized being when I was a child, the soldier I had hoped to become but had not.

The completion of this narrative was therapeutic. In the end it provided a sense of release and, even though no one else read the manuscript, a sense of sharing. My story—corrupted reality that it was—had come out.

As I read my war story, though, I realized it also contained some unintended lessons. Through the creation of the story I experienced how chronicles of war become mythologized, made romantic, heroic, and manly. While retelling the story of my year in Vietnam I gave my character a degree of control over his surroundings and reactions that I did not possess at the time of the actual events. In fiction my motives had become nobler and my strengths more pronounced, overshadowing my frailties. In conversations, the protagonist had the best lines and insights that could only have come with time and distance. Where the war had been most damaging and most affecting, I substituted a higher purpose, injecting my actions with doses of heroism, romance, bravery, and humor in places where, in fact, my memory of the events recorded no such qualities and explained nothing. I realized that by doing so I was reinforcing the appeal of playing war games as a child.

To remain efficient in Vietnam and socially acceptable after returning, I had learned not to react openly and completely to the emotional stress of the war. Now, in my written fictionalized record, I realized that many feelings were still absent or blunted and that those that were described were often controlled, contrived, or inauthentic. While facilitating release, my fictionalized tale also helped me maintain my emotional blockade and an unwillingness to fully react to the traumas of the soul. I destroyed the manuscript, unread by anyone but me, and started again. To write honestly I had to be honest.

This time I connected the trauma, events, and reactions in a story about me. From beginning to end, I was determined to describe my failures, vulnerability, worn sensibility, infidelity, ignorance, arrogance, loss of hope, and breaks in fortitude. This was much easier to write. In fact, I couldn't stop writing. Every week or so I would turn over everything I had written to my secretary, who would type it for me.

Writing this version was even more therapeutic. While I was writing I would sometimes relive specific scenes and be moved by them to the point of tears, but gradually I had less fear and anguish. Although I remained emotionally unavailable to my wife and daughters, I had fewer intrusive daytime thoughts of Vietnam, and my nightmares stopped. I was more at peace with the Vietnam War. My anxieties and vulnerabilities diminished. I had written the story for myself, and for my own reasons, and it seemed to be serving a purpose.

During the eighteen months it took me to write my war story, our third child, our son, Mark, was born. Emotionally, the birth almost took me by surprise because, characteristically, I had not participated in the spiritual wonder or celebrated the physiological marvel of pregnancy. When Joan went into labor, I took a cab from MGH to meet her at the Brigham and Women's Hospital labor suite. When her obstetrician decided it was time to take Joan to the delivery room, he directed me to the waiting area. As I waited, I replayed my father's mythology about the firstborn son. I was pleased and excited—and thinking about the meetings I was missing at work. In my rush, I had failed to bring any work with me. I thumbed through old magazines and thought about tossing a football with my father, playing war games with my friends, clumsily holding babies, and essentially meeting my girls for the first time when they were two and four years old—already little people with personalities.

After fifteen to twenty minutes, Joan's doctor came out in green scrubs, still wearing his gloves. He was flustered and told me that there were unexpected complications and he had sent for assistance from a specialist in complex deliveries. He instructed me to sit tight and told me he would come talk to me as soon as he knew more. I wanted to run into the delivery room but instead controlled my panic and took a seat. Was I needed to save my wife and son? Would I be inadequate again? I sat down like a good boy.

I spent the next two hours frenetically stopping nurses and doctors in the hallways asking what was happening. Everyone reassured me that Joan and the baby would be fine and that I must wait for the doctor to give me more details. After waiting as long as I could stand, I went into the delivery area and began checking each room for Joan.

Although several staff tried, no one could stop me. I found Joan wide awake, comfortable, and lying in a neat, clean bed suckling our baby. The complication had been solved in a few minutes, and the doctor forgot to come out to tell me. He had gone back to his office over an hour earlier. I rejoiced with Joan and then went into the stairwell and wept like a baby.

An explosive mixture of love, guilt, and regret seized me. It took an enormous threat of actual death or trauma to strike me down with a massive bolt of parental and spousal emotions. I was overwhelmed by the feelings that penetrated the shield I needed to survive and function. I must have still needed the shield that kept intimacy out and my feelings in because over weeks it seemed to return involuntarily. I didn't cry again for over ten years.

I went back to work. Joan's mother arrived, and she and Joan took over baby and child care. I sometimes put the girls to bed before going to my desk to study. One day Joan got a sitter and she and I went to New York to visit with one of her old roommates who worked for McGraw-Hill, the publisher. Joan told her I had written a book and didn't know what, if anything, to do with it now that it was finished. Her friend knew a literary agent named Gerry McCauley and offered to show him the manuscript. Gerry responded quickly, telling me he thought the book made a very powerful statement about the Vietnam War and should be published. He offered to explore possible publishers, and the book was accepted by E. P. Dutton.

I worked with an editor named Hal Scharlatt. Apart from stopping the story when I was still in Vietnam, instead of having it continue through my reentry into the academic world, he didn't change much. The book, *12, 20, & 5: A Doctor's Year in Vietnam,* was published in 1972. The title referred to the verbal shorthand sometimes used to describe the number of incoming casualties and the severity of their injuries, three numbers that told us what to expect in the next shipment of wounded soldiers—how many were not ambulatory, how many could walk, and how many were already dead. After the book was published, I remembered that in reality only two numbers had been used because military leadership went to great lengths to avoid having the dead transported along with the living. From my perspective in Triage, I had paid no attention to how the living and dead traveled to us.

When the book was released in Massachusetts, the antiwar movement was still strong. My thoughts had evolved, and I viewed my book as less about the American War in Vietnam than about war in general. The Vietnam War, even though I found it pointless, was not the major issue for me, only a symptom of a larger wrong. War itself was the issue, and I hoped my book would lead others to the same conclusion. I thought it would be impossible for anyone to read my story and not realize the futility of war. I had a fantasy that if I could add my voice to those who had shown the human face of war, it would somehow make a difference, make our country more reluctant to go to war.

I remember the feeling of excitement when I was sent a box of books. I proudly took a book to the MGH gift shop, where they had a book section, showed it to them, and explained that I was the author. Since I was affiliated with MGH I asked if they might want to display it in their store.

A few days later a member of the MGH staff told me they had decided not to stock the book because it contained sex and profanity. They did not believe that either my academic colleagues or patients' families should know that one of the MGH doctors wrote about sex and used profane language. The violence, death, and gore were not mentioned.

I gave copies to selected friends and colleagues, people I knew very well, but I didn't share the book widely. I wanted to be recognized as a writer, but after the book was rejected by the MGH bookstore I was also worried about the exposure. Some of my friends found it powerful and thought I was brave to tell my story, but most didn't want to talk about it, or talk about the impact it had on them. My siblings and Joan's scolded me for embarrassing them and belittling Joan with graphic public descriptions of my infidelity. My mother and father said nothing. Gil found it very gruesome and thought that I provided too much detail about the horror and devastation and carnage I witnessed.

I became increasingly concerned about the open display of my vulnerabilities, my infidelity, and times when I lost courage or felt inadequate
doing my job, but tried to remember that was the point of the book.
War is not romantic and heroic. There may be heroes in war, but the
substance of war is incredibly, horribly wasteful and largely immoral.

Dutton believed in the book, or at least believed it could sell and
make money. After a number of initial positive reviews, they organized
dozens of interviews with reviewers and newspaper columnists and
with radio and television stations. I had so many lunches at the Ritz-
Carlton in Boston that the maître d' began to recognize me. The attention made me a little uncomfortable. Some interviewers clearly hadn't
done their homework and hadn't even read the book, while others found
it quite powerful, telling me that although they sometimes found it
unsettling, it was an important story and they thought I was brave and
generous to write it. The war continued.

Most gratifying were the numerous phone calls from complete
strangers or soldiers who said, "You know, I just read your book and
I want to thank you." Or a call from a wife who would say, "Now I
understand my husband." Or parents who used the book to initiate
their first real conversation with an estranged son. I found these calls
very rewarding, including the ones that came in the middle of the
night.

During the flurry of interviews, I joined five other men as "walk-
ons" to try out for the Pittsburgh Pirates during spring training in
Florida. This prearranged one-week publicity stunt was designed as
opportunities for photojournalism and did result in a book* and an article for *Playboy*. The group included a poet (eventually laureate), a director of the ACLU, a *New York Times* writer, and a very successful
photographer. I wore the uniform of the pitcher Dock Ellis. The entire
team wore black armbands because of the recent death of Roberto Cle-

---

Playing Around: The Million-Dollar Infield Goes to Florida. By Donald Hall, Gerard F.
McCauley, Charles Morgan Jr., John A. Parrish, MD, and James T. Wooten. Photos
by Bob Adelman. Boston: Little, Brown, 1974.

mente, who died at age thirty-eight in a plane crash en route to deliver aid to earthquake victims in Nicaragua.

I was excited to be asked to be a speaker at the *Boston Globe* Book Fair. At the time it was a very large event and received a great deal of advance publicity. Well known authors from all over the country were participating. I was delighted to be included and looked forward to exposing my book to a large group of people, especially those outside the medical profession.

Initially, I planned to explain why I wrote the book. However, as the book fair drew closer, I knew I could not be satisfied only with telling my personal story. I felt obligated to explain the American War in Vietnam and war itself. I took my assignment very seriously and spent weeks doing research, reading books, editorials, and magazine articles, looking into the root causes of the war, the meaning of the war, and what it said about our country. I approached it not as a doctor who had written a book about his experience but as some kind of policy person or historical authority. I wrote a lengthy speech in which I tried to coalesce all my thoughts on the subject.

When I entered the Hynes Convention Center in Boston, I was surprised to find that out of the thousands attending the fair, only a few dozen people attended my presentation. Nevertheless, I began to speak.

After only a few moments I was on the verge of tears. As I read the final passage, my voice began to break.

> The human brain weighs about three pounds and contains over 500,000 years of inherited information processing capability. One big breakthrough in evolution was the ability to connect acts with both short-term and long-term consequences. From this connection, we developed the important concepts of responsibility, planning, deterrence, and morality. The mind, life, and society of modern man may be becoming so complex that he is losing this connection. Our tax money is used to make bombs, and our elected leaders tell military leaders to order pilots to fly over yellow people and

push buttons. The concept of consequences of acts or blame for suffering gets diluted. Groups and nations and races can collectively act as if not responsible as a corollary to the invisibility of privilege.

The very group of synapses in our brains that made us survive as a species may, by their loss in complexity, render us unable to survive. We may lose our collective ability to connect acts to consequences and kill each other off or pollute the planet to death.

By writing a book, I tried to expose the human side of war on a personal scale. Unless we and our leaders can see this human side of war and reconnect our actions to their consequences, we are doomed to repeat wars or at least, as of today, doomed to continue the one we have.

The thirty or forty people in the audience barely listened and at the conclusion of my talk responded with brief polite applause. The question-and-answer period was disrupted as another hundred people began noisily filing into the room to hear the next speaker. A few challenges, comments, or questions came from the audience all at once.

"Why did you go to Vietnam?"

"What if they gave a war and nobody showed up?"

"We couldn't make war if we didn't have military doctors."

"Why don't we just withdraw?"

"Did you take care of wounded enemy?"

I awkwardly tried to respond but could not be heard above the conversations of the growing crowd pressing into the auditorium. Hardly anyone noticed as I drifted to the side of the stage.

The next speaker, the actor Anthony Quinn, was introduced and talked about his recent book. Every joke, every line he uttered generated thunderous laughter or applause. Even his carefully orchestrated pauses evoked an audience response.

As he spoke of Hollywood, I sat in the auditorium and reread my speech, finding it silly, sophomoric, presumptuous, and pedantic. I felt empty, inadequate, and embarrassed. I realized that I didn't have anything new to say that I hadn't read in somebody's articles. I had only my own sorry story to tell, and it contained no coherence or theme, and no one gave a shit about it anyway.

That night when my family went to bed, I drove forty miles to participate in a late-night radio talk show in Worcester, Massachusetts. The host hadn't read my book, and neither had any of the callers. He spent two hours using phrases he cribbed off the book jacket to incite the hawks and the doves to fight with him and with each other about Vietnam, always referring to me as "the doctor here." Whenever I made a comment, he treated my opening phrases as sound bites and interrupted me to comment on what he called the "real" war (World War II), sex, "nuking" Vietnam and turning it into a parking lot, getting the hell out, staying the hell in, winning minds and hearts, goddamn hippies, cowardly conscientious objectors, wimpy politicians, lying politicians, killer marines, "real" warriors . . .

Every caller was angry at him, at me, and the other callers. Some thought I was a hero. Some saw me as a victim. Others thought I was un-American, a traitor to real victory because my host had suggested I had real doubts about the war. Most felt I was just an airhead academic gone astray.

I was exhausted. I lost track of who was blaming whom. Victims, perpetrators, heroes, cowards, might, right, bombing, winning, hearts, fuckers, fuckees.

By the end of the show I was barely participating. Actually, I was thinking of Joan and my three children asleep in their beds. Although the host seemed bored with me and the callers, he kept the show moving. He provoked and smoked, drank coffee, managed the radio station, and did paperwork all at the same time. He didn't need me, the author.

During my midnight ride back to Boston, I felt terribly alone. I promised myself not to talk about war or Vietnam anymore.

That night I had my most vivid and frightening Vietnam nightmares since my return to America.

CHAPTER 12

Some time after my book was published, a cease-fire agreement was signed. President Richard M. Nixon proclaimed "Peace with Honor" and halted the "Christmas bombing" of Hanoi and Haiphong. American B-52s had carried out indiscriminate "carpet bombing," using the greatest amount of destructive power in the history of aerial warfare. Most of the world strongly condemned the bombing. In the United States there were scattered expressions of outrage. Although there were no mass protests, there was a national campaign to rebuild a hospital in Hanoi.

Over the next several years my book was published in paperback by Bantam Books, Penguin Books, and two other publishing houses. Feedback to me diminished to nothing, and I realized my book had little impact. I joined in the subdued national relief about the end of the American War in Vietnam and pledged most earnestly to overcome my war experience.

I no longer believed my feelings were of interest to anyone. Whatever I thought and believed appeared to make no difference, and I simply did not have sufficient psychic reserve to continue to explore or confront the invisible wounds of war that were damaging to me and those I loved. I took the position that I temporarily had been a weakling who overreacted to circumstances that men had been experiencing for centuries. War happens. Doctors do their jobs. Infidelity happens—even to good people. Get over it!

As an act of will, I decided to allow myself no time for wrestling with my demons. I believed that my work would be my salvation. Again, I would leave no room for the war in my life. Hard work could save me, and I could get myself and my life back.

Over the next decade or more I made a complete and utter commitment to my medical training and research, leaving even less time for myself or my family. During meals I read textbooks and scientific papers. When I was driving, I listened to tapes of lists and notes I had made from textbooks. When I finally reached a point where I could read or study no more, I exercised.

I had been a runner long before there was a running boom and it had become popular, but in the early and mid-1970s in the Boston area, primarily due to the Boston Marathon, running was suddenly fashionable. Now I could hide in plain sight. Joan and everyone else I knew viewed my running as a normal and healthy part of my routine.

What they did not know was that for me, running was far more than a way to maintain my physical health; it was a safe way to *feel*. I began to run faster and harder, and for longer distances, trying to end my run at a sprint for one minute, then two minutes, then longer, jamming as much torture as possible into the thirty or forty minutes I could squeeze from my increasingly busy schedule. When my chest burned and my side ached with cramps and my thighs quivered from overuse, I kept going, running as hard and as fast as I possibly could, sometimes doing intervals on hills, down and up and then down and up again and again until my body completely rebelled and I would double over, nearly delirious, as every synapse screamed out in pain.

That was the goal—not distance or time but pure agony. Because when I was feeling pain—acute, severe, and tangible pain, coupled with the euphoria and light-headedness that came from oxygen debt and endorphins—at least I was feeling something, and that left no room in my psyche to process war, and no time or opportunity to confront myself. With each foot strike while I was running I somehow felt

I was somehow striking out against the war and the horror and the waste of wounded soldiers. Simultaneously I was also punishing myself for being unable to save lives, incapable of stopping wars, and a bad person—an unfaithful husband and inadequate father. I was getting in touch with how strongly I felt about the waste and the horror and the pain I witnessed. So I ran to feel, to forget, to remember, and to punish myself. At the end of the day, when it came time to sleep, I would collapse, utterly exhausted, beyond the reach of insomnia. Then morning would come and I would start again. I continued my campaign to never mention the war or my pain to anyone. I trained for three months and ran a marathon in three and a half hours. I knew I could do better and planned to train hard for several months and run again. I didn't.

As I became more frenetic about my work, I realized that I had a substantive psychological problem. Would I eventually prove to be a psychiatric casualty of war as King had predicted? When I was with patients, I was very skilled and appropriately affable, alert, and concerned, and, except for the usual competitive gamesmanship, I was comfortable at work. Outside of the workplace, though, anytime I was with anyone, including family, for even a few minutes, I felt anxious, unstable, and inauthentic. Although I did not let it show, in public places if anyone expressed hints of entitlement, indifference, arrogance, or idleness it made me furious. Ever since my return from Vietnam, to avoid acting out, I had often needed to consciously tap into the inauthentic, quiet good boy of my childhood.

I knew about the stories of World War II veterans demonstrating the alarming and pathetic symptoms of "shell shock" and descriptions of "battle fatigue," which occurred after prolonged stress, sleep loss, fear, and guilt in any war. Many victims became lonely street people. I remembered my old shop teacher, the bashful man teased by my classmates. I tried to convince myself that I was certainly not one of those pitiful, crazy, damaged victims.

In the mainstream press and in medical literature of the day, the term "post-Vietnam syndrome" was just beginning to come into use, a catchall theoretical diagnosis to encompass the vast multitude of psychological and mental health issues that medical professionals were beginning to notice and acknowledge in returning veterans. Although the last American fighting troops left Vietnam in 1973, the war had been brought back home. The press and entertainment industry were creating a profile of Vietnam veterans as angry, dangerous, hostile men with frighteningly short fuses. It took little provocation to trigger them to hurt themselves or others. They played by their own rules of justice and retribution. Many were alcoholics or drug addicts. I certainly was not one of these and didn't even know anyone who fit that description.

I found two books very helpful. *Men, Stress, and Vietnam* by Peter G. Bourne (1970), provided physiological, biochemical, and clinical explanations of the human responses to battle stress. The possibility of a scientifically understood causality and process allowed me to feel less weak, guilty, and embarrassed. The other book, *Home from the War* (1973), was written by a well-respected psychiatrist, Robert Jay Lifton.

Dr. Lifton had done the pivotal studies on survivors of the Holocaust, survivors of the atomic bomb dropped on Japan, American POWs confined and tortured in North Korea, nonfiring participants in the My Lai Massacre, and shooters participating in other massacres. His books were a sophisticated yet highly understandable blend of classic literature, empirical science, psychology, and psychiatry. He examined what he called the "psychomythology of war making" and introduced psychohistory as an important lens through which to examine human nature.

For *Home from the War,* Dr. Lifton met with over four hundred Vietnam veterans, spent over one hundred and fifty hours in forty-five meetings of "rap groups," and invested over eighty hours in individual therapy sessions with disturbed veterans. Most had been in active combat, and most had drifted into an antiwar position either before or after they returned home. Dr. Lifton felt that the extremity of the psychological and moral inversions in Vietnam could be uniquely illuminating to the study of psychological trauma. He described the effects of sudden or sustained threat to personal integrity brought about by some form of encounter with death. Excruciating feelings of separation and self-imposed isolation reinforce one another. Shattered dreams and loss of beliefs accompany loss of trust and diminished ability to be intimate with others. Emotional and psychological numbing, stoic guilt, and frozen grief can lead to alternating rage and depression. Self-confidence and self-worth are pummeled by a feeling of being tainted by the threat itself.

As he narrated and explained veterans' stories, I connected with the warriors' struggles with intrusive thoughts of war and death, inability to be intimate, withdrawal from friends and family, hypervigilance, and irritability. By empathizing with the veterans, I felt like the author understood me, legitimized my pain, and did not blame me or think of me as weak and inadequate. I was not alone in my affliction. Although I never met him, Dr. Lifton carried me through several psychic storms.

Virtually no one knew about the reality I was struggling with every day. I sent my book to Alex Roland, my old hoochmate who was now embarking on an academic career as a military historian at Duke University. After he read the book we began a correspondence, and our friendship deepened. Initially, while I would allow him some sense of the trouble I was having internally, I still hid far more than I revealed. As we continued to correspond, I became more open and eventually overdosed him with my pain. He started drowning in my angst, which he could not understand or stem. Alex was relatively unbothered by his war experience, at least emotionally, and reacted to it far differently than I did. We tended to debate the merits and causes and impact of the war obtusely, almost in a different language. I would emote, and Alex would calmly and rationally analyze. I used Alex for support, and he gave it. I asked him for answers and therapy, and he provided neither in a form I could accept. I had no other outlet but myself and my work as I struggled to cope.

As fear and ambition fused within me, I gradually became anxious even at work, and anxious about being anxious. I had no safety zone.

My world became black and white, either or, with only two possible outcomes. I would be either a tremendous, unadulterated, undeniable success or an absolute, utter failure. I decided that I would remain in dermatology as my long-term professional career and stay in academia as long as possible. I convinced myself that the only way to avoid being exposed as an emotional weakling and an unworthy phony was for me to become one of the world's greatest dermatologists. Then, I believed, no one would ever know my soul had been shattered and my roots blown apart. I was determined that my wounds would never show. Success or absolute death-dealing failure were my only options.

Professionally, it was reasonable to imagine that my new goal was within my grasp. There were only about four thousand board-certified dermatologists in the entire country. Of those, only about two hundred were committed to full-time academic medicine, and fewer than fifty spent most of their time doing research. I noticed that many of the most fundamental observations about skin structure and function were not even made by dermatologists but by investigators from other fields. I surveyed the medical literature and noted that there were fewer than a dozen serious dermatologist scientists publishing regularly in the top-tier journals. I was determined to become one of them. My mentor, Thomas B. Fitzpatrick, had consciously chosen academic dermatology for the same reasons, and he had an enormous impact.

In the early 1970s dermatology was not the most demanding medical field. Many Harvard Medical School trainees and faculty looked at dermatology as a weak specialty populated by losers, dropouts, and lazy, greedy doctors who wanted the "good life" and valued money above everything else. Ever since my premed days at Duke and certainly during my medical school studies at Yale, there was a clear bias that the best and brightest clinicians went into internal medicine, a "cognitive" specialty, while the bravest, most confident, and possibly more selfless went into surgical specialties.

As a specialty, dermatology was shrinking. Venereal diseases, rheumatology, collagen-vascular diseases, allergic reactions, simple plastic surgery, leprosy, and tropical diseases with skin manifestations that had all once been the province of dermatologists had been captured and taken over by subspecialties originally stemming from medicine or surgery. Patients whose psychoses were expressed as imagined or self-inflicted skin disorders were referred to psychiatrists.

From my perspective, the practice of dermatology had many appealing attributes. Skin diseases are usually easy to diagnose, and treatments are most often simple and effective, which provided a sense of self-worth, and I was also drawn to dermatology because, as in ophthalmology, one can develop considerable autonomy and a self-contained practice. To a large extent, a dermatologist can be his/her own pathologist and surgeon, perform a wide variety of procedures, and prescribe a wide range of topical and systemic medications. Using well-developed pattern recognition, it is often possible to make a diagnosis within seconds by simply inspecting the skin. The skin is visible and palpable, and a skin biopsy can be minimally invasive. Skin scales can be collected and examined under a microscope. One's practice can include patients of all ages; most are not desperately ill, and the vast majority get better.

My mentors at Harvard and MGH told me I could learn 95 percent of all the diagnostic skills I would need in less than eighteen months. The remaining 5 percent, they said, would require decades. I decided not to make dermatology just a sideline but to embrace it as my specialty. I felt motivated and safe there.

Many of my fellow dermatology trainees acquired great expertise in procedure-based activities, ranging from the removal or destruction of skin cancers to more cosmetic practices including nips, tucks, hair transplants, and the resurfacing of wrinkled skin, but I did not have the required patience, manual dexterity, confidence, or interest. Making use of my background in internal medicine, instead of going into private practice I became a good hospital-based clinical dermatologist. I called myself a "skinternist" because I gravitated to the cognitive, diagnostic, and medical aspects of dermatology. With my boss and a young trainee, I even wrote a book about skin, skin care, and common skin disorders intended for the layperson.

I was always engaged in thinking about the cellular, molecular, physiological, anatomical, and mechanistic causes of the signs and symptoms of skin disorders. Therefore, I became a very good teacher even though I was uncomfortable being one. Because the students had not yet accepted the assumptions, belief systems, and lingo of the medical profession, they sometimes asked very difficult, penetrating, and irreverent questions. I worried that they felt I was not only teaching a specialty few others respected but was also a phony hiding behind my white coat.

I was afraid to get too close to anyone. I had to be a warrior and could not risk any possibility of vulnerability. Family time could not influence the protective shield of professional success that I needed to remain intact and worthy of existence. I ignored my infant son. My father became depressed and unreachable. My daughters were slow to allow me into their worlds, and Joan had developed her own protective shell that expressed itself in retreat, enabling my isolation from her and our children to increase. She went back to school and became committed to feminism and theology. Eventually, I would come to stand for every power group she judged and hated.

At home I was extremely sensitive to any subtle sign of disapproval. I chose my words carefully to avoid being a target for any of Joan's growing list of "isms" or "ists." I interpreted any questioning or blank expression on Joan's face as utter rejection, judgment, and disgust. When I struggled to make contact, a shrug, a frown, or even a simple "Aw, Dad . . ." from my girls shut me down completely. Although I knew they loved me, I felt like the females in my family did not approve of the post-Vietnam me and banded together to judge me and protect themselves from me. As if unable to avoid doing so, I acted in ways to enable their displeasure. Any attempt at humor was scrotal, dark, childlike, and sexist. My son, Mark, found me more acceptable but never defended me from the women's judgments. Rightfully so, finding me to be moody and unpredictable, he kept a safe distance and did not expect much from me.

My overcommitment to work, and its accompanying psychological noncommitment and physical abandonment of family, started as protection or self-therapy but became a compulsion in itself. Initially, research kept me functional, but gradually it became a true mission, then a passion, then an obsession. My research accomplishments brought just enough reward to make me want more recognition. In my own small academic dermatology world, I was not a failure. In that setting no one knew how worthless and undeserving I really was. My research led to patient improvement, and no one died if I made a mistake.

By investing my time in research, I became even more addicted to my work. I spent my time developing treatments instead of delivering care in the trenches one patient at a time. I joined the faculty and saw patients in the outpatient clinics two days a week to earn my salary of $28,000 a year and to justify an MGH appointment. I taught medical students and dermatology trainees six to eight hours per week to earn my academic appointment at HMS. For no pay, I spent another twenty-five to thirty hours a week doing research, trying to earn my place in academia. I believed that in an academic setting I could gradually become captain of my own time, less regulated by work hours and able to escape whenever I became too anxious or depressed. In the end, I decided to remain in academic medicine and eventually retreated further from patient care by becoming a full-time researcher.

I needed freedom from patient care because, despite my decision to never speak of the war again, and my commitment to work and exercise, I was increasingly unable to keep my psychic wounds from bleeding through into the fabric of my life. While remaining highly committed to the principles and metrics of academic medicine, I developed a distrust of authority, alienation, hypervigilance, and preoccupation with violence. When I lost discipline in my rigid management of time, I could feel the presence of my war persona in Vietnam. The demons were near the surface, and much of the frenetic activity of my life was designed to deny my forever one-year war. While I had very few actual flashbacks, or visions, I would regularly become enveloped with a too familiar sense of danger, helplessness, and awareness of my extreme fragility. If I was afraid, I was, therefore, alive. In search of an acceptable normal life I had behaviors that I kept secret.

At some point while I was writing my book, I had acquired several long-playing records of the "sounds of war"—machine guns, cannons, airplanes, firefights, war cries, screams, incoming and outgoing artillery. On occasion I would listen to them before writing to conjure up my experiences and spark my memories of events. Now, even though the book was finished, I continued to listen to the recordings. I needed them to make me feel something.

Whenever Joan and the children were out of the house I would lock all the doors, sit in the middle of the floor, and listen to the recordings at maximum, wall-shaking volume. Sometimes I would yell, but usually I just sat quietly, almost in a trance, and hurt deep in my chest as the sounds of war vibrated through me. By temporarily surrendering to fear and rage, I felt more alive and real and I could break through the numbness in my life, back to a time when everything I did had significance. Being consumed by adrenaline and grief felt honest when nothing else did. Because of my addiction to work, I was not often at home, much less home alone, but I acted this way every time I was alone. I couldn't *not* do it. Occasionally, I would even get up in the middle of the night, sneak downstairs, open a beer, and listen to war sounds through a pair of headphones.

I found it impossible to pick up a book on any topic without looking in the index for the words "war" and "Vietnam." It didn't matter whether the book was a scientific volume on some obscure disease, a work of popular fiction, a biography of a sports hero, or a children's book. As that compulsion increased, I looked for those words in ever more bizarre and unlikely places, each time expecting to find useful, insightful information that would ease my pain and help me heal or jolt me into being more alive. In bookstores and libraries I moved furtively from one title to the next, flipping through the pages with high, if unrealistic, expectations. I seldom bought books I didn't read, but I did sometimes spend an hour or more sitting in the aisles of bookstores reading parts of several books.

Several times each week, I woke in the middle of the night thinking I was in Vietnam on the ground afraid of being killed or lying in my rack in my hooch hearing a helicopter approach Triage or in a bunker feeling the vibrations of incoming shells. It only took a few seconds to realize I was in a safe bed, but by then the hormone surge had already started, and it took a while to go back to sleep.

I wore my dog tags all day, every day, as if I were an active solider and would need them if I were killed in combat and my body had to be identified. Joan, the kids, and I had moved to the suburbs, and there was a wooded hiking path near our house. At least once each weekend I wore my jungle boots and ran through the woods off the paths, hiding from hikers and pretending and almost believing I was a grunt in Vietnam. At the end of my run I would sprint until I was hypoxic enough to feel a surge of fear I identified with war.

Other behaviors were more noticeable to others. I saw every Vietnam War movie, often more than once, the more violent the better. I read and reread books about the American War in Vietnam, books about the books and movies about the war, and the memoirs of soldiers, dwelling on their descriptions of carnage and mayhem. I took courses at Harvard on the history of Vietnam and the long history of wars. I audited a course called "Just and Unjust Wars" taught by Michael Walzer. Because I fought desperately to avoid combustion of my simmering psychological damage, I tried to convince myself to categorize all these activities as either education or entertainment, or tried to convince myself that these exposures and behaviors were therapeutic. In actuality, these activities were signs of a growing addiction, an addiction to war itself.

Two or three years after my hurtful marital crises, I began the first of three serial affairs, each lasting for years. Because one of the women worked at MGH, my stupidity could have cost me my career, but the risk was part of what I needed at the time. Two were in stable marriages. The single woman dated and continued her search for the perfect mate. I saw them infrequently, and all three claimed that their involvement with me brought positive energy to them and their other relationships. I believed them and tried to take the same attitude. However, I felt bad because my deception compromised my ability to be open with Joan. All three affairs ended without drama or pain. The married women returned to monogamy, and the single woman entered a long-term relationship. There was no impact on my career or productivity. At the time, that was the criterion for success.

Believing that I had not yet told the story correctly, over and over again I returned to my book. I kept rewriting a book that had been published years before. I failed repeatedly to find closure. I thought if I could only find my voice I could explain the sadness and waste and horror that surrounded the death of each soldier and the gore of destroyed bodies. Then, perhaps, my writing would have the impact I desired. For years, on weekends, nights, and vacations, never quite finding the beginning, never quite reaching the end, I edited and rewrote the book incessantly, thinking that someday I might get it right.

I still do.

CHAPTER 13

I began my dermatology research as an apprentice to Professor Thomas B. Fitzpatrick, chairman of the Harvard Medical School Department of Dermatology, chief of dermatology at Massachusetts General Hospital, and a world-renowned clinician, teacher, and investigator. While a student at Harvard Medical School, he consciously chose dermatology as a specialty because he thought he could be a superstar. He considered himself to be the most influential dermatologist in the world, and that was arguably true. I started by helping index the latest edition of his textbook, assisting him in his research on skin pigmentation and the development of sunscreens, and accompanying him in his global travels.

As a student at Yale Medical School, I had spent two summers doing research and hated it, finding myself measuring the urine output of diabetic rabbits and cleaning the animal cages by hand. It was different working with Dr. Fitzpatrick. Each summer during my residency Dr. Fitzpatrick and his assistants and I spent ten days at an Arizona state prison quantifying the effect of sunscreens on the backs of prisoners who volunteered to lie in the sun under the predictably cloudless sky. For their service the inmate volunteers were given credit in the prison store, which supplied cigarettes, cigarette lighters, toiletries, and magazines. Their apathetic toughness and bitter resignation reminded me of troops in the field between battles, and I felt a strong bond with them.

We learned a great deal about the ideal ingredients, vehicles, application methods, and sweat resistance of sun protection agents. This was my first opportunity to see research findings rapidly influence commercial products and consumer practices. We were among the first and most vocal missionaries about the importance of sun protection. Working with Franz Greiter, a collaborator from Vienna, we developed the concept of sun protection factor, the now familiar SPF index, found on every bottle of sunscreen.

On one of our trips to Arizona, our photographer was late getting to Logan Airport in Boston. Instead of going on without him, we purposely missed our flight and took another flight, causing us to miss a connecting flight for a short hop in a smaller plane. As we drove a rented car across the desert, we heard on the radio that our scheduled flight on the small plane had crashed, killing all on board. I felt an adrenaline rush as I remembered that any small or big decision may have death-dealing consequences. I reexperienced the fear and panic I had felt during a helicopter crash I had survived in Vietnam.

Dr. Fitzpatrick's major research interest at the time was vitiligo, a skin disorder manifested by loss of skin pigmentation. About 1 percent of people of all races develop vitiligo, patches of completely white skin in which, for unknown reasons, the pigment-producing cells basically stop working and seem to disappear. This condition may not be noticeable in very lightly pigmented Caucasians, but it can be a disfiguring cosmetic liability if it occurs on the face and hands of darkly pigmented people. Although vitiligo is completely harmless and noncontagious, in biblical times it was considered "white leprosy," leading to banishment from society, a stigma that remains in many parts of the world today.

Options for treatment of vitiligo are limited. Lightly pigmented people may ignore it or use sunscreens to protect the white patches from sunburn and to prevent the normal skin from tanning, which would make vitiligo more noticeable by contrast. Others may choose to apply chemicals that have been available for decades to depigment the normal skin, making all skin the same white color. The third approach is to treat the skin with a chemical compound called psoralen, which sensitizes the skin to sunlight, resulting in marked exaggeration of subsequent redness and tanning of the normal skin. After months of twice- or thrice-weekly exposure to psoralen and sunlight, patches of vitiligo may slowly repigment. This approach carries the risk of severe sunburn of the white patches, and its effectiveness is limited. Also, in many parts of the world the required daily sun exposure is impossible, inconvenient, or socially unacceptable.

I set about to produce an artificial light source for activating orally ingested psoralen that reached the skin by way of blood flow. Using lasers, monochromators, and other instruments and lenses, I determined that the activating portion of the sun was a portion of the invisible ultraviolet radiation, referred to as UV-A, or "black light" because it activated fluorescent materials and made them glow in the dark. By ingesting the drug myself, and subjecting postage-stamp-sized areas of my skin to many different durations of UV-A exposure, I determined the ideal timing. After doing this twice a week for months, my entire body, except for my genitals, hands, and face, was covered in pigmented squares labeled with ink. The pigmentation lasted for months.

Working with physicists from GTE Sylvania, we developed a UV-A source capable of activating psoralen over large areas of skin. The new UV-A source made the treatment of vitiligo safer and more convenient, but it still required months of twice-weekly trips to the UV-A source and was not always effective. The contributions to dermatology proved to be limited, but several subsequent observations and events led to a huge impact.

A colleague at the University of Michigan observed improvement in a small plaque of psoriasis after application of psoralen to the affected skin and subsequent exposure to UV-A from a small handheld device. My physicist collaborators improved the UV-A source, making it possible to safely deliver uniform amounts of radiation to the entire skin surface. Then Mr. Gregory walked into our clinic.

A forty-five-year-old homeless alcoholic, Mr. Gregory was covered head to toe with red, raw, scaling disfiguring psoriasis. He looked like a red monster and constantly shed sheets of scales, which clung like dirty snow to his ragged clothing. Because of the appearance of his skin, he was shunned by shelters and even the other homeless men and women who slept on the streets or under the bridges. He agreed to have one half of his body treated with our recently developed method for treating vitiligo. We hospitalized him in order to observe him carefully and because he had no place else to go.

After Mr. Gregory ingested the correct amount of psoralen, we carefully shielded the left side of his body with sheets, waited the right amount of time, and then exposed his right side to our new UV-A source for the ideal duration.

After eight exposures over two weeks, Mr. Gregory's right side looked entirely normal. There was no evidence of psoriasis, and he even sported a nice tan. We then treated the left side with the same astonishing result. Gregory was ecstatic, left the hospital without permission, got drunk, and that night slept in Boston's best shelter for the homeless, a very happy man.

After further testing confirmed the results in another twelve patients, Dr. Fitzpatrick arranged for the new treatment to be announced simultaneously on the front page of the *New York Times,* as the lead article of the most prestigious medical journal, and to thousands of dermatologists from the speaker's platform at the annual meeting of the American Academy of Dermatology. Initial reaction was total disbelief. Then, as we accumulated more patients, dermatologists around the world were dazzled by our accomplishment. For the next two years we were the buzz of the dermatology world. Subsequent studies by me and others showed that this treatment was effective in many other skin disorders, including severe eczema. We called the treatment PUVA (psoralen plus UV-A).

One volunteer for clinical testing was Gullan Wellman, a beautiful blond woman whose self-esteem was dependent on her appearance. Her second multimillionaire husband was Arthur O. Wellman, who had made a fortune in the wool industry. He had then turned his business over to his sons and entertained himself and made another fortune as a "wildcat" oil driller. His brother, "Wild Bill" Wellman, was no less flamboyant and was a famous Hollywood movie producer.

As an adult Mrs. Wellman developed generalized disfiguring psoriasis, primarily on her face, arms, and hands, which for her was a psychosocial disaster. She had failed to respond to multiple standard treatment regimes. Yet after a course of PUVA, she looked normal—which for her was beautiful. In gratitude Mr. Wellman became a bene-factor and eventually contributed more than $1 million to help me create the MGH Wellman Laboratories of Photomedicine. The success of PUVA and the support of Arthur Wellman launched my academic reputation.

As a by-product of our research I was also able to determine and quantify exactly which wavelengths of sunlight maximized tanning with the least sunburn, a discovery that helped launch the hugely prof-itable commercial tanning industry. Although I was presented with several opportunities to be rich and famous (or infamous, in the eyes of my fellow academicians), I distanced myself from the tanning busi-ness long before it grew to be a multibillion-dollar industry. I was satis-fied being recognized for my research work in the academic community and didn't want to be distracted. Besides, without research, and out-side the research community, I felt I was nothing. After all, that was the bargain I had made with myself.

I used our growing collection of optical equipment to develop an ultraviolet treatment for psoriasis that did not require psoralen. We found a narrow band of ultraviolet called UV-B, which was more effec-tive at treating psoriasis with less sunburn of normal skin. Again, spe-cial ultraviolet devices had to be developed. For a five-year period I managed to convert the MGH outpatient dermatology clinic into a massive outpatient clinical research facility that treated hundreds of patients, and I eventually published more than twenty papers to share the results with dermatology worldwide. This ultraviolet-alone therapy, called "narrow-band UV-B" treatment, is still used worldwide. Even today, dermatologists debate whether narrow-band UV-B is superior to PUVA.

While these research activities dominated our dermatology outpatient clinics, I converted our fifteen-bed dermatology inpatient service at MGH into a research center to study the very popular Goeckerman treatment, the application of sticky, messy, strong-smelling crude coal tar in combination with UV-B, used widely since the 1920s to treat severe disfiguring psoriasis. Because the patients remained coated with tar day and night, most had to receive the treatment during costly hospital stays of as much as several weeks, and many hospitals had specialized inpatient facilities dedicated to this treatment. In a complex series of experimental treatments, we demonstrated that the coal tar was an unnecessary part of the therapy. A costly inpatient treatment had been converted into an inexpensive outpatient treatment. Within months, MGH closed its inpatient dermatology unit, and within two years, most hospitals did the same. Another huge impact on dermatology.

As I adopted Mr. Wellman as my new father figure, I adopted an academic son. Rox Anderson was an MIT graduate who had happily dropped out, spending his summers in the woods directing a camp for troubled boys and his winters as secretary to the chaplain at Wellesley College, an all-girl Seven Sisters school. Rox and I met by chance at a book club and started talking, and that night I hired him as a research technician. He began work in my lab the next day, and over ten years Rox transitioned from being my technician and student to being my co-investigator, friend, and teacher. Our collaborations became one of the greatest joys of my professional life. We would spend hours at the blackboard thinking about how things worked in the fascinating intersections of photons and biology, sometimes with coffee, sometimes with beer, and always with great fun. These meetings usually occurred spontaneously, wrecking our intended schedules for the rest of the day.

I trusted Rox completely. On one occasion, we went rock climbing together in Arizona, and I foolishly got myself in a place beyond my skill level and had a complete meltdown of confidence. He positioned himself beneath me and talked me down the side of the hundred-foot rock cliff. He could fix my car or help me solve quadratic equations.

Based on his study of the microanatomy of birthmarks and our growing understanding of the effects of lasers on skin, Rox hypothesized the ideal properties of a laser that could remove the vascular birthmarks known as port wine stains without scarring, a feat never before possible. Because no such laser existed, we convinced a manufacturer to build one in his garage. The treatment worked, changing dermatology forever as Rox went on to develop laser applications for the safe removal of tattoos, hair, pigmented birthmarks, wrinkles, and dilated blood vessels. Using my lab as his home base, Rox continued his research while also completing medical school and his internship and dermatology specialty training at Harvard Medical School.

The explosive impact of PUVA and other ultraviolet treatments and the rapid adoption of lasers in the clinical practice of dermatology and other specialties allowed me to fulfill my goal of becoming a world-renowned dermatologist. I spent about half of my time traveling the world as lecturer, visiting professor, consultant, panelist, keynote speaker, and special guest. In my very small world, I was a minor hero.

As far as any of my colleagues knew, I was the object of adoration at the peak of my profession with an academic legacy that was the envy of my peers. I projected an image of strength and power and success. In the workplace, an environment that was extremely competitive and at times quite cutthroat, I showed no vulnerability. While being friendly, I was always tough, always in charge. By the early 1980s, only a decade after I had decided to specialize in dermatology, I appeared to have achieved my goal. My utter commitment to work had achieved the outcome I had hoped for. Apparently Vietnam was so far in my past that few of my friends or colleagues even realized I had been there.

But I had been. Although my academic and intellectual achievements were real and legitimate and I could produce data that verified their veracity, I was not. In my own home I was anything but a hero. There I was the absent father and irresponsible husband who had sold out to academic elitism, fame, and the applause of a faceless crowd of strangers to whom I paid more attention than I paid my own family. When I faced myself I still saw a wounded phony, a person who still lived a life full of anxiety and increasingly twisted secret behaviors.

All the while, via phone calls, letters, and visits, my father's spiraling sadness continued to intrude into my life. He had, perhaps unrealistically, given his growing emotional fragility, expected to be named president of Stetson University. When he was not, his mental condition rapidly deteriorated. With a great deal of anger and disappointment, he returned to the ministry of a small church in a wealthy community in Winter Park, Florida, where he felt diminished and confined. He no longer wanted to be a preacher ministering to the needs of others. He no longer found ecstasy in orating. Brother Jimmie, the man I had always known him to be, was dying a slow spiritual death that now revealed all his weaknesses and contradictions.

I was unable to help him. I sent him letters about why he should not be sad. I called and traveled to Florida to meet with various psychologists and psychiatrists who were giving him free care because he was just a "poor minister." He was placed on a series of medications that created only deeper depression, somnolence, confusion, and symptoms of Parkinson's disease. While driving to and from work I made audiotapes for him full of empty admonishments. Trust God. Be grateful. Pull yourself together. Let go of your anger. Bootstraps. Love. Trust in God. Love from Jesus.

None of it was helpful. Again, I was impotent to make a difference. However, each time he took center stage I learned to be less controlled by his sadness. When I intervened or he showed up in my life, I responded not so much out of love for him or any confidence that I could help, but largely to share the burden with my brother, Gil, and give my mother some much needed rest.

Each time my father became excessively abusive to my mother or threatened suicide, either Gil or I would go to their home. At least once a year when my mother was at her breaking point and felt there was imminent danger of explosive emotional abuse or suicide, she would put my father on a plane to Boston, where Joan would meet him and treat him as her fourth child for weeks at a time.

It was sad to see him so dysfunctional, and I also considered it a bother to my work schedule. Out of a feeling of duty I would try to come home earlier than usual, in the late afternoon, four o'clock instead of seven or eight or later, and spend the evening with him. On Saturdays and Sundays, I usually hid in my study working, but I would grudgingly spend blocks of time with my father. He was not fun or interesting.

Our children were amused that, unless he shuffled along on an outing, his entire existence consisted of short walks from his bed to his chair and back. In good weather, Joan would place a lawn chair next to a table with pipe, tobacco, and matches, in the shade of the single large tree on our lawn. Frequently he would pull his grandchildren close to him, hugging them tightly and kissing their cheek or mouth. My children would pull away. His black teeth and paunchy belly were unattractive, he reeked of pipe tobacco, and with me as their father they were not used to public displays of affection.

After a few weeks, we would send him back to my mother. The cycle would begin again, and she would soon be exhausted by trying to keep his illness from his colleagues and congregation and to protect everyone from the magnitude of his psychopathology. When he became dysfunctional and sometimes inappropriately emotional in public, the church deacons decided it was time he retired from the ministry. I flew to Florida and convinced his church to quietly send him on a leave of absence. He never returned to work.

Brother Jimmie moved to Albany, Georgia, to be near his brother and sister, forcing my mother to be uprooted from all her friends and connections and children. Thereafter, he was with my mother almost all the time, usually heaping verbal abuse and undeserved anger on her about small issues. If he thought she took too long on an errand, he would pace back and forth in the driveway working himself into a fury.

In the meantime, my brother had re-created himself, completing college and beginning a career. He committed to a wonderful woman and wanted to have a normal stable family. He had an excellent job in Atlanta working for Bell Telephone, a position facilitated by his uncle Claude. At any hour day or night, my mother might panic and call. Several times a month he would drive four hours to Albany and confront my father, sometimes bullying him into submission, sometimes carrying him from a closet or under a table to his bed, where he would then lie sobbing, begging for forgiveness and love. Gil responded to every call without hesitation. On one occasion, he made two round-trips in twenty-four hours.

During one of his Boston visits, I had my father hospitalized in a state psychiatric hospital. Several times each day I visited him as he lay naked and incontinent in fetal position on rubber sheets. He was usually asleep but could be aroused. If he spoke at all, it was to express sadness or helplessness or ask me or God for forgiveness. He sometimes looked into my eyes and pleaded, "Oh, Bubba." I couldn't help.

In 1983, when my father was sixty-seven, he refused to get out of bed and was hospitalized in a university-affiliated community hospital in Georgia. After two or three days, Gil and my mother summoned me, and I flew from Boston to join their bedside vigil. Because my sister and her husband were missionaries in Taiwan and had three children, they did not come to the bedside.

My father's doctors seemed competent, committed, and concerned, explaining that he had moderate but treatable congestive heart failure of unknown cause. Over the next twenty-four hours, however, his blood chemistries began to indicate a spiraling, multisystem failure. Since I was on the faculty of Harvard Medical School at the great Massachusetts General Hospital, the internist in charge of his care started reporting the lab results to me and asking my advice. He was hoping I would transfer my father to MGH, but I thought he was much too sick to travel. My father was dying. Without asking me and despite my passive resistance, my father's doctor made me the responsible party.

I was unprepared. I had stopped seeing patients years before, and suddenly I was expected to make medical decisions. I realized that although I loved being a scientist and a researcher, I was never really comfortable being a doctor. Suddenly I was back in Triage in Vietnam, this time being asked to save my own father. In the years since my training in internal medicine, I had been a soldier, a trainee in dermatology, and a researcher. Now, without warning, I was no longer the son. I was the doctor, the responsible party, the savior, and, inevitably, the inadequate one.

I felt totally overwhelmed. I didn't know what to do, and suddenly I had the chart, the lab tests, and my father's life in my hands. I was called upon, but it was too late. I could not save him. I did nothing. I gave in and I gave up.

In a straight-back wooden chair at the foot of the bed, I sat alone with my father in the simple, single hospital room as he died. My family and the hospital staff waited outside. He was intermittently conscious. I could get his attention and he could respond, sometimes in an appropriate, oriented manner, but in a very limited way, almost as if he were a child. He sometimes looked at me and sometimes looked far away. He was definitely aware of my presence. When he closed his eyes, his lips made primitive sucking gestures. Twice he stopped breathing only to start again. One last time he closed his eyes and stopped his pain and struggle.

"I love you." I forced the thought. "I forgive you."

Then I repeated the thought in a whisper.

"I love you," I said aloud. "I forgive you."

Maybe his brain could still record messages.

I sat quietly with him in death. I felt nothing. Here was the warm body of the man who formed my view of the world. At times I had wished for his death. By magic, had I caused the deaths of my brother and my father? I tried to conjure up some feelings, but I was completely numb, watching my dead father and myself as if looking at a black-and-white photograph. Here was the force that molded me. He was in control, and his death was a mystery to me and his doctors. His body was dead, and I was dead inside. We were comrades in arms.

I began to think of my mother and brother and was suddenly sad and anxious. I found them sitting in a small waiting room accompanied by a man I did not recognize. As I approached, my mother began to introduce me to her minister. I ignored him. "He's gone," I said. My mother rose from her chair, and as I approached to embrace her, the minister stepped between us to embrace her himself. Without speaking, I physically moved him to the side, practically lifting him off the floor. My mother cried out to me, "Oh, Bubba." To me, it sounded like a plea for help for both of us. I held her while she cried. It was the first time I had ever held her. Gil kindly occupied the minister.

Maybe my father willed himself to death. For ten years he had said he wanted to die, and he long predicted that he would die on October 10, my dead brother's birthday, the same day Little Jimmie had been buried. He almost made it. On his deathbed he got confused and missed it by a day, dying one day early. Although I celebrated that his struggle and my mother's torture had ceased, I still felt inadequate and guilty that I could not save him.

Because his doctors had no idea why he died, they asked permission to do an autopsy. My mother refused because "he had already suffered too much." Privately, one doctor asked me if they could perform a "limited autopsy," an exploratory laparoscopy, without removing any organs, testing his fluids and performing multiple small biopsies. Although curious about the cause of his death, to honor my mother's wishes, I refused.

My mother's public grief was brief. She instructed Gil whom to call to share the news and to make arrangements for moving the body and initiate the funeral plan. She wanted to go home and weep in a controlled private way.

My father's body was sent by train to Laurel, Mississippi, so he could be buried next to my older brother. Gil, my mother, and I followed by car. At the gravesite I remembered going with my father on his daily visits to my brother's grave and standing quietly while he cried. I remembered how much I hated Christmas and birthdays because of the presence of my dead brother, who participated in absentia in the giving and receiving of gifts. Brother Jimmie joined Little Jimmie. In my mother's heart she knew they were both with Jesus. I thought they were next to each other in the ground. There was no acknowledgment of my father's military service. My father had taken the secrets of his war stories into the grave with him.

Now that he was dead, in private my brother told me the extent of my father's philandering and mentioned several of his longtime relationships, most of whom I knew as family friends or relatives. I remembered being taken to play with friends I barely knew and often did not really like. Now I realized for the first time that while I kept the kids busy in the yard, my father was having sex with their mother. I realized that while I had been away continuing my academic career, Gil had been largely left alone to protect our mother, manage an increasingly abusive relationship with our father, create a stable family of his own, and try to make sense of his own life. I knew that years earlier Gil had been sexually assaulted by a man who was on the staff at the church and was sexually precocious. While I had been oblivious, Gil had figured out that as my father counseled church women about broken marriages and dead husbands, he was also using their grief as a way to seduce them. Once my father realized Gil knew the truth about him, he had become less careful about hiding his extramarital life from Gil. Knowing that if Gil said anything no one would believe him, my father bought Gil's silence by letting him in on additional secrets and then threatening him. A distant relative of my father's was one of his steadier sex partners. On one occasion when they were in bed together, in another room Gil was having sex with her daughter.

From quips, subtle statements, and occasional thinly disguised bragging, Gil also discovered that my father had loved the four years he had spent in the navy. With no wife or kids or small-minded church believers to hold him back, he had spent most if not all of the war, stateside or in exotic ports, on the winning team, side by side with God, wearing a white dress uniform, with prestige, plenty of cash, and the complete freedom to do whatever he wanted. An officer and a gentleman, my father had spent the war in complete safety, preaching on

Sunday mornings and fucking on Sunday afternoons. He was a sailor just like in the movies.

I was puzzled that Gil had not shared my father's exploits with me before now. I was angry that because of my father's teaching about the sin of any form of physical intimacy outside marriage, my sexuality had been stunted until I married at age twenty-four. I was hurt to be kept in the dark and to be on the outside of forbidden secrets, and I vowed to always be on the inside from now on even if I had to create the secrets myself.

Without looking at the content herself, my mother gave me an autobiography my father had written a few years earlier and addressed to his children. This was when I learned that my father, who preached and practiced total abstinence, had been an alcoholic by the time he was fourteen years old. Until Jesus saved him, he was a thug, brawling, drinking, vandalizing, and having secret liaisons with middle-aged and older women. For me, the awareness of my father's story was another loss of innocence, and I felt even more adrift than before. I kept the handwritten manuscript from my mother. My brother and sister did not want to read it. I have yet to finish it myself.

I was my father's son. I knew that now. I had cultivated funding for my research the way my father had cultivated rich donors at church, using flattery and praise and attention. Physically and emotionally I was largely unavailable to my family. Among my father's many sins and weaknesses, I considered his infidelity as the core of his wickedness. At some level, I must have known about my father's sexism, philandering, and hypocrisy. In families, there are no real secrets. When I thought about what my children must think of me, I drowned in shame. The sins of the fathers shall be visited upon the son a thousand times. I recreated my nuclear family of origin and then set about to destroy it.

I returned to Boston and resumed my life. As I became even more of a workaholic, other secret behaviors increased as well. With the advent and accessibility of the VCR it became possible for me to indulge in my addiction to war and violence anytime I wanted. Just as I had listened to the records of war sounds over and over again, I could do the same with Vietnam movies. I became just as enamored with films that depicted violence outside of a war context and would watch martial arts contests and underground videos of explicit pictures of death by accident, suicide, or murder.

Despite my professional success, with each passing day I felt ever more unworthy and guilt ridden. I would swear off these various behaviors like a smoker swearing off cigarettes, berating myself and throwing away a vulgar videotape one day only to resume the affair or purchase another tape a few weeks later. I tried to atone for my growing emotional estrangement from Joan by joining her in her intellectual explorations, even to the point of taking feminist liberation theology classes with her in divinity school. As I was being reeducated and resocialized, my sensitivity to power issues and sexism markedly increased. I was the rightful target of much of the anger in the classroom, and I was trying to perforate my own shield.

Except to make me even more driven, none of these behaviors adversely affected my work. With my first National Institutes of Health grant, a grant from the Department of Energy, and Mr. Wellman's donations, I was able to build a research group of ten people including three faculty members. We named ourselves the MGH Wellman Laboratories of Photomedicine, with me as director. The research continued as I traveled, but I constantly worried about long-term funding to sustain my growing group.

In 1983, the year of my father's death, President Ronald Reagan challenged the scientific community to design a shield that could protect the United States against Russian rockets carrying nuclear weapons. His "Strategic Defense Initiative," nicknamed "Star Wars," was fraught with political problems and, from a technical standpoint, not likely to be effective. It would have to work perfectly the first time because there would be no way to test it. Nonetheless, $30 billion were poured into Star Wars over the next ten years to develop a vast network of sensing devices and small guided missiles.

One of the most unrealistic fantasies included shooting down nuclear missiles with space-based lasers. In a remarkable sell, the inventors of a new laser called the free-electron laser (FEL) convinced a bevy of members of congress and military leaders that it was the technology needed for the success of Star Wars. The FEL had a fascinating, unique collection of properties. Unlike most lasers, the FEL was "tunable," producing radiation in any part of the ultraviolet, visible, or near-infrared regions of the spectrum. On very small sites, the power of the radiation could exceed the radiation at the surface of the sun. The duration of each laser pulse of light was very brief, lasting less than one-millionth of one-billionth of a second. The FEL was the champion of a growing number of lasers called high peak power, short pulse (HPP-SP) light sources.

Subsequently, the inventor and his colleagues convinced the parties responsible for the Star Wars program that the unique HPP-SP properties of the FEL were also ideal for medical applications. As a result, and to increase the popularity of Star Wars, hundreds of millions of dollars were funneled into medical research based on what I believed to be completely unfounded hope.

I was invited to be an expert witness in congressional hearings on the prospects for medical uses of the technology. I testified that I could see no possibilities for medical uses of an FEL. First, it was too big, expensive, and unreliable. Second, although I did see promise for use of other HPP-SP lasers, we knew much too little about the basic principles of HPP-SP laser effects on tissue to judge the safety or utility of the FEL. I was asked if I would be willing to study such effects. I agreed to consider it because my laboratory had already shown unique effects of HPP-SP lasers on living tissue. The successful treatment of birthmarks was a convincing example.

I met several times with the members of my lab to discuss what came to be called the Medical FEL (MFEL) Program. They voted unanimously not to accept Department of Defense money, especially from funding for a defense system mission they knew was impossible. Primarily, they wished not to be contaminated by money from the military. I overruled them and joined a multi-institutional MFEL Program. Although I never planned on housing an FEL, I thought we could discover useful information for the medical application of lasers.

Over the next twenty years the MFEL Program provided my lab with well over $100 million to study the effects of HPP-SP lasers on tissue. Recruiting over one hundred technicians, students, administrators, support staff, and M.D. and Ph.D. scientists, Wellman Labs grew into the Wellman Center for Photomedicine, a large multidisciplinary group studying the effects of near-infrared, visible, and ultraviolet radiation on biological materials and living tissue. Our growing understanding of HPP-SP effects led to over twenty new FDA-approved diagnostics and treatments with a large impact on health care, especially dermatology. My group introduced the use of lasers to break up kidney stones. We laid the research foundation for many of the surgical uses of lasers. We never obtained an FEL.

During another frenzy of domestic and international travel, as I began to believe my own success story, I demonstrated the depth of my moral degradation with an affair that ended badly and had elements of a Greek tragedy. The female lead came to my attention when a powerful and very well known colleague told me he had seduced her in his office. I immediately coveted her. She was sexy, modern, energetic, attractive, and friendly. I seduced her, but she refused to be abandoned and then she owned me.

I came to dislike this "other woman" and hate myself, but through a sick mix of guilt, shame, and lust I felt trapped in the relationship. Although she looked exactly like my mother, she was her complete opposite. A wealthy single child of the sixties, she had been left a considerable amount of money and made her own personal "fulfillment" a full-time job. She owned a luxury apartment, a vacation home, and often visited Boston. She spent her time pursuing yoga, massage, aromatherapy, enlightenment, meditation, sweat lodges, exotic travel, gurus, personal trainers, skiing, skydiving . . . and me. She insisted that she loved me and that I was her one and only lover.

On occasion, when I traveled, in the states or internationally, she would join me as a secret roommate. If I resisted, she might book her own room in my hotel anyway. I could not muster the courage to have the confrontational, firm, and painful rejection it would take to unhook from her. She picked up none of my hints about how seeing her was making me crazy. She planned our encounters with the help of Frederick's of Hollywood, Victoria's Secret, candles, and incense. I felt powerless. I sometimes looked forward to our meetings with all the enthusiasm of forced manual labor.

Although we met infrequently, the mechanics of scheduling our sex and keeping it a secret were awkward and time-consuming. I eventually stopped sharing my travel schedule and told my secretary to lie about my whereabouts. Yet because my appearances were usually publicized in advance, she sometimes found me. Even when it was untrue, I began to tell her that Joan was traveling with me. My self-loathing, passivity, and inability to reject the relationship I enabled kept me awake at night. Each time I built up my resolve to dump her, it always seemed somehow easier to just let her show up, hide her presence, and sleep with her. Although possibly too naive and needy, she was a good person and was a victim of my projection, manipulation, inauthenticity, and sex compulsion. Through the fog of my cowardice, I could not yet see that my codependent love-struck pursuer looked like my mother and stood for my father.

OW (the "other woman") occasionally manipulated me into spending a day or night with her away from work and home. On those occasions, I felt not only crushing guilt, shame, and self-hate but also a sharp pain of separation from Joan and my children. Instead of being authentic, honorable, and strong, I became a passive volunteer playing a dishonest role that continually raised the OW's already high expectations. I gave away all my personal power. Once I was trapped in New York City by a blizzard because I had delayed my return from a business meeting in order to have lunch and spend time with the OW. Airports closed and streets were abandoned. Instead of relishing an overnight stay with her in a very expensive hotel room, without overcoat or boots, I walked many blocks to the train station and felt blessed to endure a ten-hour journey to Boston. I longed to be with my family and back at my job.

The sick story ended in an ugly way. Hurt and vengeful, the OW contacted Joan after a clumsy and inarticulate phone call from me breaking off the affair. Joan and I had ten or twelve sessions of couples therapy in another attempt to salvage our marriage. The therapist understandably sided with Joan and focused not at all on my motivations or psychopathology but on my sins and possible punishments and the affair's impact on Joan. With guidance from Joan, the therapist assigned a list of home improvement and household chores that I embraced and accomplished with vigor and pain. Even so, I knew this was the beginning of the end of my family unit.

Again, I was filled with shame, both for my sins and for my inability to say no to the inappropriate demands of a needy person I did not love or respect. Still, I did see a glimmer of hope in this episode. Even before the phone call to Joan, I was thoroughly disgusted with myself and my accomplice. A few years earlier, I would have relished the affair as a great setup. Because they were centered on sex, required no maintenance, and carried no short-term or long-term expectations, I had coldly rationalized that my earlier affairs were not harmful to others—infrequent, efficient encounters. Although the connections were caring and intimate and the secrecy was bonding, the relationships had the style of a "zipless fuck" with an option to repeat, or "friends with benefits" for the adult set. With one partner, we sometimes decided to go to the gym instead of having sex. Initially stimulated by the risks, adventure, and lust, I wore a scarlet letter on the inside and seemed to be the only one who actually carried any shame.

Although I returned to a vow of purity, I remained wedded to my work. I tried to be a good doctor. I was a good researcher. Although I was a good provider, I had again failed my family. In our "picture perfect" family I was actually a traitor and a phoney.

CHAPTER 14

Twenty years after I left Vietnam my private inner core felt abandoned, abused, unheard. I was still haunted by the feelings of dread and helplessness I associated with Triage. I harbored hidden resentment, distrust of authorities, hopelessness, and cynicism. Secretly I mourned yellow and white and black victims. I found myself increasingly restless, tortured, and lonely—never more so than at social events or professional meetings where my peers assumed I was in control. Only I knew that my one-year war was not complete and that I carried invisible wounds.

When I served in Vietnam I was always afraid of being overwhelmed by the number and severity of casualties on the next helicopter. Now I worried about possible past errors in judgment or technique that might have cost young men their lives and limbs. If the boy I attended died, not only was he dead, but so perhaps was the man I did not choose to work on first. The present mingled with the past, and sometimes ugly images or smells of Vietnam lingered in my mind.

The study of war continued to be a serious preoccupation, consuming my nights and weekends. I devoured books about the history, strategy, tactics, and weapons of war. I read about nationalism, conscription, sanctioned killing, the training of warriors, and the diplomacy of fear and might. What captured me most intensely was the personal stories of the soldiers at the point of the spear.

I was angry. I wanted to attack those who were comfortable with war more than I wanted to comfort those who were afflicted. I wanted to display young men's arms and legs and viscera in churches and boardrooms and government chambers and executive offices. Sometimes I wanted revenge. At the very least I wanted an explanation.

I was embarrassed that I had bought into the American myths so absolutely. I had believed in a personal Jesus, a God who guaranteed justice and rewarded hard work, holy patriotism, manifest destiny, the sanctity of marriage, romantic love, the power of goodness, and every other Western myth—and in less than a year all were destroyed by my environment and by me. As a child I was a good boy and believed everything I was told. Most people gradually test their mythology, test power and authority, and learn reality a step at a time in their adolescence, but in war in only a few weeks I discovered that all the things I had believed were not true, in the childlike way I had embraced them. Naive magical thinking was crushed by the banality and randomness of evil and death. The fall from grace and belief was enormous and precipitous. I felt stupid.

I was too embarrassed to express the depth of my disappointment. I sought ways to explore and expose my pain and feelings of inauthenticity and inadequacy. If the answers did not come from physical exhaustion, study, and immersion in war perhaps I could find them elsewhere.

I cast about for solutions and reconnection, trying on different philosophical, quasi-religious, and self-actualization programs like so many coats, going through all manner of isms and acronyms like EST (Erhard Seminar Training) and various men's groups wrestling and beating drums around campfires, tying red ribbons on our wounds, and going through physical trials together, then getting in touch with our inner child and forgiving ourselves. But I could neither forgive nor forget. I remember coming into the kitchen in my Weston home suffer-

208

ing from forty-eight hours without sleep, wearing war paint. Joan insisted I shower before the children saw me.

I became a serious yoga devotee, practicing Ashtanga Yoga and breathing exercises almost every day. I learned deep meditation and could calm myself when agitated. I began to feel more "centered" and could sometimes observe my inner war with little or no emotional response.

I also used yoga for very nonspiritual purposes. I used it to pursue my need for excess and overstimulation. I needed another addiction. It could be running or sex or just notching up the work a bit, but I always had to be overwhelmed by some excessive behavior. I began practicing yoga to excess, doing sun salutes, a complex series of different ways to bend and stand, to exhaustion, pushing the limits. If I did ten one day, I would try to do eleven, and then twelve. At times, instead of using yoga to quiet my mind for meditation, I struggled to perform, to set personal records in strength and endurance. Pushing to one's physical limits is antithetical to preparation of the peaceful, empty mind. Yet, I needed to push the limit, in yoga, in everything. It almost did not matter what.

One of my men's groups, made up of mostly younger men, met weekly to compete in risky physical contests. With another group of men, I repeatedly confessed my sins and anxieties as we sat in a small circle. For fear of being seen as weak, I did not share my symptoms of stress related to Vietnam. One of the members, tired of hearing me confess affairs and express my ambivalence toward marriage, challenged me in front of the group to leave Joan. I promised that I would. Rather than lose face before the group at the next meeting, I told Joan I was going to try being alone. My priorities were completely inverted.

Joan had stretched, challenged, saved, and nurtured me, been my college sweetheart, first lover, and mother of my three extraordinary children, and helped me keep a measure of balance by criticizing my excesses and being underwhelmed by my worldly successes. She made a real attempt to protect me from myself and from the mechanics of family life. Yet despite all that, I came to feel diminished in our relationship. I knew my role and understood the expectations, even though I failed to meet them. I did not understand my failure to feel heroic and authentic in a relationship with someone who loved me greatly, and was always faithful and committed to me, even while she yet disapproved of the parts of me she judged to be inauthentic or inappropriate or gender-wired.

One night, as Joan sat silent and disbelieving in the living room, I made several trips taking clothes and a few other belongings to my car. Except for the sound of my footsteps going up and down the stairs and doors opening and closing, everything was quiet. Without further conversation I drove away and spent the night with my yoga teacher. I felt so awful the next day, I moved into my office at MGH. Thereafter, I kept a blanket and a pillow and a roll-out mat in my office; after housekeeping and security personnel left, I would sleep on my office floor and then be sure I was up in the morning in time to shave in the men's room before anyone found out. I kept my belongings in my car. A department chair and professor, and director of a multimillion-dollar research lab, I essentially made myself homeless. Eventually I remodeled my lab to include a shower so I that I had a place to bathe.

Communication with my children practically ceased. Joan carried on her life as if nothing permanent had happened. I continued to support my family financially.

I had never really been alone before and didn't know the difference between being alone and being lonely. I had always shared my living and sleeping space with a sibling, a classmate, a wife, or a fellow soldier. Yet I always felt alone. To be authentic, I had to be as alone as I felt.

Living alone, in self-imposed isolation, symbolized a commitment to an inward journey seeking calm and healing through withdrawal. It was also an attempt to integrate my world—to make my life more compatible with the alienation and distrust I was feeling. Aloneness was a desperate experiment, a counterphobic compulsion, and an untested fantasy.

I stopped smoking. I became celibate and withdrew completely from Sugar, Caffeine, Alcohol, and red Meat (I called this my SCAM routine). I failed and succeeded and failed over and over again. I had never realized how anchored I had been to Joan and my children. Without them, on my own, I rapidly became more erratic and unhinged. Twice I moved back into our home in Weston and then moved out again.

I moved into a tiny studio apartment alone, then moved into another apartment with my yoga instructor. I convinced myself that she was a freedom-child on a spiritual journey. After graduating from college, she sang professionally in bars and town halls, hung out with cowboys and hippies, and studied yoga. At one point, she led her own small band of musicians. She wrote and recorded songs, meditated for hours, and kept a horse and rode through the woods and galloped across fields. I was fascinated by her weird friends. She wrote poetry and constantly worked on a novel I never read. She was the perfect template on which to project all my fantasies of spiritual enlightenment, witchcraft, art, earthiness, and complete freedom from guilt of any kind. In the company of her fringe group, I learned the adolescent lessons of romance, jealousy, "breaking up," sexual freedom, and spiritual ecstasy.

I slowly learned that she had her own private magical thinking and an inconsistent, self-congratulating code of honor. She played with truth as if it were a mysterious, harmless creature subject to her higher morality. I began to distrust her intentions and recognized a phoniness similar to my own. I thought she was using me more than loving me. Then again, at this point in time, I trusted no one. I finally asked her to leave, and I abandoned the apartment myself. Several times I found another place to live and she moved in with me again. We bought a cabin on a lake in the woods, and she made it into a studio, shrine, and home. I commuted twenty-five miles to work.

I moved back into my office. I rarely experienced war nightmares or flashbacks anymore, but after I moved away from home I began to be bothered by intrusive thoughts. When I made eye contact with a homeless, physically disabled, or intoxicated man, I suddenly began to feel a painful pressure in my midchest, and my throat would swell. A picture of the Vietnam War Memorial, or any kind of war memorial, would bring me to tears. The sound of a helicopter made me physically ill. I no longer felt safe. In public places, restaurants, and meeting rooms, I had to sit with my back to the wall and have an unobstructed view of the door.

Seemingly without provocation, the same image returned over and over again. A wounded marine, well muscled, in his midtwenties, lies naked on a table. His chest and abdomen are slit open from right midclavicle to pubic bone. His skin is flayed open, exposing his organs. I can see his heart and lungs, his liver, his stomach, and his glistening intestines. He is slowly bleeding at the incision sites, but there is no blood pooled in his body cavities.

The picture I see could not be possible. In the reality of Triage he would never have been cut so cleanly open, leaving his organs on display. I know this never happened and must be some memory I have constructed, a kind of collage. He is conscious and looks at me, making pleasant idle conversation. Occasionally he closes his eyes, moans, and quivers as so many wounded men did when they were first being carried on a litter into Triage. I can move around to see him from different angles, but I do nothing. Corpsmen in jungle fatigues and doctors in white coats wait for my signal, but I hesitate.

In the middle of a meeting or a conversation or even if I was sitting quietly, reading, his image might appear. It would be there but it was also not there. It wasn't dangerous—I wouldn't walk into walls or wander into the street, and I was not paralyzed. If I was interrupted I knew where I was, but for a moment I would not be processing my surroundings. If someone asked me a question, I could give appropriate answers.

I also began to exhibit other symptoms. I was never physically wounded in Vietnam, but out of nowhere, with no outside stimulus, I would spontaneously begin to drag my right leg as I walked, as if I had been wounded and was severely disabled. In a way, I was. I made sure no one ever noticed my partially paralyzed leg.

I had alienated myself from everyone. Sometimes late at night in my office I would start to feel lonely and exhausted, but I couldn't go to bed until after housekeeping had come to clean, because I couldn't let anyone know I was sleeping in my office. When I was too tired to work, I would leave the hospital and walk the streets to kill time. I wandered randomly, sometimes sitting on benches or curbs. I desperately longed for Joan and my children. I would sometimes lie awake tossing and floundering about all night or cry myself to sleep because I missed them so. Even so, the next day I could not break through my own guilt and remorse to encounter them. There was a barrier of shame I could not climb over. I would make it through another day feeling totally alone.

Several blocks from the hospital is the New England Shelter for Homeless Veterans. I walked by it a number of times before one night I finally decided to walk in. Someone at the front desk stopped me and asked me to show him my papers proving military service, the kind of thing I had never paid attention to or even known about, because apart from my old friend Alex, I never knowingly interacted with vets. I told him I didn't have a military ID, and he said, "Well, you know, we have to prove that you're a veteran."

I stared at him. "If you could find somebody in the shelter who was in Vietnam between 1966 and 1970 and let me talk with him, he would know that I was in Vietnam." I told him that I had a place to sleep. I just wanted to hang out for a while. The guy waved me inside. A guard searched me for weapons and drugs.

About forty or fifty men from their midthirties to midsixties were watching TV, playing cards, or sitting silently alone or in small clusters. In other rooms, another forty or fifty men were lying in long rows of beds. Most were not asleep. It was moderately quiet, not a happy place, but not really sad either.

For several hours I just hung out. I didn't actively engage anyone in conversation because while playing cards, watching TV, or taking naps, everyone was in his own private space or already talking to someone in a comfortable way. Still, I lingered. I somehow needed to identify with the men, especially men in my age group, who knew what war was and what it does to people and especially people who had lost their bearings and no longer had a place to live. Being there was enough.

Occasional eye contact was brief and without expression. Over-heard conversations without substantive content seemed to start from nothing and drift away without completion. Brief forced laughter followed loving verbal abuse. It felt like it would be out of place to talk about anything serious—especially about war or Vietnam.

Unable to talk even to the Vietnam veterans at the shelter about my persistent pain, I didn't speak at all. Maybe men always lose their voices. They play games and work and don't talk about war, feelings, or responsibility. They don't talk about talk. It is not voices crying in the wilderness but voices not being able to cry at all.

On Christmas Eve Joan, the kids, and I always went to a party at a certain friend's home. It was a tradition. The same families attended each year. Because I had left the family and our friends knew the whole story, I didn't feel welcome anymore. I felt like I couldn't participate in a family-based Christmas party. One Christmas Eve I left the office, started walking, and, without conscious intent, ended up in the Vietnam veterans' shelter. I stayed in silence for several hours, listening to Christmas music from a tape deck. Sometime after midnight, I left the shelter and randomly walked about in a cold rain.

In Vietnam I grew to love and hate the rain. In rainy season, it was the last sound I heard as I fell into sleep, a natural lullaby for my cave instinct, the reminder of my continuing existence, the signal of natural forces, a symbol of my smallness, and a connection to life before Vietnam. Rain provided an unmodifiable force to which I could absolutely resign. Relentless, but cleansing and forgiving. I knew that rain could wash out wounds and create the mud that drowned the wounded.

In Vietnam the monsoon season started just like any other rainstorm. Late one afternoon it poured for an hour, then tapered off to a steady drizzle that lasted all night. It did not stop raining for two months. The baseline was a steady, cold, misty, shifting rain. On top of that were intermittent sheets of solid water that lasted for hours. The wind varied considerably. Eventually, because everyone accepted being constantly wet and walking ankle deep in mud, life went on as usual. Long underwear, fatigues, boots, and two blankets could not keep the cold, wet chill out of one's core. The patrols kept going and returning.

After a few weeks of steady rain, there was a constant feeling of cold wetness that sank to my bones. No matter what my body temperature, the number of layers of clothes, or the number of blankets, I still felt an inner primal coldness that gnawed at my brain and soul. Sometimes the cold made me angry. Yet it also reminded me of being alive and being vulnerable. Rain made me feel both safe and helpless, bathed yet exposed. An aching dampness. A teasing dankness. It gave me another chance to surrender.

I went back to my office and, in my cold wet clothes, fell asleep on the floor. It was a very restless sleep. I was cold.

And it came to pass in those days, that there went out a decree
from Caesar Augustus, that all the world should be taxed.
And all went to be taxed, every one into his own city.

The chaplain was reading by candlelight. He had a King James southern accent.

And Joseph also went up from Galilee, out of the city of Naza-
reth, into Judaea, unto the city of David, which is called Bethlehem;
(because he was of the house and lineage of David:)
To be taxed with Mary his espoused wife, being great with child.

We were under a leaky tent being used as a chapel for a Christmas
Eve pause in war.

And so it was, that, while they were there, the days were accom-
plished that she should be delivered.

The congregation was small. Four doctors, four corpsmen, two
marines, and one army soldier sitting on wooden benches with hats
in hand.

And she brought forth her firstborn son, and wrapped him in
swaddling clothes, and laid him in a manger; because there was no
room for them in the inn.

I wondered if everything was quiet up in Triage.

And there were in the same country shepherds abiding in the
field, keeping watch over their flock by night.

I thought of all those marines out in the field. Kids in the mud.

And, lo, the angel of the Lord came upon them, and the glory of
the Lord shone round about them: and they were sore afraid.

Those kids were scared shitless out in this black night and cold as
hell. I knew how cold they were.

And the angel said unto them, Fear not: for, behold, I bring you
good tidings of great joy, which shall be to all people.

My mind began to replay mortars socking into the mud. The sound was nauseating. I heard screams.

> *For unto you is born this day in the city of David a Savior, which is Christ the Lord.*

Merry Christmas, you poor bastards. God knows I wish you weren't out there.

> *And this shall be a sign unto you; Ye shall find the babe wrapped in swaddling clothes, lying in a manger.*

I wrinkled and twisted my hat. I stared down at my hands. Mud and blood.

> *And suddenly there was with the angel a multitude of the heavenly host praising God, and saying . . .*

Mortars socking into the mud. Machine-gun fire, flares, screams. Kids getting hit and drowning in the mud. I could see them plainly in my mind.

> *Glory to God in the highest, and on earth peace, good will toward men.*

I couldn't stand it any longer. I left the service and walked up toward Triage. Now it was raining in steady, heavy, solid sheets. A high-pitched whistle scared me, and by reflex I dropped to my knees and felt mud seep into my groin. A flare popped in the east, and, as it settled slowly to the ground, even in the rain it gave a luster of day to objects below. Three figures approached, silhouetted by the dying flame in the sky. I got to the Triage entrance just ahead of them. Two marines were bearing a third soldier between them. They let the soldier slide gently to the floor in front of me.

He was covered with mud; his clothes were torn and dripping with blood. A full pack and trench tool still clung to his back; he looked like a monster, skin burned a gray-black. His eyes were wide open, his nostrils were flared, and the strap of his helmet was clenched in his teeth. Rain matted his hair to his head. He clutched at a hole in his belly. His stare was pleading; his eyes begged for help. A clench of his fists and a twist of his head led me to know that soon he'd be dead. He stared straight to the sky, wiggling and twitching, trying to cry. He convulsed once and then he was dead.

One good thing about a hard rain is that nobody can tell when you're crying.

On multiple occasions, for months at a time I stopped seeing anyone other than my work associates. At those times the study of war came to be a very serious preoccupation, consuming all my nights and weekends. Sometimes while my colleagues assumed I was studying or writing a paper, I would spend days reading about war. War had revealed things to me that I would never otherwise be forced to know. Most people will never know these truths, preferring never to learn them, even choosing to refute their possibility. Unable to find adequate language and reluctant to share these deep lessons with an indifferent, unreceptive, or even hostile world, I remained quiet. Pursuing the meaning and lessons of my one-year war alone became both a disease and an attempt at a cure.

I was taking the air shuttle from Boston to Washington and by chance found myself sitting next to a colleague from the hospital I knew to be a psychiatrist.

We recognized each other and knew each other by name but were more strangers than acquaintances. Still, it was good to have someone to talk to, and we spent most of the flight chatting—sharing stories about our work, hospital gossip, and information about our lives, nothing that I recall as being very revealing.

The plane landed, and while we waited to disembark, he scrawled something on a piece of paper. Then he looked at me.

"You know, John," he said, "you're clinically depressed. You need to get help, and I'm going to recommend a couple of people to you." Then he handed me the piece of paper.

CHAPTER 15

No one knows.

I am sitting in an old wickerarm chair in a small one-room cabin on a dirt road at Bare Hill Pond, in Harvard, Massachusetts. The cabin is old, sparsely furnished, even spartan. The floor is bare, worn wood. The bed doubles as a couch. In the corner is a small kitchen—a counter and table with a telephone, two straight-back chairs, a tiny gas stove, and a small electric refrigerator full of beer and food too stale to eat. The canned food on the shelf has been there for years. The sink works intermittently. The water that comes from the faucet is brown, tastes of minerals, leaves me thirsty, and cleans nothing.

I do not know how long I have been here. From my beard, my body odor, and the number of beer cans covering almost every surface or else crushed and scattered across the floor, I am guessing it has been four or five days.

The phone rings. I don't answer. I never answer. When I try to write the words evade me.

For months I have been marching, step by step, away from my "real life," from the family-oriented husband and father, the professional, responsible person it took so long for me to create.

No one knows where I am. I barely know who I am.

Each day I swim to a small deserted island a half mile offshore. I do yoga sun salutes until I am too tired to stand, then sit in the lotus position and meditate for an endless period of time. Light-headed and weak, I long to remain still, but I know I must return to the shore before I become disoriented or unconscious. The swim back to the cabin is a struggle, laced with intermittent visceral panic and thrashing and gasping for breath. The water seems colder, deeper, almost black. The distance back seems longer than before.

The psychic pain is almost unbearable. Once or twice a day I run, seeking defense against feeling. Physical pain is more quantifiable, explainable, and honorable and distracts me from my sense of dread. In shorts and heavy boots I run random pathways through woods as brush scrapes my skin raw and my wounds sting with sweat. My eyes constantly scan the woods for safe places to hide from people or bullets or incoming shells. I stay off the trails and conceal myself if hikers pass nearby. I try to get lost. I charge up hills with burning thighs and lungs and stumble back down on jelly legs. I surrender to pain, slow to a walk, relax into a stumble, fall to the ground, roll into a ball, and cry. My palms and knees bleed. The dirt under my fingernails seems mixed with brains and blood. My nostrils harbor the smell of death; I taste putrefaction. I long for the intensity of a struggle to survive.

All is silent except for birds and insects and my heavy breathing. To break the silence and purposely risk being discovered, I scream out random profanities. Welcoming the panic and pain of breathlessness, I grunt aloud.

"Hello pain!"

"Hello fear!"

"Hello loneliness!

"Hello random death!"

There is no answer back but my own breath.

At night I retreat. Outside there is the noise of the woods, of life turning over, crickets, tree frogs, owls. As I enter the cabin, these sounds fall away. It is darker inside than out. I slump into the chair, drink beer until I am numb, and then fumble for the videotapes, slipping one into the slot on the VCR. I sit in the dark, transfixed before the images, the sound turned on full, drowning out everything. *The Green Berets. Platoon. Full Metal Jacket. Apocalypse Now.* John Wayne meets Mr. Kurtz. The screen fills the wall; the war grows to fill the room. The walls come down, and I fall asleep on the floor. I sleep and wake intermittently, lost in sound, wakened by incoming and outgoing artillery, helicopters filled with dead and dying, Triage filled with wounded boys, barking orders, and babies crying. I will myself into episodes of sobbing, moaning, and shaking.

When the cabin turns to Triage I escape and sleep on the ground in the open near the lake. In my helmet and flak jacket, I lie facedown halfway between the blast wall and the landing zone, too tired to move and too afraid to sleep. The jungle creeps through the woods. I am afraid of being responsible for others, of being called upon and found unworthy. I am the final responsible party. I can endure the pain as victim, but the pain as the final responsible party is much more difficult.

Too tired to move. Too afraid to sleep.

At night thoughts and dreams become the same.

Incoming!

CHAPTER 16

Arm outstretched, palm open upward, he waved me to a comfortable leather chair and sat facing me in an identical one, the only other furniture in the small, quiet room. The light was dim and muted. Heavy curtains hung over the windows. There was no couch, desk, or large table.

"So . . . what can I do to help you?" he said.

"My big brother died and my Southern Baptist minister father never got over it." I surprised myself with this unplanned, abrupt, and seemingly inappropriate introduction. Speaking rapidly without emotion, I felt completely numb.

"Your older brother, he died when you were . . . how old?"

"And I never got over Vietnam," I interrupted.

It just came out as if he'd stuck a pin into an abscess and the pus just squirted across the room, unplanned and uncensored.

He was silent.

Suddenly I was feeling anxious, vulnerable.

I backed off and tried to counter my embarrassment by spewing out my standard professional biographical sketch, but he seemed to already know—in some detail—who I was.

I remember nothing more about those next fifty minutes.

I began a relationship that continues to this day, undergoing serious therapy to learn how to deal with my traumas, my psychotic dad, my dead brother, my experiences in Vietnam, and the pathological narcissism that enabled me to hurt my family. In psychotherapy I felt less alone and on a path to recovery. That was the day I began to heal.

Although he did not tell me at the time, Jim Groves, my therapist, recognized that a major component of my symptomology was post-traumatic stress disorder (PTSD).

Throughout the seventies and eighties a small number of very committed psychiatrists, most of them working in the VA or Department of Defense health care system,* spent thousands of hours helping and learning from Vietnam veterans with lingering symptoms of war-related stress. Academic and community specialists had begun to discuss the similarities among the long-term psychological impacts of rape, child abuse, and exposure to violence or death.

By 1988, the official reference and standardization manual for psychiatry described PTSD as a legitimate syndrome with definitive diagnostic criteria, the only well-described psychiatric disorder that requires an outside event as part of the diagnosis. The traumatic events that spawn PTSD are varied and may involve being a witness or a victim of rape, assault, serious car accident, violence, actual or threatened death or injury, acts of terror, or any other event that is extremely stressful. If the experience is unwanted and leads to intense fear, helplessness, or horror, PTSD may occur and last for months or years.

War and combat are major causes.

The symptoms of PTSD emerge out of well-developed automatic alarm signals that evolved to protect animals and humans from danger. A sudden environmental stress (e.g., saber-toothed tiger, snake, ambush) causes the brain to release adrenaline and other hormones and biochemicals that trigger the "fight-flight" response or occasion-

---

*The Veterans Administration was superseded in 1989 by the cabinet-level Department of Veterans Affairs, with health care implemented by the Veterans Health Administration. Following common practice and in the interests of simplicity, I use "VA" throughout.

ally a "freeze" reaction (inability to move). The brain registers fear, and the body exhibits fast heart and breathing rates, increased blood flow to muscles, inhibition of digestion, and dilated bronchi, and while the pupils may dilate, attention is very constricted, focused on the source of threat. Loss of bladder and bowel control may occur as the body actually unloads its waste. These changes are involuntary and reflexively geared for immediate action. Cognitive processing may be dominated by this primitive biological surge.

These physiological shifts prepare the host to fight or flee or exhibit other protective responses. In order to avoid situations in which the threat may arise again, reminders of the threat and surrounding circumstances are stored in memory in a special way. When the stress is massive and the subject has little control over the situation, the brain connections among memory, fear responses, and triggers (associations) become "hard-wired."

In people (or animals) who get PTSD, memories, fragments of memories, or associations trigger the fear response in the absence of new threats. This fragile or overreacting and easily triggered fear response causes the symptoms of PTSD. The networks of nerves and tracks in the brain have been reprogrammed, and the ratios of chemical mediators are different. The clusters of symptoms called PTSD are all manifestations of an exaggerated fear response or learned ways to avoid, diminish, or control the fear response. This state may be useful on the battlefield but sometimes causes problems in civilian life.

The protagonist may have few or many symptoms, which usually fall into three categories: reexperiencing symptoms, avoidance and numbing symptoms, and hypervigilance or increased arousal. The reexperiencing symptoms are intrusive and unwanted and can come at any time. A sound, sight, or smell may trigger an unpleasant memory accompanied by the same fear, horror, or helplessness caused by the original traumatic event. Examples of these symptoms include bad dreams, nightmares and night terrors, envisioning distressing vivid scenes, and life-threatening thoughts. Feeling like one is actually going through the event again is sometimes called a "flashback."

People with PTSD often go to great lengths to avoid things that might remind them of the traumatic event. They may shut themselves off emotionally or physically in order to protect themselves from feeling pain and fear, or they may avoid people, situations, or conversations that may evoke reminders of the traumatic event. While emotional numbing can be useful to avoid triggers, it seriously affects relationships, especially intimate ones.

Other symptoms are forms of hypervigilance, remaining on high alert at all times, a useful attitude on the battlefield. Persons with PTSD may exhibit or seek an adrenaline rush, often participating in various risky behaviors such as speeding or provoking fights. Conversely, they may have unnecessary and unreasonable fear for their own safety or that of others. They may be easily startled and may have difficulty falling or staying asleep.

It is normal for unsettling, exaggerated components of the fear response to linger for one to three weeks after a traumatic event. If symptoms last more than a month and interfere with daily activities, the person is said to have PTSD.

Although thoughts of war continued to take a marked toll on my psyche, I had neither fully recognized nor accepted that I was in the throes of PTSD. I did know that despite my best efforts I was not getting better, and as time passed I exhibited more and more symptoms. Even as I found professional success and my career thrived, my life was getting worse. Since my professional success depended largely on a growing and tightly wound combination of excessive ambition and fear of failure, the traumas of my war experience and my childhood were spawning an ever more dangerous and toxic mix of behaviors as I struggled to compensate and heal myself. Generally, I was emotionally numb. Nothing else but my crazy behaviors could really get my attention, but collectively the behaviors were making me worse and preventing intimacy.

However, I had mixed feelings about adopting a label, especially one that ended in "disorder." Reinforced by the serious taint, tarnish, and rejection I felt after my return from Vietnam, I could not accept the stigma of being weak, contaminated by war, or in need of help. I did not want to have a common, well-known syndrome. I wanted to be special. I wanted to be an impervious hardened warrior. On the other hand, a diagnosis or label did provide a shield to hide behind, an inner beast I could blame for my ruinous behaviors. Most important to me was the hope that the collective professional wisdom surrounding the identification of PTSD would help me understand and treat my pain.

I had not sought therapy before because I was afraid my academic colleagues might discover my weakness and craziness. Now a large part of the motivation to enter therapy was the overarching guilt I felt and the specific guilt I created by hurting others. Although I talked regularly with Joan by phone, I was estranged from my children. I was beginning to acknowledge and understand the magnitude of the private pain and public humiliation I hurled at Joan. I realized that I left her primarily because I could not stop hurting her.

After decades of misery—and a push by my colleague on the plane—I had finally made a decision to seek help. All my attempts at self-treatment and trying to will myself better had only made me more numb, more depressed, and more affected by the war each and every day. I had damaged not only myself but also my family and others I cared about. If a casual acquaintance could sense my depression in the midst of an innocuous conversation, then it must be becoming obvious to others, I thought.

Jim Groves was a restless, intense, anxious, and desperate-to-help-others kind of doctor, a slightly ungraceful, slump-shouldered Texan prone to chewing his nails as our sessions got tense, often apologizing for interrupting me when he spontaneously erupted in a wonderful, loud total-body laugh in reaction to my stories, which served to release tension in us both. I did not know it when I first began to see him in 1989, but from 1975 through 1980 he had set up and run a walk-in clinic for Vietnam veterans. He was equipped to accept me as his patient.

Over time I would come to understand that psychotherapy, like Vietnam, is another country, one that I had to explore and learn about before I became effectively engaged, and I never felt completely comfortable being there. I still had images of Sigmund Freud and lying down on a couch and talking about birth trauma, but I discovered that it is very different from that. At times it was just sitting and chatting with someone who was giving me his full attention, really listening, and not passing judgment, or cutting me off. No automatic rejection or building disapproval.

Sometimes I would talk about my childhood, Vietnam, or, more often, what was happening in my life at that moment. It was rare for Jim to interrupt me, but when I ran out of words and was quiet he would do one of two things. He would be quiet for a short time to see if I would speak again, and if I did not, then he would say, "Where are you right now? What are you imaging? Why are you being quiet? There has to be something going on in your mind that's off to the side of the screen right now."

There always was, and it would be helpful to me to be able to express what was happening when I became uncomfortable or silent and my mind was drifting. The other thing he might do was say, "Well, here's what I think is going on . . ." Then he might give me some of his interpretations of why I was acting the way I was, but most often he would allow me to discover these truths myself.

It was very practical, very direct, very human and compassionate. Most of the time we spoke about real-life, real-time issues I was having, like a problem with some staff in the laboratory or with my family, or having nightmares, or just feeling depressed. He might begin by asking me about my activities or mood since our last appointment. He would ask me about Vietnam on occasion, but more often he would wait for me to take us back to war.

What Jim was beginning to do was teach me some very practical strategies to help me think differently. In psychotherapy these strategies are often referred to more formally in such terms as "cognitive therapy," "exposure therapy," and "behavior modification." We developed various ways of thinking and behaving and coping. For example, in cognitive therapy the patient learns how to think differently. In my case, for example, when I heard a helicopter I had to learn not to think it was a helicopter headed for Triage, or when I heard a muffler backfire, I had to actually learn that I was not about to die from incoming shells. Jim had to tell me again and again that my beliefs were untrue, that the backfire from a car is not a mortar. Believing it, and then learning to tell that to myself, I learned not to elicit a fear response.

Behavior modification is getting in touch with one's feelings to the point where one will not repeat unwanted or damaging behaviors. If one is captured by exploding anger, for example, instead of punching someone or breaking things, one could learn to take a "time-out"—go outside and take a walk or simply take some deep breaths. Sometimes it is simply like a recovering smoker avoiding that early-morning trigger to smoke by not having a cup of coffee but doing something different. I learned how to avoid triggers and trained myself to behave differently if I was heading toward having or causing pain.

In exposure therapy, in a safe setting one goes through the traumatic event again and again. Each time one doesn't die and nobody else dies. Eventually one can separate memories from the fear response. In exposure therapy I purposely went back to an original trauma and talked through it over and over again until I was desensitized to it and realized that it was something from the past and that when I thought about it, it was not happening again. I learned to separate memories and triggers from my fear response to inhibit the fight-flight hormones from taking effect. Jim helped me understand that flashbacks are really just a time issue, the past showing up in the present. My brain found more acceptable ways to protect itself. I still see wounded soldiers being carried into Triage, I see their wounds, but I understand that I'm not there. I can remember it, but I'm not there. I am not responsible. It is a way to deal with those memories without falling apart.

Therapy sounds simple, and in a sense it is. It's simple and practical and repetitive, but it is not easy and is often painful, and the subject has to be willing to go through it; it cannot be done without the full participation of the patient. For me, learning this did not happen overnight, and it is not over now—I am still learning. There is no single strategy, no cookie-cutter approach that works for everyone. I had waited so long to get help that my thoughts and behaviors and strategies of coping were deeply ingrained within my psyche, and getting better would not be instantaneous. In a way the entire process is about discovery, learning what strategies work. I had the greatest difficulty describing my addiction to sex and the accompanying manipulative behaviors. He accepted the person (me) I was describing with no judgment. I could not do that.

The role Jim played in my life evolved over time from therapist to literature professor, coach, cheerleader, editor, management consultant, and friend. He was addictively well read in everything from Shakespeare and Milton to early-twentieth-century novels to biographies of obscure giants of other centuries (Thomas Gresham, John Wilkes, Cato). Sometimes it seemed that the entire Western canon was trying to come into our sessions. He sensed that I would respond to that. Early on, he gave me reading assignments: Sappho (it was short), *The Rime of the Ancient Mariner* (I had killed the albatross), Freud's *Dora*, Kenneth Clark's *Civilisation*, John Rawls, and *Miss Manners' Guide to Excruciatingly Correct Behavior* (I forget what the point was, but there was one).

He also started me on a medication, which at first made me very depressed. A second medication had no effect. While taking the third medication, I had an episode of catatonia, sitting alone in my office for hours unable to move, not even able to reach for the phone. Jim then switched me to lithium, which helped a little. We finally settled on Prozac, which I have taken ever since, afraid to stop it even when I feel much better and quite stable. After some years, at my suggestion, we added Wellbutrin to fill in the occasional ditch of depression I would fall into for two or three hours several times a week.

Of course, I knew none of this that first day when I walked into his office, or when I walked out forty-five minutes later, but over the next 362 days I saw Jim in one hundred separate sessions and, ever so slowly, in fits and starts, began to turn a corner.

Still, things were going to get much worse before they got better.

My inner war had wrecked my life enough to drive me to seek help, but it was not until I was deeply afraid of suicide or insanity of the most primitive kind that I came to recognize that my own mix of survival campaigns could never work. I could attack (work harder), flee (into addictive behaviors alternating with numbness), or give up and embrace the night (give up my shield, stay in therapy, yield, relinquish my ways of thinking and forms of behavior). I needed more of the last ingredient but was not yet ready to admit how much I needed help.

Lord, give me chastity and continence, but not yet.

CHAPTER 17

OBITUARY
John A. Parrish, M.D., Dies
Champion of Multidisciplinary Collaborative Medical
Research

Harvard Professor John Parrish passed away December 15, 1992, at the age of fifty-two. In an academic career that spanned more than thirty years Parrish established hospital-based multidisciplinary organizations for the creation and application of new knowledge and technology to health care. Although this approach had been widely used for decades in engineering and physics, it was not a component of medical research prior to Parrish's work.

Parrish learned the power of multidisciplinary research as a young physician investigator. In the early 1970s he formed a team of physicists, engineers, chemists, and dermatologists to develop novel treatments for skin disorders including therapies that required the ingestion of a photosensitizing drug followed by exposure of the skin to a specific wavelength of ultraviolet radiation. This treatment was very effective in treating severe psoriasis and within two years was used worldwide to treat a variety of serious skin diseases. Parrish's refinements of other ultraviolet treatments led to successful outpatient therapies and the subsequent closure of almost all dermatology inpatient units in American hospitals. His observations continue to be the basis of improved treatments for a variety of other skin disorders and helped facilitate the proliferation of tanning salons, an outcome Parrish regretted.

Working with R. Rox Anderson, his student and collaborator, Parrish introduced methods to achieve selective tissue reactions to laser radiations, making it possible to use lasers to remove vascular birthmarks, pigmented lesions, and tattoos without scars. Parrish's team also introduced the use of lasers to remove kidney stones and gallstones nonsurgically. Their work formed the scientific platform for bloodless debridement of burns, laser-based resurfacing of aged and wrinkled skin, and selective removal of hair, as well as many of the laser-based surgical and diagnostic procedures used in ophthalmology and surgical specialties.

Parrish's passion was "translational research"—moving new knowledge and technology into patient care. He believed academic medical centers should commit vigorously to this "fourth mission" in addition to their traditional missions of patient care, research, and teaching.

In order to explore models for translational research, Parrish founded three large multidisciplinary research centers, the Massachusetts General Hospital's Wellman Center for Photomedicine, the MGH-Harvard Cutaneous Biology Research Center (CBRC), and the Center for Integration of Medicine and Innovation Technology (CIMIT), a consortium of ten Boston academic medical and technological institutions, including Harvard Medical School teaching hospitals, and Massachusetts Institute of Technology. CIMIT identifies innovative physicians with transformational ideas for improving health care and connects them to the right engineering collaborators, industrial partners, and funding sources, focusing on the discovery and demonstration of inexpensive, simple technological solutions for home health care and for health care in austere environments.

Author of several books and hundreds of scientific publications, Parrish was chief of dermatology at Massachusetts General Hospital and professor and chairman of the Department of Dermatology at Harvard Medical School. He was a member of the Institute of Medicine of the National Academy of Sciences.

Parrish was born in Kentucky and raised in Florida. A graduate of Duke University and the Yale University Medical School, as a young man Parrish served in the American War in Vietnam, treating casualties from major hot spots at the peak of that war. He never recovered from the experience.

Cause of death was severe grief and disappointment and hypersensitivity to the human condition.

I wrote my own obituary while staying in a tiny room at a small fishing and diving camp located on one of the smallest of the Cayman Islands.

It was the year of my peak craziness. I had left Joan permanently and was taking a six-month sabbatical from Harvard Medical School and Massachusetts General Hospital. Rox had taken over Wellman Labs while I was away. I embarked on a number of sexual affairs including women in my professional world, all high-risk relationships. The women were vulnerable and attractive. Some were sophisticated successful women who were misled by me or using me to meet their own conscious or unconscious needs. Like me, they found the deception and the risk-taking aspect of our relationships intoxicating.

The machinations I had to go through to keep each relationship unknown to other women required an even more complex series of lies and other deceptions, occupying whatever little remaining free time I had and keeping me from dwelling on Vietnam. Unrelated to my feelings about sex partners, the sex act itself released mood-altering chemicals I needed. I had sex more than I really wanted to. I did not even particularly like some of the women I pursued. Withdrawal from these mood-altering experiences left me feeling more isolated and lonely. Physical coupling made isolation bearable, and then shame led to more isolation. Although I was critical and judgmental of others, I accepted little personal responsibility for my own actions and mistakes. I started to believe my own lies and convinced myself that no one ever got hurt. Sex was a victory, a reaffirmation, and a comfort. I constantly tried to capture the intoxication of young love flavored with the thrill of the hunt and the heightened arousal of the forbidden, the illicit, the stolen. Each time I began a quest of seduction I expected the outcome to be different—more fulfilling, romantic, uplifting, wholesome, and fun. It never was. Paradoxically, the rubbing of mucous membranes protected me from intimacy. It was a continuous cycle—a virtual, nonvirtuous circle.

I kept these activities absolutely secret. Although sex and violence are big business, and very pervasive in our society, in my social and family circles, my interests and actions would be considered perverse and hurtful to me and others. I was convinced that there was not a single person I knew or respected who would not think my actions were inappropriate, immature, irresponsible, or vulgar for a man in his fifties.

In my work I had stepped up the pace and the stakes. I needed bigger "hits." I took on massive missions. My passion for creating multidisciplinary research environments reached enormous proportions. I sought larger platforms to demonstrate new models. This zeal was fueled by my need to add to my growing academic profile.

Although not trained in basic principles of molecular biology, cell biology, or biochemistry, and never having done basic bench-top research, I proposed to the leadership of Shiseido, a Japanese cosmetics company, that I form an MGH-based research group at the cost of $10 million a year to study the fundamentals of skin biology. In a three-month period I made eight trips to Tokyo, two to California, one to Hawaii, and three to New York. Shiseido finally agreed, and I founded and directed the MGH-Harvard Cutaneous Biology Research Center (CBRC). Ted Kennedy and James Wyngaarden, director of the National Institutes of Health, helped to mitigate the political concerns about "brain drain," a hot topic of the time. CBRC grew to be a 120-person laboratory performing research, spending well over $200 million over the next twenty years. It was the largest basic-science skin research laboratory in the world.

While I was chief of the dermatology service at Massachusetts General Hospital, chairman of the Department of Dermatology at Harvard Medical School, a faculty member at the Massachusetts Institute of Technology–HMS Health Sciences and Technology Program, I accepted several national and international positions in societies, honorific groups, and alliances. I became chairman of the MGH Faculty Committee on Research and assumed major roles in HMS and MGH committees on diversity, women's careers, care and support of postdocs and Ph.D.'s, the rights of human research subjects, industry-academia interactions, and conflicts of interest.

I led a relentless seven-year campaign culminating in MGH committing a new research building to multidisciplinary research not based in the traditional academic or clinical departments. At various times, over one hundred MGH leaders participated, working through ten committees with different lifetimes, responsibilities, membership, and leadership. At first, the department chairs and many of the established power brokers resisted a theme-based, communal, multidisciplinary approach. Eventually, the major department chairs and research leaders took ownership of the idea, and the new MGH Simches Research Building was organized around leading-edge research themes. Many people took credit and deserved it. It became a top-down and bottom-up success.

By day my life was a series of meetings. By night I acted out my addictions to war, sex, violence, risk taking, and exercise. I was in frenetic overdrive.

Foolishly thinking I had made more progress than I had, and unwilling to give up my wild life, I stopped going to therapy and embarked on my own self-directed spiritual journey. I continued my medications and self-regulated the dosage. I was taking part in more mythopoeic men's groups, calling on the gods of maleness for our salvation. I was doing a lot of reading, too, people like Robert Bly and others, all the Carlos Casteneda books and Native American writing about vision quests. I was looking for relief from my symptoms of PTSD, but in some way I may also have been trying to duplicate the military experience of being bonded to other men in combat.

I became particularly intrigued by the concept of the vision quest, a Native American rite of passage and rebirth designed to help one find the direction of one's life. The quest usually takes place in the wilderness, accompanied by a period of fasting, and the pathway is most often revealed by an animal in a vision or a dream.

The more I read, the more I became convinced that if I put myself through this ritual I might have some kind of visionary experience that would deliver insight and wisdom and help free me. I thought I should go out in the desert, confront my own death, and think about everybody I'd ever known and everything I'd ever done until I received a vision. The Native Americans used to take mescaline and other drugs to assist them in reaching that state. I wasn't planning to take any drugs but rather to confront death solely through fasting and physical isolation. According to most accounts it was important to have some real risk in the experience, some chance you might actually die, so I was determined to go to a place that fulfilled that criterion. At some level I knew that if I didn't leave Boston, I might lose my judgment altogether and possibly lose my job.

I went to a travel agent near MGH and asked the agent, "What's the most remote but accessible area you can think of, a place I could go where I would definitely not see any human beings?" She thought for a moment and said, "Well, the Lesser Cayman Islands. The bigger islands are filled with tourists, but some of the lesser islands don't have anybody there at all." I asked her how I would get there, and she explained that after flying to the Caymans I would have to rent a plane. In a matter of a few minutes she had made the arrangements for me to stay at a fishing and diving camp on one of the lesser islands that she thought was otherwise uninhabited.

I told no one I was leaving and carried virtually no luggage, just a small backpack with only a few items—underwear, a change of clothes, a pair of sandals, a few toiletries, and a notebook. Although I was a dermatologist, I forgot to pack sunscreen or insect spray. When I reached the airport my backpack weighted only twenty-eight pounds.

I was leaving everything behind. Sometime between when I decided to go on the trip and when I actually arrived at the camp, I made the decision that if I was not saved by a vision I was prepared to die. Although I had never been suicidal before, the thought of a real death began to compete with my desire for a metaphysical experience.

I arrived in the Caymans, hired a pilot, and flew to the island. It was as remote as the travel agent had described it to me, an arid, almost treeless desert island about twelve miles long and one mile wide. There wasn't a proper airstrip, just a wide, grassy field on which to land.

As soon as the plane took off, I saw a giant black snake cross right in front of me. I was thrilled, certain that this was a sign that my vision quest was ready to begin. Then I walked down to the seashore and saw a perfect seashell, a conch shell, absolutely intact, without a scratch on it. I gazed at it with wonder, completely transfixed. Again I thought it was a sign, but about thirty seconds later I saw another one, and then another one, and I realized they were all over the beach. Since so few humans came to the island, the beach had not been picked clean of shells by tourists. They were a sign of isolation, and nothing else.

Besides myself the only other people I knew of on the island were a local who operated the camp and his present guests, three male Australian divers. I had my own small cabin and only saw them briefly each morning and evening at the simple meals that were served. They sensed that I didn't want to talk, and all politely respected my need for total solitude, talking with one another as if I were not even there, as if I didn't speak their language. Over the course of several days my silence built upon itself to become a shield against the strangers who kindly ignored me.

While they left the small encampment to go diving every morning, I stayed in my cabin. Only after I had been left alone would I venture out. Most of my first few days were consumed by slow, aimless wandering on deserted scrub-wooded paths, abandoned dirt roads, and virginal beaches. As I walked I tried to characterize and summarize each of my personal relationships with all those living and dead that I had ever loved or cared for. I ate and drank very little.

At night, except for the sound of the sea and the wind, and a gasoline-powered generator, my world was reduced to a single dim lightbulb and my own inner visions. A squeaky wooden bed was covered with a thin, hard mattress. A small dresser covered with decades of stains and scratches held my backpack, my notebook, pens, an extra shirt, and a few stones and shells I had collected during my walks.

I was already physically uncomfortable, covered in sand and sweat from my long walks, and I didn't bathe. When I found relief in sleep, I was either jerked awake by a specific regret or gradually aroused by painful longings for something I could not articulate. The pain was deep and dry and familiar, and I could not predict that it would ever end. Other nights I fell into a deep paralyzing sleep that lasted from sunset to midday, then was slowly eroded by dull dehydration, hunger, and a full bladder.

During the sleepless parts of the night and the heat of the day, I wrote about my impending death in a journal. Besides my obituary, I also wrote letters to Joan, my children, and my siblings, explaining my actions and apologizing, or at least trying to. I wrote letters to my dead brother and father, and to dead soldiers whose names I never knew. I could not find the strength or the words to write to my mother. Because I did not think my professional colleagues would understand my mission, I wrote to none of them. My obituary would have to suffice.

One night when I felt complete in my writing, I put several liters of bottled water into my backpack and stashed the letters, the shells, and my wallet in a place that would eventually be discovered. I fell asleep, and at sunrise I asked the native man who ran the camp to drive me as far as his truck could go and just drop me off. He drove me down a dirt road that slowly disappeared until it was gone, the way blocked by rocks and shrubs. I handed the driver a green garbage bag that contained everything else I had brought with me to the Caymans and told him he didn't need to save my room. I had brought a wad of cash. Without counting it, I put some in my pocket and handed the rest to him. He shrugged, turned the Jeep around, and drove off. In a few moments the sound of his Jeep lurching over the rock-strewn path faded, and I was alone.

I wandered around and in a few moments found a circle of rocks, ashes from an old campfire, and a dead tree trunk that stuck up in the air like a sundial. I was certain these were signs.

Voluntary isolation was an attempt to yield to the alienation and distrust I felt when immersed in the complexities of my world. To be more authentic, integrated, and complete, I had to be as alone as I felt. Aloneness was a desperate experiment.

I walked across a large, flat mesa until it ended at the edge of a sharp cliff that rose straight up thirty or forty meters above the sea. I walked along the edge of the cliff until thick, gnarly, prickly shrubs left no room to walk. Then I climbed onto the face of the cliff. For hours I slowly picked my way along the edge, pausing frequently to reflect on my life and to watch the waves crash into the rocks far below.

Physical concerns slowly began to draw my attention away from my inward reflection. In order to move along the vertical face of the highly irregular cliff, I had to cling, climb, sit, squat, and pick my way using both hands and feet. Minutes turned into hours. A heavy, pleasant ache developed in all four of my limbs. As the sun rose higher I could feel it on my skin and sense the heat entering and leaving my body with each breath.

Slowly, a hypnotic calm detached me from my instinctual fear of heights, and I embraced the blue sky frosted with a few wispy clouds and the sea rimmed by tiny foaming waves. A small voice willed me not to float away. "If you fall you'll surely die," the voice intoned over and over. Yet it did not frighten me. The pointed rocks below and the churning sea seemed not at all unfriendly.

I climbed down the cliff a few feet, planted my feet on a narrow ledge, wedged my backpack into a crevice, and pressed my back against a giant rock. The sky and the sea were so identically brilliantly blue that there was no horizon. I closed my eyes and listened to the hot breeze, distant sea, and buzz of passing insects. There was nothing else. I wanted to remain there, immobile forever.

Slowly, deep in my head, I began to hear a mechanical rhythm within the sound of the wind and the waves, and I became afraid and nauseated. A familiar dread paralyzed me, and I began to feel invaded and afraid. Whenever helicopters approach, my primitive brain responds before I can consciously hear and identify the chopping buzz. My first awareness is an emptiness in my chest, a light-headed, dull confusion, and anticipation of impending disaster and loss of control. Then come primitive denial and flailing fantasies of escape. A surge of flight or fright hormones compete with those of immobilization. After all these years an approaching helicopter is still a call to action. Ready or not.

I waited for it to come. The sound of the sea and wind remained. An actual helicopter did not materialize. On this ledge I was not available to dead and wounded soldiers.

I could always jump. I realized that jumping wasn't needed. All I had to do was lean forward and my war was over and I was dead. Death made Little Jimmie even more special. In death I could really get my family's attention. "I'll show 'em; I'll die." I told my legs to thrust me out to my death, but they did not respond. I told the angst to go away, but it didn't respond. I remained very still.

I was thirsty. I closed my eyes and imagined water in my stomach and intestines. Too empty to feel or think and too tired to move, I was still for a very, very long time. I went into a timeless place and could not cross to safety.

By midday I was miserable; my skin burned, and my lips were dry and cracked. It was much too hot. With considerable difficulty, my limbs now stiff and sore, I climbed upward and returned to the mesa.

Now I sought out the shadows. I spent several hours lying naked under low shrubs and small scruffy trees, the only shade in sight. The ground was rocky, its surface covered by shards of sharp, jagged rock, scattered patches of dark sandy soil, and occasional tangled tufts of tough grass, mostly root and little blade. I lay on my shirt, pants, shoes, and socks to protect my skin from the unfriendly earth.

As my body cooked and sweated, my mind cycled between hyper-vigilance and stupor. Panting alternated with breathless quiet. I could not keep thoughts long enough to trust time and place.

I tried to practice yoga, but the rocky ground was so uncomfortable I couldn't lie or sit without pain or danger of cutting my skin. I tried to sit on my shirt to meditate, but my back ached and I had a headache from hypoglycemia and withdrawal from caffeine. In the late after-noon, when the heat and sun began to wane, I began to move slowly about the island again.

Time moved slowly, stopped, and disappeared.

At dusk, I tried to name and organize my personal priorities, but dull depression and a growing sense of loneliness sludged my think-ing, and my thoughts were frequently interrupted by the buzzing and biting of mosquitoes. Restless, sunburned, tired, and at times disori-ented, I sat, stood, and roamed about. Slowly moving giant clouds filled most of the sky.

As darkness surrounded me, I decided to remain still and spent several hours lying on my back. Ignoring the pain from my bed of pointed rocks, I let my mind wander. Absolute darkness was some-times interrupted by bizarre moving shapes as the clouds revealed a clear sky and many stars. I tried to observe my thoughts and give up control.

It seemed impossible to sleep. The ground hurt my bony promi-nences, and the cold of the night was bitter and deep. I was completely unprepared for the temperature and had no source of warmth. The cold hurt and made me angry. One thing I feared about death was the accompanying drop in body temperature.

The night sky became absolutely clear, and the stars moved slowly through the blackened silver sky.

I yielded to the deep insult of unavoidable cold and moved beyond shivering and hugging myself to complete stillness. Cold and helplessness totally saturated my mind. The time until the warmth of the sun seemed too long to provide any hope.

Wishing for sleep, but afraid to sleep, I heard myself saying, "If I should die before I wake, I pray thee, Lord, my soul to take." I returned to my earliest memories, lying awake waiting for my mother to attend to my older brother on those nights when he woke screaming and vomiting as I clutched Boy, Dog, and Goody. Just as I did then, I pretended to be asleep while my mother cleaned up, and soon I did fall into a fitful sleep.

I did not wake until the heat and glare of the sun began to hurt my skin and eyes and the ground pressed too painfully into my elbows, shoulders, and buttocks. I was miserable. I had walked off alone the previous day with all these romantic notions about being in the desert and having a vision, but my journey was neither romantic nor powerful; it was physical torture.

Once again I climbed down the face of the cliff, this time carefully making my way to the bottom, where I found two large rocks leaning against each other that formed a cave on the shoreline. I climbed into the cave and watched the waves for hours. At times I watched specific waves or rocks or crabs or birds, and at times I saw nothing. The sound and smell of the sea were constant. I tried to think through my whole life beginning with the earliest images.

Over the hours the tide brought in bigger waves, which broke over my feet. I tossed tiny pebbles and shells into a growing pool of water that eventually began to ebb.

After the peak heat of the day passed, I climbed back onto the mesa and ambled aimlessly about in walking meditation, either mindful of the ground several feet in front of me or absorbed in self-evaluation. I was feeling sunburned but did not seek shade because it seemed important that my wandering be random. The ache in my thighs and lower back was pleasant awareness, and the smell of my own body was comforting.

I tried to understand who I was and describe what purpose there was in my life. What were my values? What was *my* value? Again I let my mind go. I tried to watch my thoughts pass through without letting them define me. I paid no attention to time or the path of my wondering.

A giant black bird frightened me as it swooped down to the ground a few feet from me, took three quick steps, and flew off, crowing loudly, revealing nothing. The sun began to set, and I lay on my back, trying to ignore the mosquitoes and the cold and the pointy ground. I watched the stars emerge one at a time. I was no longer hungry.

For most of the night I tried to be present only to the moment, a transient, self-aware organism lying on the cold hard ground looking at millions of suns billions of miles away. I imagined being there forever, and I tried to internalize that my entire life occurred in only a flick of time.

I fell asleep at first light and slept until the heat of midmorning. The day blended with the one before and after. As I slowly walked, head down, along a small path I heard something in front of me. I looked up and there was a large black bull walking toward me. We both stopped and stared at each other for a very long time. I was afraid to move forward and afraid to turn and run.

Bored, the bull finally just slowly turned around and walked away down the path. There was no vision. I started walking again. After three—or was it four—days of fasting I felt anxious, insignificant, and hopeless. I pushed myself to try to experience a spiritual surrender, a personal death, a giving up. I felt only misery.

At dusk it began to rain. I was grateful because now the mosquitoes didn't torture me. For a few minutes I surrendered to the chilly rain, but then I got so cold that my bones hurt. A hard rain fell, and I slept again on the hard ground.

I awoke at first light still wet and cold, but by the time the sun was well above the horizon, I was hot and dry. I noticed that my water supply was getting low, and I did not know how long it might take to walk back to the camp. I had made no arrangements to be picked up, and if I failed to return no one would miss me. The possibility that my passivity itself would lead to death stimulated a mission to survive, but I wanted a more transcendent vision of hope and purpose.

Remaining motionless, I was possessed by black-and-white feelings of war. At first there were no specific memories, flashbacks, or visions but only a very familiar sense of danger and helplessness and a vivid awareness of my dark powers and extreme fragility. I realized how near the surface the demons lay and how much of the bread and circus of my life was required to deny my war experience.

Surrendering, I was invaded and possessed by the presence of war. Feelings, occasional memories, specific conversations, the wet warmth of fresh wounds. The still cold of the dead. The smells of explosives and gasoline and living, dying, and dead people. Visions of bones, blood, and sticky muscle quivering like Jell-O.

I was confused and unsure how to get back to the fishing camp, and even if I knew, I did not know if I had the strength to make it. I could not climb down to the sea to follow the shore line because I was too unsteady to negotiate the steep cliff. In any case, I had seen that in most places there was no beach; the rocky cliffs fell directly into the deep sea, which was now constantly churned by huge waves smashing onto the rocks. I could not remember any clues from the path of the sun, which was, in any case, directly overhead. I decided to begin to walk, always keeping the edge of the mesa and the sound of the sea to my right.

After many hours I reached sea level and a beach. At dusk I heard a dog, saw a house, and then, to my surprise, entered a small village complete with a tiny restaurant. I ate two three-egg omelets and a dozen pieces of toast and drank several glasses of juice.

Food could not dampen the hunger and restlessness deep within me. I walked along the beach away from the village trying to feel born again, unable to shake feeling depressed and empty. Because I had invested so much in this inward journey, I hoped my deliverance might yet come. When it was completely dark I lay on my stomach, feeling the sand on my cheek and hearing it crunch in my ear. I turned my head toward the ocean so that when the tide came in the water would wake me or drown me.

A few days later back in Boston, I reread the literature of the vision quest. Certain animals have specific meaning and significance. I looked through the list and there were no bulls. Nothing had changed.

BOOK FOUR

THE GOOD WORK

CHAPTER 18

Entering into therapy with Jim Groves provided me with a pathway toward recovery, but Jim was only one support needed for what was still a very distant goal. Barbara Gilchrest provided another. If Jim brought me to the precipice of crossing the divide from sickness to health, Barbara was a partner I needed to reach to the other side.

I first met Barbara in the 1970s, soon after I joined the faculty at Harvard. She was one of about fifteen residents in the three-year dermatology training program, so I got to know her fairly well. I taught her in individual and group tutorials.

She was one of the brightest students I had ever encountered. During her residency she spent one year as my research fellow, helping care for my patients, doing everything I did, planning research projects, writing papers, and becoming my protégé.

I remember that year very well. I thought she was pretty and pleasant, an athletic strawberry blonde with bright eyes that could be green or brown and an intense but open, inviting nature. At the time our boundaries were clear. I never saw her as a love interest—she was married, and I was trying to stay married.

She was so bright that I was intimidated. Every time we met I knew I had to be on my game. She would be able to see through any pretense, something that tapped right into my black-and-white view of success versus total failure. I had to do well because I was afraid of being exposed. Or bested.

It always seemed I couldn't teach her fast enough. It was as if each time I opened my mouth to explain a disease or a concept for an experiment, she processed the knowledge immediately and started making connections. When I looked into her eyes I could almost hear her saying, "Yes, yes. I've got it. Tell me more, faster, faster." Her thirst for knowledge, passion to learn, and ambition were undeniable and exceeded mine.

I actually felt threatened by her. I was the emerging star of the department and it was obvious to me that she was just as sharp as I was, if not sharper. She wanted to stay on the Harvard faculty and expected to. Despite the fact that she sometimes made me uncomfortable, I wanted her to stay. I liked her and enjoyed working with her and felt we would work well together. Even then, her presence pushed me to accomplish more than I might have otherwise.

Our department chairman, however, did not share my enthusiasm for supporting her professional growth. He was a chauvinist and sometimes diminished the contributions of others, particularly talented women. He only wanted to work with people in situations where he could claim a large portion of the credit for their work and accept the acclaim as their senior partner. If other members of the department ever began to outshine him, or wanted to take legitimate credit for their own work, he would begin to constrain them. The more ambitious and talented would therefore leave. He would expand upon small indiscretions or shortcomings and use that to banish anyone he saw as a rival.

I was probably the first member of the department he allowed to stay and outgrow him in some areas, but I had risen so quickly, as his academic "son" and disciple, that by the time he realized what was happening it was too late for him to unseat me. By then I had attracted too much research money and space, and many of the faculty were more loyal to me than they were to him.

He did not make the same mistake with Barbara. He sized her up pretty quickly and realized that she was sufficiently bright, confident, and self-aware that if she stayed at Harvard she wouldn't stay in his shadow very long. At the end of her residency, Barbara opted to spend an additional year training in basic science in a prestigious laboratory at her alma mater, MIT. She then accepted a faculty position at another Harvard teaching hospital and opened her own independent research laboratory. She was still part of the Harvard department but outside the chairman's direct control. At that point Barbara and I ceased to interact. After six years of objective academic accomplishments in her new setting, Barbara requested a meeting with the department chair and questioned why he had not promoted her to a higher academic rank as he had another junior faculty member with less success. He responded by belittling her accomplishments and suggested they were the work of others. She asked for my support, and I argued to promote her, but I still didn't wield enough power. The department chairman was the only person who could initiate promotion to a higher academic rank. It was not my battle, and part of me shared the chairman's concerns.

For Barbara, this was a major slap in the face. Understandably she was very angry. She deserved the promotion. At the time, I think she was probably more angry with me than she was with our chairman, because she felt I had not argued hard enough on her behalf—and she was probably right. She soon left Harvard, feeling mistreated and abused. I think it was the first time she had ever failed, the first time her intelligence and hard work had not carried the day. She had found herself in a no-win environment, fighting by someone else's unknowable rules. It mocked her. While hardly equivalent to a year at war in Vietnam, it profoundly undermined Barbara's trust and forced her to reexamine her belief in a fair world. I did not yet know it, but there were many parallels in our lives, and over time there would be more.

Barbara was born on Armistice Day in 1945. She and a younger sister grew up on the wrong side of the tracks in a wealthy suburb of New York City in the home of their paternal grandmother. Their father, a housepainter, loved guns, liquor, solitude, and hunting. He was usually out of work and spent hours every day alone in his basement making bullets and reading books about Hitler and the philosophy of racial purity and mourning the fact that Germany lost World War II. Except on occasions when he got drunk with a few cronies, the only person allowed to visit the basement workshop was a loud and obese German friend who shared Barbara's father's attitudes and philosophy.

Barbara's Czechoslovakian grandmother was strict, mean, uneducated, narcissistic, and small-minded. Neither she nor her son liked the girls, seeing them as an inconvenience. Barbara's mother, much like my own, loved her children but was dominated by her husband. She did the best she could but had no real voice in the household. Most rooms of the house, including the kitchen and the living room, were off-limits to the girls. They were expected to keep an extremely low profile and do nothing to provoke either their father or grandmother. They were expected to be neither seen nor heard.

Barbara survived the hostile environment by escaping into fantasy, and she developed a deep love of books and learning. Very well coordinated and something of a tomboy, she also fled the nastiness and unreasonable constraints of her grandmother's home by remaining out of the house as much as possible. She spent much of her time secretly doing forbidden things like climbing trees, walking about town alone after dark, going into her dead grandfather's large tool barn, sneaking into the basement to see the guns and devices and supplies for making bullets, and using the front door of the house that was designated for guests only. Not allowed to have a pet of any kind, over Thanksgiving break in fourth grade she volunteered to care for the class's three-foot-long corn snake and smuggled it home under her clothing, keeping it fed but hidden from the entire family for five days. Even as a child, she recognized that a certain amount of rebellion was a reasonable way to deal with unjust arbitrary rules. Still, to avoid confrontation and perhaps in the hope of winning her father's approval, she was the quintessential good girl by all visible criteria.

As in my family, Barbara's sibling coped with the home environment in a very different way, openly rebelling, performing poorly in school, and at age fifteen running away from home and disappearing and ultimately moving in with relatives halfway across the country. After early childhood Barbara and her sister were virtual strangers, unable to provide each other much support. As with me and my siblings, decades into their adult lives, the sisters are friends but reside far apart, in very different worlds, with the ghosts of the past between them.

Reading saved Barbara and paved the way for enormous academic success. She was the best student in the history of her high school and went on to graduate with honors as one of the few women at Massachusetts Institute of Technology and then at Harvard Medical School, the first member of her family to attend college. Upon informing her father of her decision to attend medical school after college, she was chastised for not accepting a full-time job as a computer programmer. Instead, she worked as a freelance programmer up to twenty hours per week throughout medical school, sending money home to her mother whenever possible. Better than summers on a road crew, but likely she felt a similar and inexplicable lack of appreciation for her ambitions and values by a family completely unfamiliar with the world of higher learning to which she was dedicating her life.

Noticeably bruised by the glass ceiling at Harvard, Barbara nevertheless broke through the constraints our department chairman had tried to impose. She pursued her career in the same spirit in which she had broken the unfair rules in her childhood home. She tried harder and never looked back.

We went in different directions. I focused on building laboratories and fostering collaborative research. Barbara combined patient care with clinical and basic research and did very well. Three years after leaving Harvard, she was recruited to be professor and chair of dermatology at Boston University. Harvard was the top dermatology department in the world, while BU was, out of a hundred or so dermatology departments in the United States, somewhere in the middle. Barbara changed that. She built the department into a very competitive top program, increasing the faculty twentyfold and the budget fortyfold.

In addition to heading the BU department, she directed joint residency and research training programs with Tufts University, thus expanding her academic domain.

A decade after she had been my student, she was chair of dermatology at BU and I was the chair at Harvard. During that same decade, she bore three children and struggled with the classic work-family conflicts virtually unknown at the time to professional men, such as myself.

On at least two occasions, I reached out to Barbara across the BU/Harvard divide to suggest teaching or research collaborations. She refused outright, afraid that the Harvard name would dominate everything. From her perspective I represented the white male chauvinist Harvard that had shown her the door. Because she was not a white male and the name Boston University did not carry the same cachet as Harvard, she didn't feel either she or her department would be respected. Based on her experience, she had every right to think so.

As heads of the two academic dermatology centers in Boston, we competed for trainees, faculty, patients, fame, and power. I did very well in academia, published some key papers, and was considered a big name in the field. Locally, I usually had the upper hand, but largely because my platform was Harvard and, unlike Barbara, I did not participate in raising a family. Even so, the people I had worked with and trained with saw me as a kind of deserter, because I had abandoned straight basic science and established a lab with a Japanese cosmetic firm and another lab in photobiology, which involved many organs besides skin. I didn't go to most of the major dermatology meetings and I stopped seeing patients.

Strategically, Barbara took a different track. She became much more influential in dermatology than I and much more successful than I in national and international academia. She held leadership roles in all the dermatology societies, coedited leading professional journals, maintained a high-prestige clinical practice, and managed a financially and academically successful large department. She made numerous fundamental contributions to the science of dermatology, aging, and cancer. She was fiercely loyal to and supportive of her faculty and trainees, her chosen academic family.

Barbara and I were on the same national and international lecture circuit and ran into each other occasionally. We were not close and did not socialize together, but we were superficially friendly, albeit with a touch of professional jealousy and competitiveness thrown in. We each always knew how the other's career was going.

Unlike me, however, Barbara had managed to maintain an outwardly successful home life. She had married a former classmate from MIT, and her husband became quite well known and successful on his own. By force of will and an abundance of energy outside work, Barbara functioned as wife, homemaker, hostess, and mother, managing to raise three boys while keeping her career on track. She was a woman who appeared to "have it all" before most other women even thought that was possible.

At least that's the way it looked on the outside. Like mine, a great deal of Barbara's success was fueled by the circumstances of her upbringing. While perhaps not as traumatic as my own, her childhood endowed her with a powerful need to succeed, and while she seemed to be more successful in her family life than I, all was not quite what it seemed.

Outwardly, she and her husband did very well. They owned a lot of property and were a power couple in and around Boston, close to the social center of local politics, business, and academia, friends with the locally rich and famous.

Then, in a very sudden, brutal, traumatic, and public way, Barbara's marriage fell apart, causing a great deal of pain and damage to all members of the family. There was a very ugly divorce. She was shattered. As I had found with my experience in Vietnam, it changed her understanding of herself and challenged all her beliefs. She tasted massive failure, self-loathing, and shame.

Like me, she was able to maintain her professional standing and continue her career, never missing a deadline or a day of work. However, over the course of a year or two her life became very unstable.

Her children were devastated and acted out in various ways; one son broke off all communication. There were also major financial repercussions. She lost far more than money in the divorce, including the friendships she had built up over the years, largely with the wives of her husband's colleagues. For many months, she could not sleep or eat normally. She was emotionally isolated, overwhelmed with grief, and on some occasions suicidal.

Boston is a very small community in many ways. I had heard a lot of rumors about the breakup and knew she was not doing well. Neither was I.

Although I had resumed seeing Jim Groves and was in some ways making progress, I vacillated. On occasions I felt stable and in control, and then, perhaps overconfident and impatient with the process, I would see Jim less frequently. At times, as if I missed all the destructive behaviors I had developed over the years, I acted like an alcoholic falling off the wagon and would start up all over again. When Barbara was at the nadir of her depression and pain related to her broken home, I was living by myself on Beacon Hill in the throes of another period of frenetic and promiscuous behavior.

A colleague suggested we might have a lot in common—clearly knowing each of us better than we wished to be known—and I suggested to Barbara that we have coffee after a local dermatology meeting "to catch up." In the back of the hospital cafeteria, we talked for hours. Because we used to know each other, because we each believed we were being honest about our feelings and situations even if generally closed with other friends and acquaintances, because we were starved for understanding—for whatever reasons, we poured out our stories. It seemed to each of us like a lifeline had been thrown out, but how could a former supervisor and trainee, current competitors, proceed?

We started meeting to play tennis. It was physically exhausting, a plus for each of us, and allowed us to focus solely on each other and the present. It was also fun. Barbara was a very good athlete and beat me most of the time, so it was challenging to try to keep up with her.

We really enjoyed it. There was no pretense, and neither of us had to hold back. After playing we would go out to dinner and talk. Then the next weekend we'd play tennis and go out to dinner and talk. At a certain point we started playing less tennis and did more talking. We became lovers—but that's what I often did, and at the time I didn't think much more of that relationship than I did of other relationships I was maintaining. I set boundaries, who could call whom, when, and at what number.

Our first night together awakened and released us physically the way our first conversation had emotionally and intellectually. We got up the next morning and went to our separate places of work. In the middle of the day Barbara called me and said, "I miss you. I'm in love with you."

My heart sank, and a familiar sense of panic set in. I said to myself, "Oh my God, what have I done now?" That was exactly the kind of situation I tried to avoid, and when it reached the point that a woman wanted a monogamous, enduring commitment, I usually left and moved on because I believed I was incapable of a real relationship. I didn't know how to have one.

Barbara was different, though. Part of it was that Barbara was absolutely relentless and had decided we were right for each other. Another part of it was that she knew my story, or much of it, and that did not stop her. She told me she was mine and I was hers and that was that, she was not going to go away.

I continued my complex but increasingly empty nightlife. For months, as Barbara and I continued to see one another, her denial and my deception preserved her self-esteem, but after a while she began to inquire about my whereabouts and expect more of my time. I insisted that I was unable, or unwilling, to tolerate any assumptions or judgments about my private life. I could not (would not) be bound by any expectations about the company I kept or where I ate or slept. No one should depend on me for anything. Because I knew my capacity to hurt others, the more I cared for someone the more I retreated from commitment. In addition, I could not depend on myself, never knowing when I needed to party, walk the streets, hide, or spend hours in bed in fetal position under my blankets. For months, except for a few awkward arguments, we danced around the topic of monogamy. I repeatedly insisted that, outside of the workplace, I refused to allow anyone to have expectations about my communication or presence. I had gone to great lengths to construct that kind of life.

Barbara continued to state her progressively confining expectations. It reached a point that I felt I had to be with her each night or make up a lie about my whereabouts or need to be alone. On occasion I disappeared from her life.

One day Barbara bluntly stated her absolute need for monogamy. I surprised myself by agreeing with her, and then surprised myself even more when I discovered, after a while, I was able to stay committed.

Little by little, all the work I had been doing with Jim started gaining some traction. I did not need to keep my past out of my present by filling it up with all manner of risky behaviors, at least not as often and not nearly as much. It snuck up on me. At a certain point, as my relationship with Barbara built, slowly, over time, I began to heal more rapidly. My need for other women or the circus of drugs, sex, and rock and roll diminished.

In a way Barbara and I saved each other. I had been crazy for years, hurting people needlessly—the women I dated and my family. For the two years before we connected, Barbara had been nearly as miserable as I was. I am probably the only person who knew how troubled and insecure and driven Barbara was; and she, for a long time, was the only person that knew what a damaged person I was. In private we were two lonely people who discovered that by clinging to each other neither of us was as damaged as we had been alone. We understood each other. In response to her ex-husband's taunt that "we deserved each other," Barbara wrote me a poem:

D *riven by ghosts we cannot name*
O *ppressed by others' hurt and blame*

W *e reach out toward a mirror image*
E *xpecting somehow further damage.*

D *etermined strangely still to find*
E *xistential peace of mind*
S *atisfaction not maligned*
E *xplanation*
R *omance of a different kind*
V *alidation*
E *cstasy and love not blind*

E *ver at the edge of pain*
A *pologetic and isolated*
C *oping some days, safe and sane*
H *opeless others, immolated*

O *nly judged by love we've slain*
T *orn by what we can't regain*
H *onest when allowed to be*
E *vasive by default, are we*
R *eaching out once more in vain*
?

It was not in vain. Barbara was a stabilizing influence on me and I on her. We moved in together in 1995, and since then my mental health has been better than it had been for years. I find her endlessly fascinating, and I'm never bored. We like the same entertainment; I really enjoy her intellect and humor. She has a broad, classical education, speaks three languages, and is far my superior in arts and classics. The competitive tension is almost gone, and we seamlessly support each other.

Most critical for me, however, she loves me for who I am, which is something I had never experienced. Or allowed. I always felt like I had to earn love, even the love of my parents, especially my father's, but I never quite pulled it off. Joan was never really happy with me, and rightfully so, because I was a workaholic and gave her all the home duties. I left her to go to school, then to war, and then to work. I was unfaithful. When I lied, she cried, and a part of me and the relationship died. I was not enough for her, and in some ways I was too much for her. I was always tiptoeing around, trying to earn her approval, yet always felt like I was going to say the wrong thing or do the wrong thing, or worst of all want the wrong thing. I often did.

With Barbara I can be sick, tired, or depressed. I can be wonderful or I can be an asshole. She treats me with complete understanding and with respect. She shares my childhood isolation and rejection, need to prove myself endlessly, willingness or perhaps compulsion to work hard, redeeming love of learning, and inability to always be the person I aspire to be.

We have bonded physically, emotionally, and spiritually. I saved her from self-destruction, and she prevented me from continuing and

John Parrish and Barbara Gilchrest at a tennis court.

expanding the hurt and ruination my personal life was bringing to me, my family, and others. I was clearly headed for an ugly, possibly public, crash. Barbara is my soul mate. With her, I have reached across the chasm created by my Vietnam experience and reassembled from the prewar and postwar pieces a person capable of helping others . . . and myself.

CHAPTER 19

During my treatment, Jim Groves had his own traumatic event. After work he had hailed a cab outside his office to run a Christmas present over to a friend. It was an older cab and lacked required seat belts, but Jim thought nothing of it at the time. Suddenly the cab lurched forward and markedly increased its speed. The driver yelled, "No brakes, no brakes!" As the cab accelerated, Jim pounded the Plexiglas shield between him and the driver, screaming, "Stop, stop," but the driver panicked, jumped the median, and eventually crashed into oncoming traffic at more than forty miles an hour. Apparently he never thought to shift to another gear or turn off the engine.

For the eight-second ride, Jim sat in the back of the cab in dissolving disbelief as it bore down on the approaching cars. He could see them coming closer and closer. He knew he was about to die, but he braced himself anyway, scooting down into the seat, spread-eagling his arms and legs, trying to position his head so it wouldn't hit the metal back of the cab's front seat.

At impact he felt no pain, just noise and bright flashes of light—then utter silence. He was unhurt, or so he thought.

Except he couldn't move. Somebody at the window said, "Holy shit, look at that." Then he heard a deep gurgling sigh—the driver's last breath, a sound Jim would remember for years. He smelled gaso-line and heard it dripping onto the ground under the cab.

The body is an amazing machine, more resilient than an aging 1972 Chevy Capri taxicab. Jim broke all the bones that could absorb the energy of a shock wave. The bulletproof Plexiglas shield of the cab had closed around him, decelerating his body over a distance of about a foot. By the time the shock wave traveled up his legs, arms, and torso, the impact was dissipated.

He had no head injury but had broken both legs and his pelvis, spine, sternum, and ribs. Yet with two surgeries, a couple of weeks in the hospital, and some rehab, Jim was back in the office in a month see-ing me. He had to use a wheelchair for a period of time, but mentally he appeared as good as new.

Or maybe not. Regardless of his training in psychiatry he devel-oped "full-blown PTSD," complete with flashbacks of the wild plunge into oncoming traffic, an involuntary stepping-on-the-brake motion of his foot when people mentioned cars, anxiety, depression, and re-curring nightmares, brief, iconic, terrifying images that startled him awake every night, three or four times a night. It was always the same: He was falling off the balcony of his apartment in a high-rise building. Falling, falling—the lights of windows going by faster and faster until he awoke panicked and startled.

Years earlier, he had worked for the VA and had seen dozens of patients with PTSD related to combat. He knew exactly what this was, had a good idea how to treat it, and managed to effectively treat himself.

Some years later I read one of Jim's publications on the nature and evolution of traumatic nightmares in PTSD. Although they were as-cribed to "a patient," I knew that the patient was Jim. He came to un-derstand that the accelerating lights in the falling dream were a "video" of the "acceleration" of streetlights as the cab gathered speed. He no-ticed that as the dreams became longer and acquired details—a plant on the balcony, a curtain in the window of the building—his anxiety seemed to be modified, soaked up the way spilled oil is absorbed by sawdust on a garage floor. The dream acquired color, tempo, and eventually a narrative structure. The plots evolved from absurd to less absurd to plausible. Evolving night after night, they slowly lost their horrific quality as his psyche absorbed the impact of his trauma. After months of these dreams, he had the last of the series:

He was driving a gray Ford station wagon through a snowy afternoon, going up to a ski resort in New Hampshire. The road was utterly empty of other traffic, and the couple of inches of snow on the road made it quiet and soft, the ride gentle and smooth. He would go up gentle hills and slide gently down into valleys. As twilight fell, he slipped off the road onto a muddy shoulder, where the car settled into the ooze and sat perfectly still.

Jim volunteered this traumalogue as it related to my therapy. I recognized symmetry in our relationship and our experience; two men with PTSD, bonding in empathy like combat buddies.

Jim knew the psychiatry literature and had vast experience and great instincts. At most times he seemed to know what I needed. When I would choose to return to therapy, his approach to me was an agile mix of many techniques, some of them now embraced by the current PTSD-treating community. All the while, he gauged his level of treatment against how much I could stand (or, just as important, how much he could stand), and tension was neutralized by our work together on my writings about Vietnam. He considered it basically a psychoanalytically inspired treatment with several supportive parameters added. Many of the modern-day research findings on the pharmacotherapy of PTSD he had already learned about empirically while working for the VA.

At one point Jim organized a men's group consisting of six driven, professionally successful, bright, interesting patients he had been seeing for months or years. For two years, I joined the group every Tuesday morning from 7:15 to 8:45. I shared my stories, anxieties, and weaknesses and listened thoughtfully to others. I gained more compassion, self-awareness, and insight into the spectrum of men's relationships to women. I tried to be helpful to others. I tried to be authentic, but could not decide if I was hero or victim, good or bad, dominant or submissive. At times I was too assertive, trying to be co-leader of the men's group. I even organized meetings "off campus" in the absence of Jim. At one of these meetings we discussed the possibility that Jim was gay and decided none of us were willing to bring that topic into our group meetings with him. In my psyche, I fell back into Hooch 75 and my feelings for King Price. At that time, because we actually feared for King's professional status or even his life, my Vietnam "men's group" absolutely avoided the topic. This time I agreed to bring the question to Jim in one of our private sessions. Jim was receptive and actually relieved. I became part of his support as he "came out" to the men's group, his family, friends, and professional colleagues. Decades later, the men's group continues. I dropped out after two years because I was getting better and had learned to carry the perspectives and support of the group in my head.

Jim, and to a lesser extent the men's group, brought out the parts of me that did not like or trust women. I felt he was especially judgmental of Joan (or the Joan I brought into our sessions). I even met with Jim in separate couples sessions with Joan, and once with my yoga instructor. I found these sessions helpful. They made Jim very anxious.

Jim was always very supportive, finding none of my thoughts or actions evil or unacceptable unless they caused me pain. He could find humor, kindness, and even love in my most manipulative, selfish, and hurtful behaviors. His unconditional support enabled me. At times it gave me permission to pursue my addictions, and at other times a logic and reason and a strategy not to. Over time the reasons not to began to take hold. Although there would be moments when I felt I was getting better despite my complex relationship with Jim, whenever I took a long look back, I knew he was a major force in my recovery.

Although we lived apart, Joan continued to be my wife, mother of my children, and a faithful, if critical, friend. We co-owned our home in Weston, and I provided financial support. She was still family. Joan is unable to lie, and her penetrating honesty often knocked me down, but each time I struggled to my feet, I stood taller. Over time she also became an increasing force in my healing.

Joan remained angry because she saw my Vietnam "stuckness" and the Vietnam War (hers and mine) as part of the sexism, classism, objectification of women, and power imbalances that doomed our marriage, making us both victims. She felt that we were both to blame for buying into unrealistic myths and overacting our given stories. Because I was the first to break and to break our contract, she blames me more, but accepts that because there are so many subtle, complex, indirect, and convoluted ways to make or break unspoken and legal and emotional contracts, blaming is destructive and endless, and retards healing. She was, however, very clear and consistent in her disappointment that we could not heal together.

It made Joan sad to know I could not get joy from my life. She constantly reminded me that the existence of our children and grandchildren should be enough to make me happy. I should feel marvelous and be in wonder. She told me it was very sad that I found so little joy in my wife and girls when I returned from Vietnam. I could have balanced the suffering if I had been able to let my family in. She told me I was in the painful vise of objectifying women. She felt that for me, a companion, a woman, and an orgasm were all the same. Women just didn't count. She felt it was sad for me not to have the comfort of women. Not to take them seriously. Not to let them be important.

I remember her exact words: "Suffering is in the world. Suffering is the world. Suffering is in the world in many forms. We all have our suffering with different content, in different ways. Yours is loneliness. Yours is your inability to connect, to give yourself up. Yours is your Vietnam. Ask for grace. Ask for peace."

Joan pointed out to me that I was less addicted to work than I was to the professional and professorial power inner circle role made possible by my hard work. She regularly named the sexism, racism, elitism, classism, and closed networking that supported the MGH and Harvard senior academic network, especially in medicine. She opined that I was so impressed by my role as professor, chairman, academician, and leader that I had become an actor who became his role. For a poor boy from the South, the role was actually above my station and talents, and I became a self-deceiving phony. I usually disagreed with her but knew she always spoke the truth.

As I healed and let Joan in, she kept me connected to my children until I was able to reestablish my own relationship with each one. Joan is the glue that held us together. She even tried to include Barbara in holiday celebrations and vacations, but that proved to be too uncomfortable for everyone. Even though my children love me, they do not completely trust me because of my history of withdrawal and instability. Still, I have begun to learn to find joy in my children and grandchildren. When I arrive in our Weston home or my daughter's vacation house on Cape Cod, my children and grandchildren are always glad to see me and barely notice when I leave. When I consider the pain I have caused, that arrangement feels good—or as good as it can be.

Of all the men I had known and worked with in Vietnam, the only person I maintained an ongoing relationship with was Alex Roland. I saw Alex two or three times a year—either he and his family visited me or my family visited him. Our kids and wives knew each other well. Of all the people I knew, apart for Jim Groves, the only person I would speak or communicate with about the war on a consistent basis was Alex. After Vietnam Alex had gone on to a successful academic career, becoming a professor of military history and eventually chairman of the History Department at Duke University. As a military historian, war was at the center of his studies. As a friend, he was essential.

For years we generated fitful bursts of dialogue, sometimes angry and pointed and other times understanding and empathetic. Our best arguments lasted hours or even days and grew louder with each drink. We debated the meaning of the Vietnam War and war in general, both to us as individuals and to our society, sparring with the same passion with which we had once relieved tensions by wrestling on the floor of our hooch. We never did this by phone but either spoke to each other in person or exchanged letters.

Alex's written responses to my letters would sometimes take on the shape of a seminar discussion or a lecture, filled with facts, intellectual analysis, and suggestions for reading. He would question my conclusions, both about the war and myself, and spur me on to undertake ever more honest looks at myself and my behavior. Alex played the role of the professor who was never satisfied, who always expected more of me, his student. He parried my search for easy answers.

My letters to him, on the other hand, were more emotive and desperate. As I became more comfortable in therapy and with my diagnosis of PTSD, I shared that knowledge with him. In one letter I wrote:

Dear Alex,

The lingering invisible wounds of war have been given a name: The "post-Vietnam syndrome" has become the post-traumatic stress disorder (PTSD) and entered into the official diagnostic roster of psychiatry as a legitimate diagnosis.

I have had almost all of the menu of symptoms listed in textbooks and journal articles. I am not sure what to think about that. Does it mean that now I have a legitimate complaint? Is my pain now justified? In dermatology, the naming of a constellation of descriptors makes it quicker for professionals to communicate but may impede curiosity about underlying causes. Naming something makes one feel better. I sometimes think a dermatologist is a doctor who translates the patients' descriptions into Latin and both parties feel better.

Should I be relieved that I have a defined disorder? Am I a disorder? Was I flawed both before and after the stress? Should I be proud of my invisible wounds and be reassured that I have a real documented disorder? Should I be ashamed to be among those weak enough to have permanent residua of nature's important fear response?

Somehow I feel labeled and invaded but not understood or supported.

Now that I was beginning to understand myself, being understood by others took on greater urgency. That was what I sought from Alex—his understanding and support, all the while knowing, but not admitting, that since he had a different experience in Vietnam, there was perhaps no way to gain what I was looking for from him. Perhaps there was no way I would ever gain that from anyone.

Still, Alex was always a caring, consistent "backboard." He was a soldier and a scholar who had moved on—I was a wimp who used my psychic wounds to manipulate others. We exchanged views with a full quiver of sarcasm, irony, anger, condescension, acceptance and rejection, manly love, and tolerance and intolerance. We broke off communications for months or years and then resumed as if there had been no interruption. I composed my letters carefully, often working through several drafts. I thought each letter had a unique twist or new insights. Reading them years later they seem both repetitive and competitive. Alex dashed off his letters in one sitting without organizing or editing. I thought he was the better writer, and he had the advantage that his whole career was centered on the study of war. Where I emoted he analyzed and rationalized. Whether we actually corresponded or not, I knew he was always available, and that made me feel less alone and lonely.

> Dear John:
>
> The greatest difference I see between our senses of Vietnam is that you still feel the experience intensely. I have thought about it and I have had ideas that I felt strongly about. But I still don't feel very much about the war . . .
>
> You may be more haunted than I because your experience in Vietnam was more traumatic than mine. You were up to your ankles and wrists in blood throughout much of the year. I walked around the hospital through pools of blood, hosed out my ambulances, carried my share of bodies and parts of bodies. But I don't think I ever became emotionally invested

in those bodies, the way you obviously did. Even when one of my classmates appeared one day in the hospital to have multiple pieces of shrapnel removed, I was undisturbed. He took his wounds in stride and so did I. You could not or did not or would not . . .

Of course, you live periodically in Vietnam. You write about it. You read about it, though it seems to me more for immersion than understanding. You watch movies about it. You obsess over it. But you don't do anything about it. You don't put it behind you. You don't think about it constructively. You don't do compensatory service to expiate your guilt. You don't campaign against racism and sexism and all those other "isms" to which you ascribe responsibility for the war.

You simply keep it warm and young in your memory—a place where you can go and hide . . .

You do indeed have lots to answer for, but it is not complicity in the Vietnam War. Rather it is appropriating the Vietnam War to license a ruinous behavior that seems to be the only relief you find from your demons. I think that you love war . . .

Every once in a while I feel as if you are, of course, right, and I am simply a dried prune . . .

But I resist. I just can't buy it. It doesn't parse. You retreat to Vietnam when you have a current crisis, not when Vietnam sweeps over you. It is where you go to hide—from yourself and from your real demons. But now you and they are clothed in camouflage, virtually indistinguishable from the Vietnam you have conjured. You say Vietnam won't let go of you. I say you won't let go of Vietnam . . .

I fear we are headed for a divorce. Like Joan, I cannot give you all that you want in our relationship. Your letters call out for more engagement than I can muster. Always you are drawn to a wider audience for our dialogue, just as you were drawn away from the monogamy of your marriage. Perhaps

CHAPTER 20

I suppose it was somehow a measure of progress, but at a certain point, after years of relative silence and isolation, I decided to reconnect with some of the other men I served with in Vietnam.

I forget what I was doing, but it began one day when I started thinking of Parker Powell, the surgeon I worked with in Phu Bai. I had only seen him once since Vietnam—he had a meeting or conference in Boston about five years after the war, and Joan and I had gone out to dinner with him and his wife—and we had since lost touch.

It was strange, but for a couple of days I just could not get Parker out of my mind. They were fond memories, too, because I always thought he was a terrific guy and he had been of great help to me, showing me the ropes in Triage and building my confidence. At one point he had even tried to convince me to become a surgeon. I hadn't, obviously, but to hear him say that had been a great boost at a time when I was questioning my ability to do my job. He was a steadying influence. Off duty he never seemed bothered or distressed. He just sat in the corner of the hooch reading a novel.

The last I had known was that after the war Parker had returned to Fresno, California. I did some homework and discovered that he was still there, still apparently working as a surgeon. I got a phone number and called one evening, hoping to catch him at home. His we will just separate, forever to stay in touch as you seek communion with others who can give you what you want . . .

You treated patients as best you could, you voluntarily and at some risk comforted and treated the indigent at the TB hospital in Hue, and you spared some other poor soul who may not have been as brave or as strong or as lucky as you were to get out alive. You were neither John Wayne nor Mr. Kurtz, but you did more good than harm.

Early on in our correspondence, we signed the letters formally: "Sincerely, John" and "Best, Alex," "Your friend," etc. Even as we jousted, disagreed, and sometimes argued, our friendship deepened. After a while we ended each letter "Love."

wife answered the phone, and when I identified myself and asked for Parker, something in her voice didn't sound right. It wasn't.

Since returning from Vietnam Parker had been a successful surgeon, and for the last twenty years he had never missed a single day of work. He had a nice career, and he and his wife were active and prominent in the community—Parker loved music and had served as president of the Fresno Philharmonic Orchestra. A few weeks before my call he complained about fatigue and chronic pain in his back and abdomen. Apparently he had been bothered by the symptoms for several months but had never said anything and had never gone to see a doctor himself.

He did, and it was discovered that he had a rare form of lymphoma. The diagnosis was terminal. He had entered the hospital two days earlier and was already in intensive care. His wife was beside herself and wondered if his illness was the delayed result of exposure to Agent Orange, the defoliant that had been widely used in Vietnam.

I could not believe it. It was one of those "Oh my God, there is such a thing as clairvoyance" moments. I wanted to speak with him, but he was too ill. I called several more times over the next few days, and his wife said that while Parker occasionally told her about his hoochmates, he otherwise never spoke about Vietnam. When she told him I had called, he was aware enough to smile and nod his head. A few days later he was dead.

Many months later I visited Parker Powell's widow at her home in Fresno. Prompted by hundreds of photographs and documents, we spent more than two hours reviewing Parker's personal, family, and professional life and had a conversation that was surprisingly close and intimate. She was a bright, classy woman, and I liked her enormously. When we parted I kissed her on the cheek and gave her a warm total-body hug. Then she kissed me on the mouth with a fervor that left me breathless. I was confused, aroused, and titillated as I drove away.

Learning that Parker had died before I had a chance to see him affected me deeply, and I decided it was time to track down my other close relationships from Vietnam before it was too late. I was able to locate King Price in San Francisco and began to include him in my correspondence with Alex. I even sent him a copy of all our past correspondence, something Alex found upsetting, as if I were breaking a trust. Still, Alex respected King, and we both found his occasional contributions to our dialogues always entertaining and sometimes helpful.

Alex, in fact, thought that King provided some of the best insights into war he had ever received. King thought the most frightening experience we can have is one in which we feel that we have lost control of events. If we survive the crisis, by retelling we try to reestablish control, to remove the fear and terror by convincing ourselves that we were somehow still directing our own destiny. In this way war stories become a method of healing. Their purpose is not so much to tell listeners what really happened as to convince the storyteller that he or she was in control at a time when he or she actually was not. As in the old telephone game, with each retelling the stories change as the storyteller becomes more central to the event and moves ever more confidently from crisis to crisis, in command, under control. By the time they have served the teller's purpose, they are often so boastful, incredible, and self-satisfying that no one wants to listen.

Alex thought that I was trying to relive my war story over and over again so I could gain control of it. I probably was, and still am.

Before I had a chance to see King I had the opportunity to visit Stan Myers, the division internist. He still lived in Memphis, and when we met in the airport his full-body hug surprised me. He had aged, as had I, and gained weight but had the same warm face, big smile, and deep, slow-flowing southern accent.

He seemed nervous, telling me repeatedly how glad he was to see me. Although I was staying at his home he drove to a hotel, and we found a corner table in the restaurant. It was 3:00 P.M., and the room was empty except for us. He seemed uncomfortable and immediately began talking nonstop.

I was stunned by what I learned. While we were in Vietnam Stan had seemed pleasant and untroubled, big-hearted, sort of the quintessential good old Southern boy, smart but also simple in a way, very open and straightforward. His "goodness" and tolerance were often the butt of jokes and barbs in our hooch, particularly those delivered by King, whose dry wit could sting, but Stan always seemed to take the abuse good-naturedly.

Now he spoke in a way I had never heard him speak before, urgently, unloading, sharing, confessing. Before he went to Vietnam he had been totally and completely out of control. An alcoholic, he was also addicted to intravenous use of hard drugs and had to give himself several injections a day. His friends in the medical community kept him afloat and out of trouble before finally making arrangements to have him sent to Vietnam to see if it would be possible for him to "dry out" and beat his addictions. He agreed to go to war in a desperate attempt to pull his life together and avoid losing his wife and family, his medical license, his reputation, and his sanity. Stan went to Vietnam to heal.

Before he left he went on a huge bender, spending eight days in San Francisco and two days in Okinawa completely intoxicated. Just before his plane touched down he set down his whiskey glass and decided he would not touch either drugs or alcohol while he was in Vietnam.

He didn't. He spent his entire year stone cold sober. His first time ever away from home, for Stan, Vietnam was a test, a turnaround, and a passage. While he was in country his wife had their third child.

I was as surprised by this as I had been when I learned that Parker Powell was dying. Stan apologized for never sharing this with me before. My story, compared to his, seemed inconsequential.

He went on, telling me that after he returned from Vietnam he dealt with his addiction to drugs, alcohol, sex, cigarettes, and caffeine through various step programs. Although he stumbled and relapsed several times, it was his successful one-year war against addiction that showed him he had the strength to recover. He had just celebrated his fourteen-year anniversary free of all destructive addictions.

His confession complete, we left the hotel and drove around Memphis for hours. He showed me his childhood home, his schools and churches and the places he hung out with Elvis Presley, his boyhood buddy and high school classmate. Then he took me to his weekly meeting of Sex Addicts Anonymous. I joined the confessional introductions and told parts of my story. After dark, when his staff had departed, he conducted a forty-five-minute detailed tour of his one-person medical office.

The next morning on the way to the airport, Stan repeatedly asked me how he could help me with my pain about Vietnam. He stated that he felt no pain or anxiety over his one year in the war. Vietnam had been good for him.

A short time after I saw Stan, I made arrangements to see King Price, who was living with his partner in San Francisco. I was scheduled to attend a meeting in Palo Alto and was able to schedule a day off to visit King.

Of all the men I had served with, I had been particularly eager to speak with King. Not only did he seem to have more insight into the war than anyone else (except, perhaps, Alex), but now that I was in therapy, I looked forward to picking his brain for that insight. I thought he might be helpful and interesting because he was a very, very bright man. He had jumped right into our correspondence, but there were certain things I wanted to discuss with him in person.

I knew that King had worked at a VA hospital for a time after the war, and I assumed that he had had a lot of patients from Vietnam with PTSD. I also wondered if he suffered from PTSD himself. I had learned from our correspondence that right after he returned to America he had talked his way onto a freighter and gone to sea essentially as a stowaway for weeks. For a time he just couldn't deal with human beings unless they were total strangers. He described himself as crazy at that time, but his experiences during the war were far different from mine. He was never on the battlefield or in Triage. All the carnage he witnessed, talking with people who had lost balance emotionally, was psychological. It was always his decision to select whom to treat in Phu Bai, whom to send back to their units, and whom to send to a navy hospital in Vietnam or the States. As head psychiatrist for the whole 3rd Marine Division he was the ultimate authority. He had the power to send people home—some probably begging to go home who weren't really in bad enough shape, and others who were in bad shape begging to stay because they didn't want their record marred. It was an awesome responsibility.

I had never really known why, of all the people he encountered in Vietnam, I had been the only professional colleague to whom he offered a "no questions asked" chance to leave the war zone.

Now, as I made my way to King's apartment, I felt uneasy, insecure, awkward, and intrusive. I also knew that I would not receive the answers I was looking for. Two years before, King had suffered a stroke.

When we met he looked surprisingly healthy. He was taller than I remembered, and thinner, with a tidy trimmed mustache. He did not hug me or even shake my hand.

His speech was slurred and labored but understandable. He had to struggle to find the words to express himself, although given time and encouragement, he could ask simple questions. He understood everything, but the man who had absorbed so much of the psychic pain of others now could not emote himself.

His partner, Felix, hovered nearby, supportive of his needs. I tried to intuit what King was trying to say and, guided by his eyes, help him say it. King understood everything I said and probably things I didn't say, but his own responses were limited.

I talked slowly and almost constantly, responding to his nods and frequent smiles. I told him about my job and what I knew of our other hoochmates. I told stories of various high jinks and absurdities, and we both laughed. When silences became comfortable, we both retreated into private memories and reflections. Felix was quiet, but attentive.

King no longer had copies of our correspondence. They had been destroyed in a fire. When I mentioned his proposition, he responded in a way that let me know he remembered, but his reasons remained hidden away.

I stayed only about an hour. King's struggle for words seemed to make him tired, and we had had our "visit." Although he was polite and gracious, smiling and nodding frequently, I don't know what he was really thinking.

As I left, he stood with difficulty. We hugged. I said that I would see him again, knowing that I probably would not. Felix walked me to the door. I turned to King as I left.

"Peace," I said.

He gave an asymmetrical tolerant smile and, not even trying to search for a word, turned to gaze out his window at the Golden Gate Bridge.

I called Jim Veesar, a physician who was my hoochmate in Dong Ha. When we first met we realized we had actually flown to Vietnam on the same plane. Later we spent one alcohol- and sex-fueled week together in Thailand on R&R.

We had not spoken for over twenty years. Jim had dealt with his tour in Vietnam by fully embracing what he called the "great surgical experience" the war provided; it kept him busy in between occasional but regular "wild and crazy" weekends in Da Nang. In Vietnam I had been nurtured and distracted by his good-natured humor and his sincere if somewhat frenetic immersion in the care of casualties. Because he planned to be a surgeon he sometimes volunteered to take my place in the OR if it was a "good case"—usually an amputation that required more than big shears and strong arms.

Shortly after returning to the States Jim became psychotic, requiring repeated hospitalizations. He developed the delusion that he was still in Vietnam. After years of therapy, though, he finished his surgical training, married, fathered children, and established a practice. About ten years later he began to have serious difficulties with Vietnam flashbacks and alcohol abuse. One day during an amputation, he became catatonic and had to be helped out of the operating room. He joined AA and at the time we spoke was running a successful rehabilitation center.

I briefly shared with him that I had difficulties letting go of Vietnam.

I asked him if he wanted to talk or visit or read any of the correspondence I had accumulated.

"No," he said quickly and rather nonchalantly, as if I had mentioned a random unimportant topic that did not happen to interest him. "I don't want to think about Vietnam."

After an awkward silence, I invited him to call me if he was ever in Boston.

"Same for you if you ever get to this part of the world. Gotta go. 'Bye."

Then he hung up.

In November of 1996 I arranged for a reunion of sorts, inviting Alex and Stan to visit me together in Boston. After an awkward greeting we began to share stories of our civilian lives, quickly realizing that we had lived more years since our lives together than before. Several months earlier, I had sent Stan copies of the correspondence between Alex and me, but he made no mention of the letters.

We told brief war stories without feeling. "I remember the time . . ." and "I'll never forget . . ." and "sometimes I can still picture . . ." and "do you remember . . ." and "you always . . ." and "we usually . . ." and "I wonder whatever happened to . . ." Bound by a common history, we interpreted some events very differently, as if they were different stories.

We were comfortable with long silences. We took walks. We ate too much. Alex and I drank too much. None of us smoked anymore.

Stan was accommodating, yielding, self-deprecating, and tolerant. I fell asleep on the floor during Stan's confessional autobiography of addiction and failure and salvation. At some level I was listening, but I could not focus on the style and content of Stan's seven- or ten- or twelve-step successes.

Alex educated us about many topics and then studied our reactions.

We contributed loving, cynical, and tender reminiscences of Parker and King. We marveled at the consistency, steadiness, inner wisdom, confidence, reliability, and thoughtfulness of Parker. We laughed at recollections about King and remembered what a large, strange, inter-esting, and intelligent man he was. We laughed about King's frighten-ing scream the time he sat on a lizard after running nude to our bunker during incoming shells three decades earlier. His sexual orientation and loathing of Stan were not mentioned during our tour or during this reunion.

I complained and challenged my hoochmates. "Did we learn any lessons? Is there any shared meaning?" I reminded them that grunts often recited, "It don't mean nuthin'." I expected more from myself and needed more from Stan and Alex.

Alex belched and said, "It don't mean nuthin'."

Through an unspoken contract, we avoided present feelings and vulnerability but trusted enough to share past failures and mistakes. We treated each other with warmth, respect, support, and a graceful growing distance. We were separate and alone together. Forged by the same fire, we had strong camaraderie, a kind of love that only men can understand and never discuss lest it be tarnished.

Alex Roland and John Parrish, 2008.

Alex and I expected something to happen—we knew not what. We wanted to be distracted and educated and entertained with new content or new feelings, but during our gentle recollections and vague reminiscences, we gradually lost energy and connection. We filled the ever-enlarging spaces within our slowing conversation with short verbal family portraits. Children, grandchildren, and parents, living and dead, were more present than Vietnam.

Our wives were not only absent as participants in the conversation, but they barely entered as subjects. Stan's was alone somewhere in the city waiting for him. Alex's very carefully selected second wife was at home with her children, his children, their children, and the present selectees in a line of foster children. I remained separated from Joan but was beginning to forge a lasting relationship with Barbara, who essentially hosted the reunion while staying out of sight.

In silence we were present to the moment and not present at all. We were like men fishing or watching football on television. Speaking was like taking a turn at cutting bait or going to the fridge for beers.

There was no intensity to our talk, no focus. We were safe. We were home. We recognized that a part of us remained emotionally and spiritually exhausted and sought rest in the safety of old familiar caves and modern diversions. There was no need to go back now. No desire to return to war. No requirement to look backward. No real obligation to look inside.

I fell asleep again on the floor. These nice men, these old friends, these war buddies couldn't prevent nightmares, but they were there each time I woke.

When it was time to go, Stan embraced first me and then Alex, and we responded by slapping his back, and for a moment we were all quiet again.

We agreed to try to get together again someday, but we never have.

A year later I was invited to attend a reunion in San Diego organized for the 3rd Medical Battalion, 3rd Marine Division. Several months before the reunion, I asked the organizers if they had planned any time for attendees to share reactions and feelings about their war experiences. The thought had never crossed their minds. When I told them of my reactions to Vietnam, they barely understood what I was talking about.

"Of course it was awful," responded one. "All the shit funneled to us. It was carnage. But now it's all over. If you are lonely, my wife and I will include you in our dinner plans."

Another one said, "My war experience doesn't bother me. I still treat trauma for a living. In our busy emergency room, I still treat AK-47 wounds, stab wounds, fragmentation injuries . . ."

Still, I convinced the organizers to forward a letter from me to all attendees.

January 24, 1997
TO: All Members of the Third Medical Battalion Third Marine
    Division Who Served in Vietnam 1965–1970
FROM: John Parrish

Dear Colleagues:

First, I wish to thank those of you who reconnected us and organized the upcoming reunion. Being together more than thirty years after working together in Vietnam is a special gift and opportunity.

I also want to share with you that over the last three decades, I have had a great deal of difficulty integrating my Vietnam experience into my subsequent life.

My lingering pain is difficult to describe and changes form from time to time: Soft, blurry flashbacks; nightmares involving carnage and blood and guts, but mostly centered on feelings of inadequacy—fatigue or paralysis while being overwhelmed by casualties; episodes of hypervigilance and feelings of impending doom during which I sense the sights, sounds, and smells of mass casualties in Triage and feel the physical fear that used to clutch my chest and throat when helicopters approached. Sometimes images of specific wounded soldiers stay with me.

I have intermittent intrusive thoughts and memories and unwelcome and uninvited preoccupations with the Vietnam War. I think about the American War in Vietnam more than I want to.

I am successful in my work and my professional peers would be surprised to know that I sometimes spend my time alone watching Vietnam movies and reading books to try to find some meaning, explanation, cause, justification, or understanding of what I experienced in Vietnam.

Do you have any advice for me?

Do you wish to talk about how the American War in Vietnam affected you?

I will be arriving late Friday afternoon and would be happy to meet with anyone who wishes to talk together about what the Vietnam experience meant to them and how it affects them today. We have eight hours of scheduled lectures about military medicine and trauma. Looking at the program, there are two times that do not conflict with any scheduled meetings:

5:30–6:30 p.m. Friday

5:30–6:30 p.m. Saturday

Maybe real men and savvy physicians don't talk about these things. Or, maybe no one else feels unfinished.

In any case, have a wonderful reunion.

Sincerely,

John

After the reunion, I met Barbara at a resort at Cabo San Lucas at the southern tip of Baja where the Sea of Cortez meets the Pacific Ocean. As I sat alone on the patio of a plush apartment, I watched a line of eight or nine Mexican men about fifty meters away dig a wide shallow trench and throw the sand slightly uphill away from the ocean. Another row of men threw the sand farther up the hill. Slowly, day by day, they made small changes in the contour of a dune just out of reach of high tide.

They moved slowly. There was no shade, and the sun was very hot. Their skin was dry and brown and red. A steady breeze off the ocean removed the sweat as soon as it appeared. Every hour or so, they all stopped to rest and stand perfectly still at even intervals in the baking sun.

As I sat watching I imagined that in a few months the men would have prepared the earth for another group of oceanside bungalows for American tourists. I though of the enormous power and technology of the U.S. war machine. With heavy equipment the U.S. Army Corps of Engineers could finish the earth-moving project in one day—by 1630 hours—and have time for a couple of beers before chow and movies. Awesome power. Impressive capabilities. I thought about the reunion of military doctors who served during the peak of their war in Vietnam. In order to get CME (continuing medical education) credits and tax deductions and to avoid unstructured noncocktail time, the men sat together all day listening to each other give lectures about the causes and care of tissue trauma and watching personal Vietnam War slide shows presented by some of the more dominant males.

In many ways, the doctors attending the reunion were ordinary people. They accepted war and their support roles in war. They were proud of their surgical skills and their ability to innovate and survive in primitive settings. They had a tough job and they did it well. They were throwing sand uphill, one shovelful at a time. They experienced the fellowship developed while pursuing a common goal under difficult conditions. They appreciated the respect, support, encouragement, and teamwork of their colleagues. They felt that it was good to see each other again after thirty years.

Old men told stories about the wounded and shared memories of specific injuries and pathways of fragments through multiple viscera.

They remembered heroic attempts to repair exploded livers and spleens and lungs and hearts and recalled simple creative measures to preserve life and limb. Many successes, many failures. Some memorable. All day, every day.

Not once in Vietnam did I have structured or spontaneous discussions about our activities in Triage or about individual or collective responses to unusually stressful times in Triage during mass casualties, incoming rounds, large numbers of civilian casualties, or epidemics of malaria. When individual severely wounded marines were discussed it was in the O-Club over drinks or in the chow hooch over dinner. Bragging, descriptions of anatomy, fragment paths, and procedures, or even jokes replaced any serious debriefings or discussions of an individual doctor's fear or response to horror.

Several of the doctors at the reunion had been back to modern Vietnam for brief visits as tourists, capitalists, returning warriors, curious observers, or attendees at medical conferences. They created slide shows for their church and civic groups. They interpreted the good service and accommodating spirit of the Vietnamese merchants and guides as love and respect for Americans and soothing affirmation of Americans' (especially American doctors') righteous and superior position in the world. To the doctors, the selected Vietnamese who sold them a thinly plated forgiveness for past bombs represented all Vietnamese and all peasants and nationalists everywhere. It may have taken a long time to win Vietnamese hearts and minds, but finally the American way was being appreciated.

To me the doctors' dramatic stories of reconciliation with strangers, clever travel tips, tourist vignettes, and biosketches of the forgiving "natives" reeked of self-indulgence, the blindness of privilege, arrogance, racism, and proud demonstrations of their own emperor's travel clothing. They all made the point that despite great effort, they and their "hosts" could find no evidence of the fact that the 3rd Medical Battalion had ever been anywhere in I Corps. Not at Phu Bai or Dong Ha. No landmarks at Quang Tri. Nothing at Khe Sanh. Only rice fields at the sites of every battalion aid station. I was somewhat pleased at the touring doctors' surprise and disappointment at not finding shrines or markers to Americans or nostalgic scenes.

From the attendees I had known in Vietnam, I was surprised to hear that my humor, quick wit, and steadiness were a source of sustenance for many of my fellow doctors. I may have lost that part of myself. When I shared my continuing postwar pain, I received quick, reflexive expressions of support, a few crumbs of sympathy, and a lot of social space.

Not one of the doctors accepted my written invitation to meet to grapple with the meaning of the war or its impact on our individual lives. A few of the wives told me that my invitation letter was "lovely"— then they seemed at a loss for what to say next.

I love, admire, fear, and avoid those Mexican men working to move the sand.

CHAPTER 21

By 2005 my life was beginning to take on a new and more comfortable form. My relationship with Barbara was strong, and my friendships with Jim Groves and Alex were deep and sustaining. I was again close to Joan and my children and felt joy in being a small part in the life of my grandchildren. My children were always cordial and pleasant to Barbara, and I had a growing relationship with her three sons. Nevertheless, my children (and therefore my grandchildren) would not spend prolonged time (trips, vacations) with me unless Joan was included and Barbara excluded.

Although she occasionally initiated meetings with lawyers to discuss all forms of separation and divorce, I was unable to divorce Joan. We agreed upon what resources were needed to guarantee her and our children a comfortable life, and I will always gladly provide for them. Barbara wanted me to divorce Joan and marry her. Each time I prepared my income tax return or when I sat alone and studied my enlarging folder of facts, figures, and logistics of divorce, I got depressed and confused and did not act. I was unable to find the psychic energy. Something nondescript, large, and frightening paralyzed me. This was evidence that I still had a long way to go in order to heal and be a whole, integrated, responsible adult.

Although I relentlessly continued to work on my written war story,

I was feeling more balanced and strong. I had fewer episodes of intrusive thoughts and visions of Vietnam, but I continued to choose to think about war. Instead of being an addiction and escape, my work was beginning to contribute to my health in a more direct fashion.

I was beginning to ponder retirement from my academic responsibilities, but I felt a deep abiding commitment to a project started five years earlier. In the mid-1990s, I had begun to meet with a few highly motivated Boston-area physicians and technology innovators who were convinced that the breakthroughs in modern technology could, and should, deliver more effective solutions for unmet needs in patient care.

During the time I was directing the MGH Wellman Center for Photomedicine, huge advances were being made in the technologies serving consumer markets, manufacturing industries, and national defense needs. Yet the migration of those technologies toward the service of health care needs was slow, stymied by the difficulties of collaboration between those who knew the clinical issues well and those who knew available technologies well. In most situations, the clinical innovators did not possess the skills or the resources to surmount all the obstacles of moving ideas "from bench to bedside," ultimate dissemination, and commercialization. Similarly, the developers of the technologies themselves often lacked the skills and expertise to deliver the technology to the health care business quickly and efficiently.

Academic medical schools and teaching hospitals did not provide the best environment for technologically based improvements in health care. Peer review funding processes, such as at the National Institutes of Health, had devolved to low-risk profiles, leaving early-stage ideas starving for support. Thus, the first challenge was to develop new locally informed mechanisms for funding promising early-stage work and talented neophyte innovators. Even when early-stage, higher-risk funding was available, new concepts often ended at the publication stage, satisfying the academic imperative. Yet publications are not an adequate means to assure adoption, dissemination, and implementation of effective new paradigm-shifting technologies and practices. Multidisciplinary and interdisciplinary collaborative work was not adequately rewarded by traditional granting mechanisms and academic promotion processes.

We had faced this obstacle in the MGH Wellman Center, but over two decades my colleagues and I had developed strategies, approaches, and structures to reduce the time it took to bring new technologies from concept to ultimate clinical application. Although the Wellman Center only worked with one technology—photonics—a multidisciplinary team was committed to each project. I had gradually recruited chemists and biologists with training and expertise related to the ultraviolet, visible, and near-infrared regions of the electromagnetic spectrum and added physicists who had developed lasers and other sophisticated sources of energy. I insisted that all projects be led by a physician even if he or she had very little research experience. We provided the remainder of the multidisciplinary team with equipment, technical help, industry partners, and funding. This approach was working. Rox Anderson and our colleagues in dermatology had taken several novel ideas through FDA approval and to clinical practice. For applications of light to organs other than the skin, we recruited gastroenterologists, cardiologists, ophthalmologists, obstetricians, gynecologists, and surgeons to lead research teams formed around their specific needs.

I set out to extend this approach beyond photonics to other technologies. I combined forces with like-minded M.D.'s and Ph.D.'s and created the Center for Integration of Medicine and Innovative Technology (CIMIT), a voluntary collaboration of Massachusetts General Hospital, Brigham and Women's Hospital, Massachusetts Institute of Technology, and the Charles Stark Draper Laboratory (a nonprofit engineering institute supported largely by defense and other government contracts) working together to improve health care by accelerating the capture of emerging technologies. CIMIT invested heavily in building a powerful, dedicated facilitative infrastructure of experienced individuals from multiple backgrounds, each of whom had decades of experience in bringing technological ideas of clinical importance to full fruition, serving as a functioning management team. We decided to focus on biomedical devices, procedures, systems engineering, and technology—because, compared to drug development, the timeline from idea to "first-in-human" use could be short, allowing CIMIT to have impact in a few years. Eventually, CIMIT grew to include thirteen Boston-based institutions with enormous combined capabilities.*

CIMIT proved to be astoundingly effective at bringing new ideas to commercialization and clinical implementation. Forty new companies were formed or redirected, and CIMIT-funded investigators generated over $200 million from industry, government, and foundations to continue the research launched by CIMIT. Twenty-five percent of projects resulted in FDA approval, commercialization, or clinical use. On average, for every dollar CIMIT invested in research, the individual investigators generated another ten dollars from other sources. In biomedical research that kind of success is extremely impressive. We found that the most beneficial impact is derived when biomedical applications of modern technology are driven by unmet clinical needs (clinical "pull"), not by a random search for medical applications of new technological capabilities (technology "push").

My interest in war influenced CIMIT to be receptive to trying to meet many of the needs of military medicine, and my status as a veteran and combat surgeon helped CIMIT compete for funding in these areas. Largely due to the efforts of the late Congressman John Murtha, an ex-marine and chairman of the Armed Forces Appropriations Committee, and the late Senator Ted Kennedy, the largest single source of money for CIMIT was congressionally mandated funding from the

*Boston-based institutions: Beth Israel Deaconess Medical Center, Boston Medical Center, Boston University, Brigham & Women's Hospital, Charles Stark Draper Laboratory, Children's Hospital Boston, Harvard Medical School, Massachusetts General Hospital, Massachusetts Institute of Technology, Newton-Wellesley Hospital, Northeastern University, Partners HealthCare System, VA Boston Healthcare System.

Department of Defense. CIMIT's trauma care program was easily translated to the unmet needs in combat casualty care. While serving as director of CIMIT, I still retained all my academic duties at Harvard and MGH. In many ways I was the same workaholic I had always been, and my days were full of meetings that never seemed to end.

I was taking a rare break and was on vacation on a small, remote Caribbean island with Barbara when my usually quiet and stoic mother, age eighty-nine, began to complain about severe pain in one of her knees. My sister took her to a teaching hospital, where she was put to bed and treated with pain medications for six days. The "observation unit" had no bathroom and was not staffed for usual in-patient nursing care, so my family took shifts as her attendants and comforters.

My mother was miserable, literally writhing as she constantly changed her position to relieve escalating back pain that resulted from being confined to bed. Her knee pain and related swelling increased. Still, believing that this was nothing more than a routine hospitalization and that she would be discharged in a few days, my brother decided not to tell me that my mother had been hospitalized.

My mother's primary physician was away on vacation. As my sister became more involved in my mother's hospital care, she grew resentful toward the physician in charge. She felt that his daily rounds were abrupt and superficial and that he neither listened to my mother nor spent any time explaining things to her or my family. Issues surrounding Medicare "rules" and "length of stay" seemed more important to him, my sister said, and despite my mother's lack of improvement he made arrangements to transfer her to a rehabilitation center.

Early on the morning of her scheduled discharge from the hospital, my mother called and pleaded with my sister to take her home, telling her she did not want to go to a "nursing home." In a clear strong voice, she said something that at the time seemed entirely inappropriate: "I want to die at home." After reassuring our mother that no one died from knee pain, my sister came to the hospital. She was alarmed to find our mother's condition had deteriorated rapidly from the previous evening. She knew who and where she was, but her speech was slurred, with occasional clumsy choice of words. She was very sleepy yet restless and anxious.

My sister went back and forth between various nurses in the hallway and at the nursing station and kept telling them, "Something is wrong with my mother," but was essentially ignored and told that our mother was just "tired" and that her present condition was the result of a generous dose of morphine given to quiet her down during transport. No one came to check her mental status or vital signs. Finally, despite her protests, the transport team arrived to move her.

She lost consciousness intermittently in the ambulance, arrived awake and in acute distress at the nonacute care facility, and was immediately sent back to the emergency ward of the hospital she had just left. Jostled about for three hours by strangers' hands lifting, pushing, probing, and inserting needles and tubes, my mother died, alone, essentially abandoned. She ended her life in a swirl of strange voices, conflicting commands, frenetic activity, alarms, and mechanical devices. Not touched by a calm loving hand, without glimpses of loved ones, absent prayers and communion, she died afraid and confused among strangers.

Except for a few activities in the church, my mother had lived entirely for and through her family. A full-time wife and mother, her role as a minister's wife was her profession. She knew the lives of her children, grandchildren, and great-grandchildren in detail. She was rock solid in her absolute love for and commitment to each member of the family, often expressing acceptance when nobody else would. Her living room and kitchen were plastered with photographs, and she was constantly writing letters and mailing small gifts for birthdays and special occasions. All three generations of our family were always eager to tell Grandmother about every event, large and small, in their lives. She made us all feel special, and she alone had provided comfort during my earliest years. In our childhood, in her soft, stately way, she did her best to protect her children from their spiritually abusive father. As I grew up I tried to protect her. We were intimately bonded in many unspoken ways. Yet none of us were with her for her unquiet death.

My mother's death was not personal. My mother was the first to know she was dying and wanted to be in her own bedroom surrounded by her family. Deeply religious, she was not afraid of death, and for years she had her small estate, funeral, and burial arrangements completely organized. Sadly, her request for a quiet death at home did not fit into our mindset and was dismissed by everyone. Instead, the end was clumsy and impersonal. She was an unknown player on the stage of an empty theater. The health care system had her surrounded.

I didn't even know. It was only after my mother died that my brother contacted me. Had I been in Boston instead of on vacation, I would have flown to Atlanta when it was clear the diagnosis was uncertain and the hospitalization was lasting more than two or three days. While my mother's providers might have ignored my sister, would they have listened to a chaired professor at Harvard Medical School and department chairman at MGH? Would my discussions with her doctors and nurses have resulted in more communication among them? Would I have personally tracked down her primary care physician and the cardiologist who was most familiar with my mother? If I had been there, would I have participated in decisions about definitive care, assignment to a fully staffed hospital room, and better regulation of pain medications? At least I could have checked her pulse and looked for signs of shock or drug overdose before she was removed by the ambulance team. I was convinced I could have saved her life.

Knowing Joan would want to come to be with my siblings and their families, I left Barbara at the resort. This was not a time to increase personal stress. It took me thirty-six hours, traveling by jeep, boat, and plane, to reach Atlanta. I spent the entire time writing an obituary for my mother. I listed her loving qualities and unselfish devotion to her family. I praised the bravery she showed overcoming the family traumas. I wrote and then deleted a section about forgiving her for not protecting us from my father.

When I arrived just in time for the funeral, I found that Gil, based on instructions left years earlier by my mother, had already orchestrated the funeral and arranged transport of the body from Atlanta to

Laurel for burial. There was no time allowed for me, the eldest living son, to deliver a eulogy. To preserve my fragile ego and protect me from possible public embarrassment, my brother asked me to read my intended oration to his family and my sister's family as we sat next to the casket in the funeral home. I did my best to read aloud but interrupted myself several times by short, embarrassingly loud, guttural bursts of crying. Gil called a stop to my agony, and my sister decided that my mother needed her glasses and a different shade of lipstick.

We had been planning a surprise ninetieth birthday celebration for my mother. Her three children, eight grandchildren, and sixteen great-grandchildren were to be among the guests planning to join us from all over the country. My mother never knew about these plans and never experienced this culminating moment in a life devoted to loving her family. One week after her death, we had the celebration in her absence.

After my mother's death, I retired from all my academic responsibilities. I gave up all MGH and HMS titles and administrative positions and resigned from eight committees enabling the careers of women, minority groups, Ph.D.'s (in an M.D.-dominated environment), trainees, junior faculty, research animals, and research volunteers. I had completed nine years in leadership positions representing the research faculty, at first to the MGH trustees and then to the MGH administration, a four-year process to establish cross-departmental research centers at MGH, and a year with a research leadership role for Partners HealthCare System.

I committed full-time to the development and direction of CIMIT, the most fulfilling role of my professional career to that time. Ten years earlier, as director of the Wellman Center, I had already decided not to put my names on publications or patent applications. I wanted to have no conflicts of interest and concentrate on making an ideal environment for junior investigators. When I had decided to step down from that position, a committee conducted a worldwide search and found that Rox Anderson was best qualified. I was very pleased and proud. It took HMS and MGH two years to identify and recruit the new dermatology department chairperson. It also took considerable time for me to completely separate from committees, work groups, task forces, and advisory roles. By 2008, I had only one job: director of CIMIT. Instead of constantly reacting to administrative problems, I had time to initiate and be thoughtful and creative. I felt this was the position for which I had been preparing for since 1961, including my tour in Vietnam. After forty years of work I had a job I wanted.

I could not save my brother. I could not save all the wounded soldiers. I could not save my father. I did not even try to save my mother. With CIMIT, though, maybe I could make a difference, and once again I found myself involved in the care of wounded soldiers.

As I shed jobs, I was also being released from my addictions to sex, violence, exercise, war, and academic accomplishments. Even my writing became more of an enjoyable and compelling project and less like punishment.

CHAPTER 22

In the spring of 2008, Alex and his wife, Liz, were visiting and told me they had accepted an invitation from the Duke Alumni Association to host a twelve-day organized tour of Vietnam. They often went on similar overseas trips sponsored by the association, serving as co-hosts, and Alex gave lectures and answered questions about local history. In exchange Alex and his wife were allowed to make the trips for free.

After Alex described the trip, in a very matter-of-fact fashion he added, "You and Barbara ought to come along." He didn't pose it as a question or even a request. It was a very gentle way of letting me know the invitation was open. There was no pressure. I was noncommittal, but I thought about it for the next several weeks with quite a bit of approach and avoidance, testing how the notion resided within me.

I had never intended to return to Vietnam and had always been skeptical and critical of those who claimed an easy peaceful closure to lingering war stress. However, the more I thought about returning, I began to feel a kind of titillating anxiety, more anticipation than dread, more curiosity than fear. Another appeal was that I would be able to spend more time talking with Alex, which I always found stimulating. We had been debating the meaning of war and the meaning of Vietnam for decades, and the prospect of returning to Vietnam with my old hoochmate, both of us for the first time, was just too good to pass up. I didn't know what to expect, but I knew I had to go. Barbara and I cleared our schedules and made plans to meet the group in Hanoi.

We flew first to Hong Kong and then, after a layover of several hours, caught a flight to Hanoi. As the plane began its approach to the airport I realized that I was landing in a place that had been the headquarters of the enemy. Had I arrived there forty years earlier I would have either been killed instantly, tortured, or put into a prison cell so small it would have been impossible to stand or stretch out. Now, from the air, Hanoi looked like any other sprawling Asian metropolis.

We were met by our tour guide, a pleasant, young Vietnamese man who spoke English very well, and he escorted us to our hotel. He would travel with us for the entire trip, which would involve bus excursions into the countryside as well as air travel to Vietnam's other major cities, including Hue, Da Nang, and Saigon. Over cocktails in a reception area, we met the other members of our group. Among them were two other veterans, one man who had been stationed in Saigon, and another who had spent his year in another safe place working with U.S. Military Intelligence. There were six couples and six singles. At age sixty, Alex and Liz were the youngest in the group.

Our four-star hotel was like every other nice hotel anywhere else in the world. Apart from the staff there was no way of telling that we were in Vietnam. I could no longer understand a word of Vietnamese. I had never spoken the language after leaving Vietnam and had lost my language skills entirely.

We spent much of our time in Vietnam like other Westerners in tour groups. Most days included scripted experiences—trips to floating markets, pagodas, beaches, and limestone caves. Our Vietnamese guide shepherded us on walks through farms and villages and cycle-cab rides through ancient parts of the cities. Beautiful Vietnamese women narrated our visits to handicraft factories demonstrating the production of silk, marble statues, lacquerware, bricks, incense, rice paper, and snake wine. Each tour inevitably ended in a gift shop where some of our group, encouraged by clever and assertive locals, succumbed to shopping frenzies. To sample local specialties, once each day we were served delicious fixed-menu meals accompanied by explanations of the ingredients and their preparation.

For about half of our waking hours we were free to create our own excursions. While many in our party chose to shop or simply rest in the hotel and take advantage of the swimming pool and other amenities, I chose to explore the cities alone on foot. I was obviously an American, and as I tentatively began to walk the streets, I expected the people I encountered to show bias or distaste toward me. After all, I had already learned from Alex that the Vietnamese people refer to the war as "the American War in Vietnam," just as they refer to earlier conflicts as "the French War in Vietnam" and "the Japanese War in Vietnam," never forgetting to note that in each instance foreigners had invaded and brought war into their country.

Instead of feeling any hostility, however, I felt just the opposite. As people passed me on the street, many made eye contact and smiled. Some spoke a little English and were curious, welcoming, and eager to communicate. They seemed busy and happy and were well dressed. The streets were neat and clean. It all felt very genuine, and I did not feel as if I were being played or taken advantage of. I felt my guard dropping and soon realized that I felt safer walking the streets in Vietnamese cities than I did in large American cities like Chicago or New York City. The fear, distrust, and disdain for the Vietnamese I had felt so strongly every time I walked the streets alone or accompanied by armed marines in 1968 had completely disappeared.

There was no evidence of the war anywhere, no bombed-out buildings or empty, rubble-strewn lots. The only evidence of the war was carefully displayed in special museums. There, despite the lack of overt anger toward Americans on the street, it was still clear that the Vietnamese people viewed the American presence during the war as evil, that we had been just another group of powerful foreigners who had come to bully and torture them.

In Hanoi we visited the simple hut where Ho Chi Minh had lived and from which he had run the war. Adjacent to the former French governmental palace, it was just a simple village hut with a straw roof supported by wooden poles. The contrast with the palace was striking. I began to understand the reverence the people still have for him. There are pictures and statues of Ho Chi Minh everywhere in the cities and the villages in both North and South Vietnam. Quotes from him appear on signs and posters. His face is on all paper money of all denominations, and in both the North and the South he is revered as the true father of the unified Vietnam, the man who led them to overcome and defeat not only the Americans but also the French and Japanese.

We also saw the "Hanoi Hilton" prison, where our prisoners of war were held in appalling conditions. During the war the existence of the Hanoi Hilton had loomed over our soldiers like a nightmare; particularly among pilots, who were most often held as prisoners of war, it was the absolute last, worst place to be. Not much of it remains. Where the Americans were held was torn down and replaced by a skyscraper. What little that does remain has been turned into a museum and, of course, scrubbed of its more horrifying aspects. What is left behind seems almost benign and unthreatening, even artificial.

To me the most surprising and memorable museum was the Vietnam Women's Museum dedicated to the "Mothers of the Country." All women whose sons died fighting for liberation are considered privileged citizens, and all Vietnamese are expected to nurture them. There are portraits of some of the mothers on the walls and large leather-bound books dedicated to their sacrifice. On each page is a picture of one of these mothers, a picture of her son, and then the story of who they were, what they did in the war, and how the son had been killed.

It was very quiet inside, like a church, and there were guards on duty to make sure people remained quiet and respectful. It was sad to think of how many lives had been lost on both sides, because each dead soldier, whether Vietnamese or American, was truly some woman's son. It made me even sadder to realize that I could not remember ever meeting the mother of an American soldier who had been killed in Vietnam.

After a few days in Hanoi we boarded a plane for Hue. There had been no specific plans to go to Phu Bai, but the airport that served Hue was there. In fact, the airport was constructed using the runways built by the American military, the same ones that brought the wounded to me and my colleagues. The visions and smells had been irrevocably burned into my brain. I could not believe I was returning and I could not believe I had ever left.

It was both disorienting and strangely familiar. Here was a place where I had spent six months of my life taking care of casualties, yet there was no evidence that that had ever happened or that anyone was even aware I had been there at all. When I had first come to Vietnam the base was on the outskirts of Phu Bai, which at the time was only a small village. Now, the airstrip was surrounded by urban sprawl. Yet it was even more disconcerting to look around and see no evidence that there had ever been a military base there—not just a medical compound but any military base at all. I thought I would see some structure I recognized, but there was nothing. Every building had been razed, as if the Vietnamese were determined to erase all evidence of our presence in their country. All that remained was the airstrips, and even those had been lengthened and paved over. By looking out over the landscape and getting our bearings from features on the horizon, Alex and I were able to locate where the medical compound had once been. I saw only empty fields, small cement houses, and water buffalo grazing placidly.

During the war I had been an intrusive spectator pulled into participation by forces I did not fully understand. Now I was a tourist standing on a site where I had lived with men I grew to support and depend on, learned Vietnamese, had a Vietnamese lover, and felt my inability to make a substantial difference. It was here I began each day by pronouncing the dead that had been accumulated during the previous night and continued the day by caring for wounded warriors.

I stood next to Alex and looked toward the ghost of the medical compound. His face was inscrutable, and he apparently felt nothing. In contrast, I purposely conjured up as many images as I could: bullet holes, shrapnel wounds, smoldering burns, punji stake injuries, and splintered bones. Missing fingers, toes, arms, and legs. Blood squirting out of cleanly severed vessels or oozing out of stringy, jellied stumps. Torn intestines, lungs, shattered livers, and burst bladders. Small entrance wounds, massive exit wounds.

The *whump-whump* rattle of a landing helicopter made it difficult to hear, and in the dust I could not see Alex or anyone in our tour group. Several marines, one of whom had a stretcher, ran out to meet the craft. They pulled a man off the helicopter and it was gone.

The scene was familiar. It was the young man I had seen on my first day in Phu Bai, the young man on the stretcher who was so black that the mud on his skin looked pale, with the small, leaking wound on his washboard stomach. His body still glistened with sweat as he stared straight up, then arched his back in spasm and tried to speak. Once more he could not, and for the hundredth time, the thousandth time, I saw the muscles of his arms swell as he gripped the edge of the stretcher and a streak of red and brown fluid seeped from the hole in his body; I saw his mouth open as he tried to speak. His mud-covered hand reached toward me, and I looked into his eyes as the litter was placed upon two metal sawhorses.

There, too, was the boy whose thigh pointed toward the sky, with the boot containing his foot and lower leg lying next to him. He was still bleeding.

Dressed in shorts and sun hats and carrying cameras around their necks, Alex and the tour group waited for me in the bus. They had no idea that the airstrip was being assaulted and the headquarters of the compound was in danger of being overrun. The NVA was using mortars to surprise and pin down the marines sleeping nearby and to distract them from protecting the airstrip. A Med was between the airstrip and 3rd Marine Division Headquarters. The waiting room was beginning to fill with casualties.

When shrapnel and dirt began to spray the room, I ordered the marines to carry the severely wounded to the Triage bunker next to the blast wall. Others limped, crawled, or dragged themselves. The mortar explosions got closer together in space and time. After several deafening explosions behind the blast wall, the wall itself exploded under the assault of two direct hits.

I threw myself to the ground just outside Triage and, holding my helmet on with one hand, slithered toward the blast wall. I could hear mortar shells whistle toward battalion headquarters. When it was clear that the mortar shells were "walking" back our way, many people continued toward the Triage bunker. I was afraid to move.

The long, crunching sound of the incoming explosions was interrupted by the sharp crack of our own guns as our troops returned fire. With the shells streaking above my head, I became confused between the sounds whistling in and those whistling out. I lay frozen on the ground about halfway to the crumbled retaining wall.

My face in the dirt, I was paralyzed. I could taste dirt in my mouth and feel sweat rolling along the side of my nose. I thought of the Code of Military Justice and wondered, *Is this what happens to people when they are declared cowards? When they are unable to "advance in the face of the enemy"? Unable to retreat? Unable to move?*

Intermittent bursts of small-arms fire grew louder and more continuous. I could hear men yelling but could not understand what they were saying. Helicopters whizzed by overhead and unloaded their furious destruction. I heard the hollow *whump* from mortars exiting their tubes until a blast deafened me and I felt the spray of dirt or shrapnel hit my helmet. I could feel my heart fluttering against the ground and pounding in my throat. Time slowed, then stopped, then disappeared. I left my body. At that point, King should have sent me home or my CO should have put me in the brig.

Now, as a healthy and wealthy tourist, I stood on the precise spot of my paralysis and probed the wound. Feeling empty and exhausted, I shuffled back to the bus and sat down.

No one noticed that I had just gone to war.

The fighting in Hue, especially the struggle to recapture the old city, the Citadel, was savage—foot-by-foot, house-by-house street warfare. Tanks, artillery, and napalm bombs destroyed ancient temples and palaces. The rubble itself was then booby-trapped by the NVA. Snipers were everywhere. It took three marine battalions and an ARVN division twenty-five days to finally force the NVA out of Hue. Fourteen thousand civilians died in the cities of South Vietnam in the first two weeks of February. In Hue alone, almost three thousand civilians were executed by VC, shot in crossfire, or killed by American artillery. In the mass of confusion and bodies, it was impossible to reconstruct exactly what happened. All this loss of arms, legs, and life reestablished a fragile equilibrium.

I left the tour group and took a walk through the city with Alex and Barbara. Although I saw no familiar landmarks, guided by vague intuition and spatial memory, I found the small one-story building that had been the Vietnamese Provincial Hospital staffed by volunteer doctors from Germany and France. I also found the one-story stucco-and-concrete building that had once been the TB hospital, the place where Alex and I had been warned to leave by the nuns just as the Tet Offensive was beginning.

It was now a school. Dozens of preadolescent boys and girls were in the playground. They were holding some kind of celebration or holiday festival with balloons and ribbons, and they were singing and dancing. It was very happy and festive. They were all smiling.

I wanted to look inside the building, and I left Alex and Barbara on the sidewalk to watch the celebration. I just walked in. No one stopped me.

I walked the corridors for so long that Alex and Barbara got tired of waiting and returned to the hotel. I was ignored by almost everyone because they were busy and seemed engaged in their activities, but some of the children recognized me as an American and tried out their English. My answers made them giggle and run away.

I knew I was in the right building, but either my memory was flawed or it had been changed inside, partitioned, because I couldn't

CHAPTER 23

After leaving Phu Bai we visited the old imperial city, Hue, staying in another generic four-star hotel. We walked the streets where, during the 1968 Tet Offensive, civilians were killed by the hundreds. At the time Vietnamese students had provided intelligence and other information to the NVA and acted as guides in a house to-house search for the families of ARVN soldiers, as well as family and friends of those who worked with the Americans. Those people were either killed in their homes or marched into the streets for mass slaughter. One day over a hundred civilians were lined up against the outer wall of a Catholic church and mowed down with machine guns.

The urban civilians learned lessons about the American War that the peasants had known for years. The primary method of survival was to avoid involvement. Punishment for ties with the Americans was quick and final. Some of our interpreters and house mice were killed. North Vietnamese soldiers captured the ancient Vietnamese capital but paid a high price. Then our marines helped return the city to the stalemate of the week before. American boys were scattered among the decomposing bodies lining the streets of downtown Hue. In the brutal house-to-house battle to reclaim the city, women and children were caught in the fierce crossfire. Liberating the city, American tanks, mortars, and rockets destroyed whole buildings and their occupants.

find any rooms that looked like the wards or other rooms with which I was familiar. For a long time I couldn't find any familiar evidence of the hospital at all. Then I found the room where Alex and I had been having tea with the nurses and nuns to celebrate when the NVA attack launched the Tet Offensive. With their help, I had made it safely back to Phu Bai. I never saw the sisters from the TB hospital again and no one knew where they went. I suspected they went into Hue to find and care for any of their patients who escaped execution. I assumed they were also publicly executed because they had worked with me, an American doctor.

I was approached by a Vietnamese man about my age. He was wearing a uniform and appeared to be a security guard. He looked at me in a stern way that said, "I wouldn't hesitate to kill you." He walked up close to me and in broken English asked me what I was doing. As I stammered a response he said, "You must go," but the expression in his voice was much more harsh, as if he were saying, "Get the hell out of here," and he pointed toward the door.

I tried to explain to him that I was friendly and why I was there, but he was very sharp and very curt. His English was so poor I couldn't tell why he wanted to throw me out. Maybe it was just part of his job, but given his age and the way he looked at me, I began to wonder if he might have been Viet Cong, and I remembered the young man on the back of the bus who glared at me while Alex and I had been driving into Hue the day that the Tet Offensive began.

Several teachers came over to see what was happening. One of them spoke excellent English, and I told him that this had been a hospital back in the time of the American War in Vietnam and what I had done there and why I had come into the building. He didn't know the building had been a hospital. He repeated my story in Vietnamese to his colleagues, and they nodded with understanding and support. I told the teacher that the guard was very upset with me and I didn't understand why. All the while the angry guard stared into my eyes. The teacher then started to try to hustle me. He was a part-time guide, I was an American tourist, and suddenly he was very friendly and spoke in phrases he had practiced and knew well, offering to take me here and there. I told him I already had a guide, and he reluctantly backed away. It was very strange, the whole forty-year story acted out in only a few minutes, from unwelcome invader to healer to wealthy tourist.

The morning after the Tet Offensive began, the wounded and dead marines had arrived in Triage faster than we could respond. Over the next five days the triage system broke down completely. Triage and the airstrip were covered with wounded warriors.

Fixed-wing aircraft took large numbers of the stable wounded to the rear, and choppers moved some to the hospital ships, but the flow constantly increased. The hospital compound was jammed. All the ORs were full, and all the hallways were lined with wounded awaiting X-ray and surgery. Triage had a wall-to-wall carpet of wounded bodies with doctors and corpsmen stepping over, between, and around them, kneeling, sitting, and standing, then moving on. A sea of litters spilled out onto the road and covered parts of the helicopter pad and airstrip. Many of the wounded lay on the ground. Dead lay with wounded, and some wounded joined the dead. Each individual doctor stepped among the bodies, choosing who could be saved, who could wait, or who would be a waste of time. Rapid, scientific, and professional appraisal of the torn bodies replaced responses to the emotional tug of an outstretched begging hand or a trembling cry. All the doctors knew that the greatest compassion was expressed by efficiency. While all cries were acknowledged with a squeeze of the hand or a sympathetic glance, after that some had to be ignored. The corpsmen fell behind the endless flow of rapid-fire commands. Several marines who came to help fell all over themselves with too much good intention and not enough medical training.

Our CO screamed above the tumult, "Will you please station a marine at the chopper pad to keep those goddamn bodies out of here and send them directly to Graves." The CO was working as he gave orders. "Leave those goddamn civilians alone; there are dying marines all around you. I'll court-martial the next one who touches a wounded civilian!"

I walked back to the hotel. Later, with a group of tourists in baseball caps and straw hats, I visited the site of the two-thousand-year-old imperial walled city. Xuân had once escorted me through the imperial city, explaining its historical, religious, and political importance. Now there was nothing but a vast open field—no remnants of the four hundred pagodas, shrines, throne rooms, and altars. No golden statues, regal courtyards, or splendid buildings. American firepower and bombs had made the walled city disappear in a few hours. The ancient imperial city was now an empty field, left to memorialize both two thousand years of grandeur and the destruction and death caused by American bombs and artillery.

CHAPTER 24

It felt familiar and made me remember. At various times during our trip we took long bus rides out into the countryside, what we had called in marine vernacular the "bush." Our bright, articulate, knowledgeable tour guide shared his own story with us. When Saigon fell to the NVA in 1975, his father, who worked with the South Vietnamese Army, managed to escape to America by boat. Years later, as an adolescent, our guide repeatedly tried to escape Vietnam by boat to find his father. After his third failed attempt, he was jailed and brutalized for months. He was released after the Communist rule became more flexible and liberal, but he was not allowed to go to college because he and his family were labeled by their former relationship with the puppet government of the Americans. Despite that, he told us that now he felt free, optimistic, ambitious, patriotic, and successful in his role in the growing American tourism.

While the cities of Vietnam were very different than in 1968, from our air-conditioned bus the countryside looked exactly the same. I saw mile after mile of fields, mountains, jungle, children riding on water buffalo, old men and women moving slowly in the rice paddies. I floated back forty years. I thought about the luscious beauty of the Vietnamese countryside and about the ugliness of defoliation and bomb craters. I thought of the millions of Vietnamese whom we had killed, wounded, or resettled.

Compared to the U.S. military bases, the bush had always smelled different. Less diesel fuel and asphalt. More dirt and fresh air. Fresh and old water buffalo shit. Fresh and rotten vegetation. Unwashed men. I smelled different also. In the field, a new kind of chronic fear had driven different chemicals into my brain and armpits, and I had grown to like my smell. Sometimes in Vietnam I could best fall asleep lying on my stomach, one arm above my head, my nose directly in my armpit.

During our bus tours I saw no evidence of the larger military bases we called "the rear." To decrease the likelihood of being shelled or assaulted by NVA or VC, the U.S. military bases had been located next to villages. Construction was not meant to last more than a few years, and the utilities were portable. The villages had grown to be small cities, and the Vietnamese had seen to it that no remnants of war remained.

On dikes and dirt paths, our tour group walked through fields, scattering chickens and children, to visit a "typical family" who also spoke English and had a small gift shop in their home. Our bus drove across rivers and streams and through fields, villages, and rice paddies.

Riding in an air-conditioned bus, I stared at the horizon for hours recalling the places where I treated seriously ill Vietnamese peasants with aspirin and soap while marines protected me from suspected Viet Cong sympathizers, if not VC themselves. In 1968, when I was used as a temporary replacement for doctors who were sick, on R&R, or resting in the rear, I had spent four months moving about in these fields serving with an engineering battalion, reconnaissance units, and infantry in camps or in the field and walking on patrols in the jungles. I was sure I had seen more of Vietnam than the people now selling me trinkets.

I remembered going to Da Nang . . .

One of the machine gunners sat on the floor so I could sit on the metal seat of the UH-lB helicopter. The pilot and copilot were up front. We rattled, vibrated, and lifted straight up into the air. I leaned out the open door and looked straight down to the earth below. Vietnam was a beautiful green carpet scarred by an occasional artillery shell crater. There seemed to be enough green for everyone.

BANG!

A single loud, metallic, cracking noise burst just above my head, and the engine stopped. My heart exploded in my chest.

Our helicopter began a free fall through the air in a nose-down position. The seat belt dug into my waist. Sliding backward, the machine gunners grasped for straps, frames, and seats—anything—as we increased our heavy-boulder plunge toward the earth. Objects on the ground rapidly loomed larger and larger as we fell in total silence.

Basic animal fear stuck in my throat and tore into my belly, but it quickly gave way to an unreal numbness. Although I was not able to move, my thinking was accelerated. I didn't review my whole life as a flash before me. I didn't cry out.

I was pissed!

I was twenty-eight years old and had a lot to do—and I was dying. My bones, skull, guts, and soul would be smashed and soak into that green carpet. The solid parts would be collected into a green bag for return to my family.

Shit!

We began to rotate backward as we raced toward earth. We were going to hit bottom down. Our vertebrae would collapse on one another and explode like chalk. Our heads would drive into our necks and chests as our legs broke in ten or more places beneath our busted buttocks.

My anger passed. An emptiness was left—exhaustion of thought and of emotion.

Wait! We stopped accelerating. In fact, we were slowing. We were still racing toward the ground, but our speed was decreasing. The pilot had the controls in his hands. He was somehow keeping us bottom down and slowing our fall. Although there was no engine noise, the blades above my head were making whirling noises again. A familiar and wonderful vibration returned to the craft, still without the noise of the engine.

"Hang on, Doc, we're going to crash." The machine gunner leaned to my ear from his position in front of me. "We're going to hit down."

I didn't respond. I knew we were going to crash. My only thought was that now we had a chance of surviving. All I wanted was a chance. Some high school kid pilot somehow checked our free fall. There was no need to prepare for the crash, as every muscle was involuntarily tense and spastic. The ground rushed up toward us but at less than lethal speed. We crashed. The noise was made by metal, but it felt as if it were my back breaking. My head snapped forward. The electric jolt that shot to both feet confirmed that I was alive.

The machine gunners were immediately out of the craft and kneeling in the grass, carrying their heavy machine guns with them. The pilot and copilot unstrapped and leaped to the ground with M-16s in hand.

"Everybody out!"

I unstrapped and jumped out.

The pilot spoke sternly and loudly. "We're in unfriendly country. Get away from the craft."

"Doc, can you shoot an M-16?"

"I can," I said. It was only a partial lie. I was sure I could figure out how to work the weapon.

"Here." An M-16 was thrust across my chest. Crawling and looking far into the distance, the machine gunners were now twenty meters from each side of the craft. The pilot and I went in front, and the copilot moved to the rear of the craft.

We could see men moving in the tree line two hundred meters to our left. The land was completely flat in all directions. The copilot threw a smoke grenade. As the green smoke lifted toward the clouds, all the enemy and friendly within miles knew where we were, and they knew we were alive.

For about ten minutes we knelt in our circular perimeter far enough from our crippled helicopter to avoid shrapnel if it was mortared. The pilot was constantly talking on his portable radio. I could not understand most of what he said, but it was said with urgency. His build was slight, but he looked strong. He was busy in a determined, self-confident way. He had already saved my life. He had somehow averted a certain fatal crash. I felt confident now that he would get us out of this jam.

Who was in that tree line? ARVN? VC? Peasant farmers? Marines? Army?

A single-engine spotter plane approached from our rear, circled once, and swooped down over us thirty feet above the ground. The pilot threw an object out of his window and disappeared to the south. The pilot crawled to the message. *Hold your position. Chopper en route to extract you. You are in unfriendly territory.*

Minutes later a beautiful H-34 marine helicopter with ugly eyes painted on its front came in low from the southeast and landed beside us. We ran toward the chopper. I arrived at the side of the chopper before the pilot and one of the machine gunners. I stopped, turned around in a half crouch, and, pointing my M-16 toward the tree line, gave a head signal for the others to enter before me. I was going to cover the rear. I was the star of *War Comics*. I was playing the game like a champ. I was alive and I was living.

The pilot, copilot, and machine gunners ignored me and leaped into the craft. I followed. When I was two steps from the open door, the craft began to lift. I leaped, and my upper body and weapon flew into the helicopter as its rising floor caught me in the midsection and lifted me straight up from the earth, legs dangling ten, twenty, thirty, forty, fifty feet above the earth. Two marines caught my arms and pulled me in.

I lay on my belly in the helicopter. Its vibrating floor cut my lip and nose, but I felt no pain. The blood that ran down my chin was mine. We circled around the crippled craft. Round and round. Circle after circle. I didn't ask why. I didn't care. Finally two other helicopters arrived and landed on either side of our downed helicopter, and we left. I was strangely euphoric.

This trip to Da Nang, the city of my entrance into and exit from Vietnam decades earlier, was less eventful. I associated Da Nang with Xuân and my own growing failures in judgment. In Da Nang, Xuân encouraged me to take risks that could have cost both of us our jobs and, possibly, our lives.

Now I felt safe leaving my hotel and walking alone in Da Nang day or night. This was in sharp contrast to the times I visited Da Nang during the war and went off-limits to sleep with Xuân instead of sleeping on a military base surrounded by U.S. Marines. On my surreptitious overnight visits to Xuân's home, I slinked through the narrow streets and intermittently hid in the shadows. A lone American soldier in the streets at night could be a prime target for assassination, and my foolishness led to frightening encounters with civilian and military Vietnamese men. I carried my .45 and drew it on one occasion, not knowing if strangers wanted to sell me something or kill me. As a wealthy tourist, I could feel but not understand the connections between my wartime actions in Da Nang and the addictions to sex and danger that overtook me years later. A noisy river of motorbikes and people moved through the streets in an unending stream, as if oblivious to history. I scanned the faces. Was Xuân, or possibly a son or daughter or grandchild I never knew, among those I passed on the streets?

Xuân was a simple woman who accepted fate and bowed to destiny, but I also saw her as a survivor and the master of the small world given her. Now, as an old man and tourist in the city where we parted, I tried to put my relationship in some perspective and evaluate my actions. When I had been weak, she had been strong.

CHAPTER 25

Very early one morning, after I ate and drank too much and subsequently slept poorly in another luxury hotel room, I joined our tour group on another comfortable new bus. Except for scattered groggy mumblings about the need for coffee, we rode in silence.

Looking over flat fields, I became distracted and very vigilant. I wanted off the air-conditioned bus with its padded seats and high-performance shock absorbers. I wanted to be in the trench between the road and the rice paddies.

On my belly, my boots in mud, I am sliding sideways ever so carefully, seeking a better vantage point to peer across the field. Protecting my wounded brother, confident the tourniquet is correctly placed, I dare not fire unless it is kill or be killed, because my buddy can't run. If I have to give away my position, I'd better be able to kill them all. Stay until dark, then crawl and drag? Smoke grenade? Run for help? Run to where? The radioman is dead and his radio destroyed.

Suddenly, from behind me, a black soldier jumps into the ditch next to me. Without looking behind us he gives a hand signal, and several more grunts scramble into the ditch and quietly position themselves at regular intervals on the bank. I know they will do the right thing at the right time and have the skill to do it well. I trust them with my life and, at great risk, will do anything they ask of me. I am completely bonded to these men I have never met.

The people in the bus can never understand the brotherhood and adrenaline high I long for. Therefore, I can never completely trust them or bond with them. Peace and security seem an entitlement to those who do not know war or love a warrior.

The man next to me raises his rifle, but before he can fire, his nose explodes and is replaced by a dime-sized hole. His helmet flies up onto the road and tumbles front over back until, with a brief wobble, it rests top side up. His hips and knees bend at unnatural angles as he slams to earth on his back with a loud thud. The back of his head is gone, and the brain tissue spattered about is slowly covered by the growing circle of blood soaking into the dirt like a red halo.

As if the head shot is an anticipated signal, the marines rise in unison and charge across the rice paddy, occasionally flattening and firing bursts of bullets. There is no return fire.

I let the marines go on without me. I want to go with them and be prepared to treat them as they are wounded and acknowledge their individuality, record their deaths, and mourn their absence from the dining room table. In the bus I am empty and of no value. No chance for heroism or glorious death sitting on a tour bus. I want to be a marine in Vietnam in 1967 in jungle fatigues and tightly meshed jungle boots with steel soles. I want my weapon, flak jacket, and helmet; I want a cigarette dangling from my lips and a canteen filled with cold black coffee. I do not want to share my feelings or the events in the field with tourists dressed in shorts and sunglasses and cameras. I certainly do not want to be one of them.

I am in awe of war, its permanent role in biological and social evolution, its capture of psychology, philosophy, and theology, its role in historical, political, and technological progress. Through its own independent organic growth, war creates its own culture. War creates and uses the state monopoly on, and protection from, killing.

I am susceptible to the mind-altering extremes of war. Exoticism, eroticism, excitement. Big guns and explosive afterburners. I have an appetite for the spectacular. Awesome power, hot technology, and volcanic emotional intensity. Rapidly expanding highs and paralyzing lows. I feel a strong, hideous fascination and embrace the thrill of the proximity of death. There is a certain pleasure in demolition, a mania of complete autonomy and a freedom from social contracts.

War is not merely a means but a highly attractive end for which there is no substitute. War is a chance to put everything at risk, concentrate all faculties, and test one's ultimate worth against a worthy opponent—and against oneself.

Men love fighting and I love men and I love fighting. The true warrior fights less because he hates who is in front of him than because he loves those behind him, at home. Most of all he loves and trusts the warrior beside him. In the fury of battle, it is about survival and the brotherhood of soldiers. There is a fusion of terror and love.

War brings clarity, energy, and freedom never found in ordinary life. Danger makes war exhilarating. Past and future are equidistant and equally unimportant and unattainable.

I have a secret passion to witness more war. In war I can be the ultimate voyeur with exposure to the darkest and deepest corners of human behavior. The ugliest beauty mixes with violence. Ultimate good and ultimate evil. The contradictory blend of complete loss of freedom and total freedom to dominate and kill. The rational and irrational are simultaneously overwhelmed and become indistinguishable.

Alex has pointed out to me that the American War in Vietnam was not a particularly good or effective war. Nor was the war on my soil. I was an intruder. Still, it was my war—the only one I had. This war had been my chance to intersect with history. My chance to laugh at hideous, random brutality and the ugliest distortions of the human form. My chance to participate in the ultimate sport and confront death. Men have been doing this for thousands of years. This was my war. War has addicting and pleasurable qualities, as if it were a forbidden lover and powerful object of the most primitive and powerful lust. War and the preparation for it make me hard.

War gives an opportunity for absolute commitment, more palpable than dedication to art, transcendence, or spirituality, more available than the gradual accumulation of power and fame, and more immediate than psychic investment in family, religion, or culture. Heroism can be achieved quickly with a single act. Explosive sacrificial action of permanent impact may erupt at any time.

Our tour ended in Saigon. For decades after the war the former capital of South Vietnam was called Ho Chi Minh City. Now it is again called Saigon, and it is the center of rapidly emerging Vietnamese capitalism and commerce. I recognized buildings I saw forty years earlier when I explored the city alone on foot. At that time, by day I was shocked at the sharp transitions from opulence to street markets to extreme poverty and back to large French colonial structures with smartly dressed American and Vietnamese guards. By night I was hustled by pimps, prostitutes, and black marketers and hassled by American military police insisting that I get off the streets.

The wartime home and work place of the president of South Vietnam, now called Reunification Palace, is now primarily a place for tourism, formal government meetings, and parties. When Vietnamese children learned I had been a soldier, they were eager to have their pictures taken standing with a tall white American in front of the NVA tank that crashed through the gate in Saigon to complete the Communist takeover of Vietnam in 1975.

Northwest of the city we visited the Cu Chi tunnels, an enormous network of underground passages the VC hid and moved about in during the war. Now they are a tourist destination, and visitors can fire an M-16 at an aboveground attraction, eat a meal like those served to the Viet Cong soldiers who lived in the tunnels, and gawk at ersatz booby traps designed to kill and maim American soldiers. The rats, spiders, and other vermin that once infested the tunnels have been eradicated.

Because Western tourists are taller than native Vietnamese, some of the tunnels have been enlarged to allow visitors the opportunity to experience them. Still, they are small and cramped with very low ceilings. An old Vietnamese tour guide led us in.

Too tall to crouch and walk, I crawled in behind our guide. After we advanced about ten meters, the tunnel got smaller, and I became wedged in complete blackness. Before entering we had been told that where the tunnels branched, one tunnel led to an exit within another ten to twenty meters. The other tunnel went on for hundreds of meters with no place turn around.

I tried to follow the sound of the broken English and occasional laughter of the Vietnamese guide. I began to imagine that he was a former VC who hated me and would find great joy in my suffering, and I recalled the old wartime adage that although we ruled the air, underground the Viet Cong ruled.

With the earth pressed against my back and sides, I took short quick breaths. There were old smells I had not experienced in decades, the smells of Vietnam and death. My arms were extended in front of me as I lay on my stomach, and I could not bring them to my sides or under me.

From deep inside a familiar feeling rose up inside my chest, expanded, then retreated, then rose again. Claustrophobia gave way to paralysis. Panic. Animal fear. Helplessness.

I reviewed my PTSD training: *I am not in a war zone. My life is not in danger. A panic attack has been triggered, and it will end. Deep breathing will help.*

It took all the self-control I could muster to advance like a worm a few inches at a time until, after an eternity, I could see light at the end of the tunnel.

CHAPTER 26

In 2007 the Boston Red Sox rapidly dispatched the Los Angeles Angels and the Cleveland Indians in the playoffs, and swept the Colorado Rockies in four games to win their second World Series in four years. Several months later, on February 27, 2008, team members, accompanied by ownership and other staff, went to the White House to be honored by President George W. Bush. After the usual photo opportunity and gift of a Red Sox jersey to the president, at the suggestion of team physician Dr. Larry Ronan the entourage followed their visit to the White House with a trip to Walter Reed Army Medical Center to visit with service members wounded in Iraq and Afghanistan.

It was a meeting of two very different kinds of American heroes with very different images and futures—young men and women, most of whom served in anonymity in a foreign country under terrible conditions, now missing limbs and bearing other wounds and wearing standard-issue hospital pajamas, and healthy young athletes, many earning millions of dollars, accustomed to being cheered by thousands of fans for comparatively insignificant acts—catching a ball, stealing a base, hitting a home run.

The Red Sox spent several hours shaking hands, having their photographs taken, and chatting with the service members. The contrast in their station was not lost on the visitors. "I think the most rewarding part of the trip—I think you can ask anybody that went on that trip yesterday—was visiting the hospital," said Red Sox pitcher Josh Beckett. "I know I got to hear several stories, and as terrible as those stories are, it's something like that that you get to hear that puts everything in perspective for you and makes you realize how fortunate we are to have people like that who will go and do stuff like that. Those are heroes."

After the visit, the Red Sox went to Florida for spring training; the wounded warriors, the spotlight gone, remained behind to continue their recovery. While the Red Sox prepared to defend their world championship, the men and women who defended their country faced an uncertain future as they continued their slow progress toward recovery. That disparity was not lost on the Red Sox. During their visit to Walter Reed Army Medical Center, Tom Werner, chairman of the board for the Red Sox, met with Colonel Cam Ritchie, who told the group of the challenges returning warriors faced, particularly those with PTSD and traumatic brain injury (TBI). Some were so withdrawn they could not bear to meet the Red Sox players in person and had surrogates ask for autographs. A short time later Werner chose to address the problems Colonel Ritchie pointed out. He challenged Dr. Ronan to find a way that he and the Red Sox could help solders afflicted with these problems. Ronan, who was my friend and colleague from Massachusetts General Hospital, approached hospital administration and told them of Werner's challenge. MGH gave permission to find a way to build a partnership with the Red Sox to address it. Dr. Ronan asked me to help him organize a way to help. He knew that I had held many leadership roles at MGH and that CIMIT was coordinating PTSD and TBI research at several member institutions, including the Boston VA hospitals. At that time, neither Dr. Ronan nor anyone else involved in the program knew that I had PTSD.

Collaborative programs between two enormous organizations don't just start with a wave of a pen, the writing of a press release, or the show of hands at a meeting. We had to start from scratch to identify a course of action and create the structures to support the program, determine how it would work, and coordinate our efforts with those already in place at the Departments of Defense and Veterans Affairs.

Over the next few months we met with psychiatrists, DoD officials, federal and local veterans groups, and leaders and doctors from the Boston VA Healthcare System. Our goal and our challenge was to find a way to add value to existing efforts, to set up a program that would not supplant programs already in place but would enhance existing efforts and take on some tasks and responsibilities that were difficult or impossible for other groups.

The political turf was as complex as the medical issues of wounded service members. At the time the Department of Defense was reacting to damaging press about conditions at Walter Reed Army Medical Center. The public and their government representatives were expressing growing concern about PTSD and TBI resulting from the wars in Iraq and Afghanistan. Reports from the RAND Corporation and the Institute of Medicine stated bluntly that the VA Healthcare System was not keeping up with increasing demands on its services. We realized that a high-profile initiative by MGH and the Boston Red Sox could be controversial and make things worse in an already well publicized and politically charged arena, but we were determined that our efforts would be seen as opportunities for collaboration. I volunteered to organize a research component of the new initiative, and several committees made up of equal numbers of MGH and VA personnel explored opportunities in medical care, education, family support, and outreach.

After a period of initial exploration, Tom Werner and Peter Slavin, the CEO of MGH, asked me to lead not only research components but the entire program. The offer caused me no small measure of pause.

Personally, I had made a great deal of progress over the last decade. I was generally less driven and preoccupied by war, happy directing CIMIT, and more stable and predictable in my ability to relate to others. Barbara and I lived on Boston Harbor, both worked full-time, and each tolerated the other's antisocial leanings and high-output work ethic. I continued to support Joan in the home we co-own in Weston and was still the first person she turned to in times of need. I had a sometimes awkward but always loving relationship with my three children and six grandchildren.

Although I never trained in psychiatry, my understanding of PTSD had expanded. I now understood its root cause lay not only in the trauma I experienced in Vietnam but also in the traumas of my upbringing that left me more susceptible to be affected by Vietnam. I understood my problems included intrinsic depression compounded by a disorder of memory. The past was sometimes in the present and made me fearful because I never quite knew when the past was going to open up and I was going to fall into it again. A certain part of me was always wondering, *What's going to set me off? How much can I insulate myself and control my relationships in order to make my world so predictable that nothing is going to fly in under my radar screen to throw me off kilter?*

Although my role would primarily be administrative, the request to organize a new, ambitious program focusing on TBI and PTSD in returning warriors threatened to upend the delicate balance I had achieved. It presented me with the threat that my involvement in the program might not only rekindle and escalate my own inner war, but it might also make my own wounds more visible and expose them to those who were unaware of my past. I wondered if I should confront my demons again from a different perch or just enjoy the acceptance that comes with time and age.

On the other hand, I also realized that my experience might contain lessons that could be useful and, moreover, underscore the need for the program. I realized how vital it was for returning service members to have the opportunity for treatment, so their issues are presented to them as something that can be overcome and not challenges that they will suffer with alone, forever. They need to know there is help and life can change for the better. It took me thirty years to realize this truth.

For two weeks I pondered these questions, measuring the risk to myself against the possible good I might do. The warrior in me decided I was already involved and ready to adopt a new mission. I decided to serve and accepted the job.

Our society makes the decision to wage war, and by making that decision it must also accept the responsibility for the soldiers it breaks. We can complain about the ways they are broken and how difficult they are to fix, but they are our responsibility. Whether one agrees with the mission or not, every soldier who serves means someone else does not; someone else's child either doesn't get sent overseas or doesn't join the service. If they serve instead of our children, they become our family.

The problem we face, bluntly put, is this: Despite the best intentions and efforts of our government, the two ongoing American wars in Iraq and Afghanistan are creating more disabled men and woman than the present DoD and VA health care systems can treat and help to assimilate into a healthy family, society, or career. Protracted large-scale call-ups of National Guard and reservists, repeated deployments, and widespread exposure to blast injury are causing enormous strain. Insufficient funding and legislative constraints—the VA, for example, except for couples therapy in certain situations, can only treat service members themselves, and not their families—have combined with a growing problem to create an emerging crisis. In a recent estimate the RAND Corporation concluded that as many as one-third of all service members returning from Iraq and Afghanistan exhibit symptoms of PTSD, depression, or cognitive limitations from TBI. The familiar scenes we remember of damaged veterans from the Vietnam War living in the streets may be repeated in another generation.

Dr. Ronan and I went back to Washington to get additional advice from senior leadership. We met with Lieutenant General James Peake (Ret.), former secretary of veterans affairs; Dr. Ward Casscells, assistant secretary of defense for health affairs; and General Fred Franks. All were very receptive and provided valuable advice about successful navigation of the relevant government systems. We also met with General Eric Shinseki, at the time the newly appointed secretary of the Department of Veterans Affairs. Shinseki understood the problems from the perspective of a warrior. He was wounded in action during the American War in Vietnam.

Dr. Ronan and I met with General Shinseki late one morning in his office in Washington. After negotiating several layers of security we were escorted into the general's office suite. The general greeted us in full military uniform with one exception; he was wearing a Red Sox cap. A few minutes into our scheduled ten-minute meeting, I mentioned to General Shinseki that I had been in Vietnam, still a rare admission for me to make. The general now addressed me directly. As veterans of that war, we shared a special bond. For the next hour we shared our experiences. In particular we both lamented being abused by the public when we returned from Vietnam. Scorned by the flower children and labeled as losers by the hawks, we were never formally welcomed home. We discussed how my research might help in the treatment of PTSD and blast injuries to the brain. We proposed that by cooperating with the VA, an MGH and Red Sox initiative could add value to the care the VA Healthcare System offered. He listened intently, was very supportive of our plans, and agreed to help. He shared that he had enormous concern that an epidemic of PTSD would grow during and after the present wars. As we left his office, he put his hand on my shoulder and said, "Welcome home." This was the first time anyone had said that to me.

On September 17, 2009, in Fenway Park, the Home Base Program was officially introduced as a partnership between the Red Sox Foundation and the Massachusetts General Hospital. I was one of the men and women invited to stand on the field as Tom Werner gave a brief speech introducing the program to the public. Although General Shinseki was scheduled to throw out the first pitch, he decided instead that he would escort a veteran with the invisible wounds of war to the mound, hand him the ball, and request that the veteran do the honors. Shinseki handed the ball to U.S. Navy Chief Bryan P. Zimmerman, a veteran of the Iraq War.

Zimmerman, only thirty-six, served as a physician's assistant in the Second Battle of Fallujah in November and December 2004, some of the heaviest urban combat American marines experienced during the Iraq War, treating service members in the field. I imagine that in some ways his war experience mirrored my own. As he later told a reporter, "When I first came back, I felt normal, as if I were just like everyone else." Several years later, while working at a medical clinic, he became violent and aggressive, the *Boston Globe* reported. Still, afraid that admitting to a problem would adversely impact his career, Zimmerman waited another year before seeking help. "I didn't want to seem weak," he explained.

Shinseki handed Zimmerman the ball, and he made a strong throw toward home. The Home Base program was officially under way.

Home Base is a nonprofit organization supported by philanthropy. The mission is to identify, motivate, and treat, on an outpatient basis, American warriors and their families with invisible wounds of war. Although no U.S. warrior will be turned away because of period of service, location of duty, status, type of discharge, or ability to pay, the program's focus is on veterans who have been in the battlefield since 9/11.

America is conducting its longest wars. Unfortunately, PTSD, TBI, depression, and suicide among America's warriors are major, but not surprising, unintended consequences. The problem is likely to get worse and to swamp the resources of the VA and DoD health care systems and become a major societal issue.

Fewer than 1 percent of citizens are in the modern military class. They are all volunteers. At the peak of the surge in Iraq in 2007, fewer than one out of every one thousand Americans was actually on the battlefield executing the part of foreign policy requiring force. These volunteers hone their bodies and minds, and they are willing to leave their home, kill people, and risk being wounded or killed. After the horror of battle, some of them have great difficulty reassimilating into their family and social structure. The nature of military training and war experience often makes it difficult for the service members to seek help. In many cases, those needing help the most are least able to reach out for it.

The scope of those affected is enormous. Well over two million Americans have served in Afghanistan or Iraq. It has been estimated that more than six hundred thousand of them have serious difficulty reentering family life and civilian social structure. Our clinicians estimate that seven family members per service member are affected, some of whom are children.

Home Base serves all of New England and hopefully will be a model for similar programs nationally. With a staff of forty people, including psychologists, psychiatrists, social workers, outreach workers, research fellows, and nurses, Home Base has five highly integrated and synergistic components located at Massachusetts General Hospital.

The Clinical Program is the portal of entry for evaluation, diagnosis, and treatment. Those who choose to enter the program receive the best state-of-the-art treatment at no cost to the patient. The close interactions of the Clinical Program and Research Program provide unique options for use of novel diagnostics and treatments, including some that are still under investigation. Based on the judgment of the clinician and the wishes of the informed patient, these experimental treatments may be made available. No apparent or actual coercion will occur.

The Family Program treats families by direct care and by acting as consultants and coaches to other care providers. In addition, the Family Program conducts needs-assessment research, develops new approaches to family and warrior support, and, by acting as a model and by publishing and lecturing, disseminates knowledge nationally. The strong emphasis on families is one aspect of the program of which we are particularly proud. When my father returned from his service in World War II, and when I returned from Vietnam, there was absolutely no support available to our families. To a degree, the pathology of my father's childhood and war experience was passed down to me. Family treatment is critical to prevent this from happening to another generation of warriors and their loved ones. Often family members are the first to seek help, and parents, children, and spouses may be in the program for months before a warrior chooses to participate. At times, family members are coached or treated even though the warrior never comes to Home Base.

The Education Program increases awareness of battle-related PTS and TBI. By direct and indirect methods, it provides materials and approaches that help to improve the lives of warriors and their families. It develops new content and also uses best-of-breed existing national educational materials and contributes to their reach and effectiveness. The initial target for the program is health care providers.

The Research Program has the single aim of developing novel diagnostics and treatments for PTSD and TBI. The research functions within CIMIT and is therefore supported in part by Department of Defense funding and builds on the relevant fundamental, applied, translational, and clinical research in all CIMIT member institutions. Home Base funds are used only for novel collaborative investigations that accelerate the near-term (within two years) development of new diagnostics and therapies. The Home Base Research Program and CIMIT use their research portfolio and clinical excellence to attract additional research funding from government, industry, foundations, and philanthropists.

Another important aspect of Home Base is the Outreach Program. It includes battle-worn veterans who have been successfully treated for PTSD and now work full-time to search out warriors and motivate and encourage them to seek help; they often even accompany the veteran to the Home Base Clinic. Even the most self-isolated service members will talk to other battle veterans. Members of the veterans outreach team may spend many hours with individual troubled warriors. A decorated former Special Forces fighter may be able to help warriors overcome the stigma associated with asking for help. They organize social and athletic events and reach out to family members.

The Clinical Program, Administration and Operations, and Veterans Outreach Team are located in an identifiable, appealing, appropriately designed, and welcoming MGH site, which acts as portal for entry for veterans and their families.

We work with the VA Boston Healthcare System, which includes professionals who are among the world's leading authorities in diagnosing and treating patients with PTSD. Access to clinical care at the VA compares favorably with the private sector. Access to care should not be conflated with access to the compensation and pension (C&P) disability evaluation process. The press has elaborated on the slowness and bureaucracy of the C&P process. This is a national problem that is being addressed at all levels by the Department of Defense and the Department of Veterans Affairs. To make access quicker and easier, General Eric Shinseki has recently changed the requirements and process for veterans with PTSD and TBI to enter care and obtain health care benefits.

The Home Base Program was established to reach out to a group of veterans who might not otherwise seek and receive the care they so desperately need and deserve. Although Home Base offers another portal of entry to care, we can provide evaluation to only a fraction of the vast population the VA can serve. Some of those veterans who come through Home Base will be cared for at MGH. Others, after considering patient preferences and geographic, logistic, and administrative issues, will be referred to other locations, including sites within the New England VA Healthcare System, for treatment.

Additional features distinguish Home Base from the Boston VA Healthcare System and other regional programs. Veterans with other than honorable discharge status are accepted. The veterans working the Home Base Program are full-time employees ("boots on the ground") who have been successfully treated for PTSD in the VA Boston Healthcare System. Another distinctive feature is that Home Base is supported by philanthropy. Although hundreds of employees at Boston VA Healthcare System are veterans, by law they cannot recruit patients, advertise, or participate in fund-raising events.

By providing care for one veteran at a time, Home Base can enrich the quality of life for individual warriors and their families. The Family, Education, and Outreach programs create new processes and develop new techniques for enlisting and treating veterans. Hopefully demonstrations of feasibility of new approaches will be instructive to other programs and institutions. The intent of the Research Program is to develop better diagnostics and treatments for worldwide use. In the long run, the most important contribution Home Base provides might be to serve as a model and testing ground for effective private-public partnerships. Home Base hopes to be a living laboratory for helping government, industry, academia, and health care providers develop models of collaboration. As leaders of DoD and VA reach out to the community, Home Base wishes to participate vigorously in exploring novel and effective processes for private-public partnerships. We can be a relatively neutral place for dialogue among the key players. Home Base is committed to being a "convener," joining others in matching a growing nationwide willingness to help with the needs of warriors.

We will make a difference!

I expected my involvement with the Home Base program to alter my own symptoms of PTSD, either make me worse or make me better, and I thought it would probably do both. I've found it therapeutic from the very beginning. My kids and people around me notice that I seem to be happy and energized.

I've always approached my profession by considering all my activities as a way to stay in school, both because I love learning and training and because I want to avoid having a steady "real" job. I feel like I have trained all my life for this one. At age seventy, after forty-five years of training, I've finally found the job I was meant to have—and I like it.

CHAPTER 27

The military tattoo ceremony is a tradition with roots that can be traced back to the Netherlands and the British Army of William the Third. When King William's troops were housed in Dutch villages, drummers were sent through the streets to call the soldiers home from local inns. Over time the ceremony evolved to include bands and other instruments.

In the American military tradition, tattoo ceremonies are held to commemorate special occasions and events. Shortly after the creation of the Home Base Program, a special tattoo ceremony was held at Fort McNair in Washington, D.C., on June 2, 2010. With other members of the Home Base team, I was invited to attend. Our host was General Peter Chiarelli, the vice chief of staff of the army.

I watched from a review stand as a forty-piece band in full military dress marched onto the freshly cut grass of the drill field at Fort Mc-Nair. Selected students from ten regional high schools filled temporary bleachers that encircled an area slightly bigger than a football field.

Outside the bleachers I could see buildings important to the two-hundred-year-old army fort—the National War College and other components of the National Defense University, a place for high-level training of officers and selected Washington civilians' education, including advanced degrees in the development of national security strategy.

In another direction was the first federal penitentiary. The conspirators accused of assassinating President Abraham Lincoln were housed there until they were hanged. The first woman ever executed under federal orders was among them. The post dispensary and visiting officers' quarters occupy the building where Major Walter Reed conducted his research on malaria. Large homes in a row on the bank of the Potomac River are the residencies for the most senior army officers.

The music stopped, and the band came to attention as General Chiarelli approached a microphone at midfield. General Chiarelli introduced Tom Werner of the Boston Red Sox and me among his guests and explained that this special tattoo ceremony was to honor the Home Base Program.

A veteran under care for TBI and PTSD gave a brief but stirring testimonial, and the ceremony began. Placed widely apart in military dress and with roving microphones, servicemen and -women sang solos, duets, and quartets about heroism, patriotism, and bravery. The voices were beautiful and true.

Rousing marching music came from large speakers, and a deeply resonant voice-over described the history of the U.S. Army. As each nation-saving war for freedom was mentioned, warriors in uniforms of that period ran onto the field and took up their places in lines bisecting the entire field.

> The army of the United States has served this nation for 233 years. It has answered every call to duty and put its boots on the ground in our national interest. The traits, values, and ethos that you see in today's army began on 14 June 1775.

> *Music goes solemn*

> The defeat of the British at Yorktown brought the nation not only a great victory but even more challenges as our

young nation grew . . . Lewis and Clark's expedition into the Louisiana Purchase in 1803 . . . War with Mexico in 1847. The ongoing debate over states' rights and slavery divided the country, and brother faced off against brother in a bitter four-year civil war.

Music gets happy

Peace came on a spring day at Appomattox, Virginia, when the two armies met to end the fighting and begin binding up the nation's wounds.

This new birth of freedom would usher in the industrial age and spur on the western settlement.

The cavalry boots of the "Buffalo Soldier" would walk the picket lines on lonely outposts of the American West. They built roads, strung wire, mapped the land, and provided security for the onrushing settlers.

As the new century began, army boots had left our shores. We went to France to fight in the war to end all wars. The world now knew that America and our army would go to the aid of others in the cause of freedom.

Unfortunately, it was not the war to end all wars, as economic depression spread around the world.

Then on December 7, 1941, Japan attacked Pearl Harbor—(*guns fire*)—the day that will live in infamy.

Drums

The full resources of this nation responded, and the boots of sixteen million men and women went on the ground around the world. This call to duty would bring an end to the largest war in the history of the world.

The world entered into the nuclear age as man created weapons of mass destruction and the world became polarized between the forces of democracy and the menace of Communism.

The first test came in a faraway land. The army as part of a United Nations fighting force put its boots on the snowy hills of Korea.

Music softens

Heartbreak Ridge, Pork Chop Hill, and Chosin Reservoir became familiar names. The Korean War ended after three years of hard and intense combat. To this day American soldiers still stand on those hills guarding in the name of freedom.

In Vietnam another call came. The army went into those steaming jungles in the name of freedom. The soldiers who served in Vietnam did so with distinction and honor.

The end of the draft marked a significant period of change in our army. We shifted from a conscripted force to an all-volunteer force. This volunteer army answered our nation's calls again in Grenada and Panama, rescuing thousands from the fist of brutality. The fall of the Berlin Wall marked our victory in the Cold War. New threats emerged in both the Middle East and Europe. In Desert Storm our army needed only one hundred hours to liberate Kuwait from the occupying Iraqi forces of Saddam Hussein. In Europe, the army intervened to protect innocents caught in the violence following the fracture of Yugoslavia in Bosnia and Kosovo.

Screechy music

On September 11, 2001, war came to America as al Qaeda terrorists attacked the World Trade Center and the Pentagon. Our army responded rapidly, defeating the oppressive Taliban in Afghanistan and toppling a dictator in Iraq in a devastating attack on Baghdad. Even now, our army continues to pursue and defeat these threats during our time of persistent combat in Southwest Asia, the Pacific Theater, and the Horn of Africa.

Our army remains at the point of the spear, keeping America and our freedoms safe for this generation and beyond. The call to duty has come once again. Ladies and gentlemen, our army is in the lead in this new way of war, and with your support and understanding we will not let you down.

We will protect this nation and keep for you life, liberty, and happiness.

Several precision drill teams then performed with perfect execution. When the ceremony ended, high school students ran to talk with the soldiers, some seeking autographs and photo opportunities. The veteran with the invisible wounds of war was swarmed by adoring girls, some of whom were crying.

I approached General Chiarelli to thank him for the great honor of being his guest as his troops ceremoniously expressed gratitude and respect for the Home Base Program. I also wanted to thank him for the extraordinary powerful leadership he has shown in helping reduce the stigma and raise awareness of PTSD and TBI. Overcome and surprised by a giant lump in my throat, I couldn't speak. I shook his hand and moved quickly away.

CHAPTER 28

Of the thousands of wounded soldiers I saw and treated, I remember one more clearly than all the others.

I was in Triage, and there was a call on the portable radiophone set hanging on the wall: The men in Graves were washing down bodies, preparing to send them home, when one moaned.

"I don't know how long he's been here," explained the Graves marine. "Two legs and an arm are missing, and he's full of holes, but he started making noises. The guys are bringing him up to Triage now."

He arrived on a litter, barely half a man. Both legs were missing, one at the knee, one at midthigh, and one arm was gone just below the shoulder. There were several penetrating wounds of the abdomen and chest. None of the injuries were bleeding. His skin was pale, and there was no pulse. I put my hand on his chest. After two or three seconds, I felt a heartbeat . . . then another . . . then two coupled beats. His pupils were dilated but reacted sluggishly to light.

I put tourniquets on what was left of his legs and arm. We started a stream of Ringer's lactate into his good arm and into a neck vein. On the second try, I punctured his femoral artery in his groin and got blood for type and cross-match. In the time it took to put a chest tube into his left chest, secure all the tourniquets, and tilt the stretcher with head down, the blood had been typed and cross-matched and was ready for administration. After two units of blood were pumped under pressure into his one arm, the marine actually began to wake up. He had a rigid abdomen and was still hypotensive when we started surgery.

Parker Powell and I operated on the abdomen while others debrided and reamputated the extremities. Although the large bowel was perforated in three places, we found no shrapnel and no evidence of a through-and-through penetration track. A flank wound confined to the retroperitoneum essentially exploded one kidney, which had to be removed. We didn't open his chest because X-rays showed expanded lungs, normal size and location of the heart, and no shrapnel. The radiography also showed some fluid accumulation on one side and the chest tube I had placed earlier in Triage.

Four hours later the marine's trunk had many more tubes than extremities—two drains in his belly, a catheter in his bladder, a tube to drain his flank, two intravenous tubes, a chest tube, and a central venous pressure line in his subclavian vein. One of the orthopedic surgeons said, "Maybe we shouldn't have wasted precious time on this guy. He has little chance of surviving, and if he does he will be confined to a wheelchair."

Parker spoke up. "If this kid wants to die later, that's his business. If you want to play God, that's your business. Right now, I'm in charge and we are going to give this kid a four-plus effort. John, you close. I'm going to start another case."

We finished the case and transported the head and trunk with its jungle of tubes into the recovery area, where we assigned one GMO to be special duty nurse for the night.

The next morning the patient still had dangerously low blood pressure, and after sixteen units of blood he still hadn't made a drop of urine. I rolled him over on his side and put a stethoscope on his back. He opened his eyes and groaned a string of profanities. I asked if he could hear me.

"Yeah." He raised his head for a second, and then it fell back onto the bed. "Where am I? Am I dying?"

I told him he was okay. That was all I could think to say, and it certainly wasn't true.

"Help me." His eyes closed again. He probably didn't know he was missing three extremities.

During the day I returned often to the recovery room to regulate his fluids and to help the corpsmen with his drains and wound care as he waited to be transferred by fixed-wing to the hospital in Da Nang. He woke up again for several minutes in the midafternoon. He never reacted to the absence of his legs and arm but seemed concerned only with pain and death. He grunted, groaned, cursed, asked for help, and tried to move.

No urine. If he didn't make urine soon, I thought, we would lose him to renal failure.

Parker disagreed. "We'll fly him out to the hospital ship and put him on the artificial kidney. Hemodialysis. He's still got one kidney. Maybe it will work later."

Many soldiers had lived and died under Parker's care. Some could be salvaged. Some could not. Why such desperation and drama over one more who was damaged beyond repair? We could only do so much.

There was no dialysis machine at the hospital in Da Nang. Our radioman contacted the hospital ship and discovered their artificial kidney wasn't working. The closest hemodialysis unit was in Saigon. No plane was scheduled to fly to Saigon until eight o'clock the next morning, and that was not a medevac flight.

"I want a direct flight to Saigon—a fixed-wing—right now." Parker spoke as if he could actually get one. He couldn't. With much radio traffic we found that there was a plane available, but no crew.

We went to the air force O-Club. Parker walked up to the bar, still dressed in wrinkled, blood-spattered green scrubs. His face was drawn and unshaven. It was clear he had barely slept in days. He banged on the bar until everyone stopped talking and looked his way. "I'm Dr. Powell from A Med. I have an urgent need of a C-130 crew for a medevac trip to Saigon. I have a soldier with one chance to live, and that chance is a trip to Saigon—now. We've got a plane but no crew."

"Is he a senator's son or the brother of a VIP?" A voice from the back of the room asked.

"A senator's son wouldn't be here." Another comment from someone.

There was a long and uncomfortable silence. Then one man stood up to volunteer. Then another, and another. Finally a full bird colonel wheeled around on his bar stool and stood up.

"I'm going to fly it. I'll fly that bird to Saigon. Get me a crew. No cargo. No hitchhikers. Just a doc and the soldier." I volunteered to be the doctor. The colonel put his finger on my chest. "I'll get him to Saigon, Doc. You keep him alive."

This soldier was going to get our maximum effort.

As we prepared to take off, the patient was oblivious to the vibrations and noise. He opened his eyes and turned his head toward me. I told him we were going to Saigon.

He nodded and closed his eyes. His pulse was strong but rapid.

After a long flight he was still alive, and we were taken by ambulance to the emergency entrance of a large military hospital. I explained that he needed hemodialysis.

My patient was now in the hands of a multidisciplinary team of experts. Our flight back to Phu Bai would not take place till the next morning. By now it was well after midnight, and I could not remember my last meal. I went to the O-Club, sat in the corner, and ordered a beer.

After finishing a second beer, I left the club and went to check the legless soldier. He was in intensive care. He was not connected to a hemodialysis unit. A new tube had been added to the network that sprang from what remained of his body. He had had a tracheotomy, and the trach tube was connected to a respirator. He was unconscious. I watched the respirator labor through several cycles with hypnotic regularity. His urine bag contained about 50 cc of red-brown fluid. Several severe burn victims had just arrived from Tan Son Nhut Air Base where a Phantom jet had crashed into a C-130, and no one was paying attention to him now.

His blood gases were terrible, and even with oxygen he was hypoxic. In addition to his known injuries, the attending doctor worried that his lungs had suffered a blast injury. His prognosis was even more grim than before.

The patient died during the night, one of dozens of men and boys on both sides who died that day. Within hours an officer in full dress uniform would knock on the door of his parents' home and tell them he died in a hospital of wounds from hostile actions involving an explosive device and ask where the family wished the body returned. It would be accompanied by a military escort from a hospital mortuary to the family's chosen cemetery, and his family would receive the U.S. flag after it was used to drape his coffin.

No one would tell them that a bunch of guys who had never met their son made a hell of a try to save him. They would not know that he had spoken and lived for a few days after being wounded. They would not know that one navy doctor was heartbroken when he died. They would not understand just why he had died. Neither would I.

I had thought about this soldier for years. I could remember the details of his wounds and our trip to Saigon. For years he remained just another image from the war seared into my brains, a vision I could not avoid and did not want to.

Now, after examining this war for almost forty years, I finally felt that I could look it in the face. I had to find out who he was. I thought his family might want to know these things, that we had done all we could to save him.

I knew people. I started writing letters and making phone calls.

August 15, 2007

Ward S. (Trip) Casscells
Assistant Secretary of Defense

Dear Trip,

I served as a Navy physician assigned to the Third Medical Battalion, Third Marine Division.

During 366 days in Vietnam I personally treated well over 1,000 casualties and pronounced dead (examined the wounds and filled out the forms) over 300 Marines. I have never known any follow-up on a single one of them. I saw them once and they were medevaced to hospitals (or morgues) or returned to their units.

The circumstances surrounding the treatment of one particular serviceman should make it possible to search the records for his name.

Wounded in I Corps October 23, 1967.
Nature of Wounds:
Triple amputation (2 legs, 1 arm). Multiple shrapnel wounds.
Medevac #1 from the field to Phu Bai.
A Medical Company 3rd Med 3rd Mar Div
Surgical Procedure:
Three surgical amputations
Multiple debridements
Partial nephrectomy
Partial colectomy
Medevac #2 Phu Bai to Saigon October 25–26 by fixed-wing accompanied by John A. Parrish Lt/MC 690677.
Died of wounds October 26 or 27, 1967.

I am particularly eager to find a family member of one warrior. For me, he represents a connection to the world I re-entered after the war. Is it possible to find out his name and anything about his family? I am driven to pay my respects to them. I don't need to share gruesome details, but it is my one chance to let someone know how much the military doctors cared and gave their all. I need to do this.

Also, I am curious about the details usually provided to family members about extent of injuries or circumstances of fatal encounters.

Were autopsies performed on soldiers who died of wounds? I appreciate your help.

Sincerely,
John A. Parrish, M.D.

September 7, 2007
Dr. Parrish:
Summary:

1. There were 5 Marines identified as DOW during the dates in question in the I Corps AO, but no Army. Of the five, 1 died on a hospital ship, 3 died in Da Nang, and 1 died in an unknown location.

2. Attached are the Marines' casualty cards. Notification Officers used discretion in what they told families, so detail varied from marine to marine.

3. Apparently, not all Vietnam KIA and DOW received autopsies. Criteria for who did is unknown. Current policy is an autopsy on all OIF/OEF KIA and DOW.

V/R,
George W. Weightman, MD
Major General
Commanding General
Medical Research & Materiel Command
Fort Detrick, MD 21702

September 11, 2007
Dr. Parrish,

Based on the broader search dates that you have sent, I am appending a list (24-28 Oct 1967 Casualties.doc) of all the personnel identified as casualties either died of wounds or killed in action. There are 151 persons identified for those dates. Of these, 15 are listed as died of wounds. Of those 15, 11 are identified as being casualties from military province 1 and 1 is identified as being from an unknown location. I have appended all 15 individual records in a second document (24- 28 Oct 1967 Died Of Wounds.doc).

We do not maintain health records for deceased soldiers. Those records were retired to the National Archives and Records Administration, National Personnel Records Center in St. Louis. You will have to request copies of their records using a Standard Form 180. The form and instruction for requesting records can be found at their website.

V/R

Lewis L. Barger, III

MAJ, MS

Medical Historian

OTSG Office of Medical History

September 12, 2007

Dr. Parrish,

I have no further information about the two Army casualties, but CPL Dissinger, USMC, was pronounced dead at 3d Field Hospital, Saigon. His casualty card is at the top of the third page of the attached adobe document. We received this from the US Marine Corps Historian's office. I hope this helps you.

V/R

Lewis L. Barger, III

MAJ, MS

Medical Historian

OTSG Office of Medical History

September 19, 2007
National Personnel Records Center
Military Personnel Records
9700 Page Avenue
St. Louis, MO63132-5100

To whom it may concern,

I am a physician who served as a Navy physician with the 3rd Marine Division in Vietnam in 1967-68. My service number is 690677.

I am seeking a copy of the medical record of a patient I treated in A Medical Company, 3rd Med Bn 3rd Mar Div in Phu Bai and accompanied (Medevac) to Saigon where he died. The part of the record important to me is the record of his care in the 3rd Field Hospital, Saigon, where he was pronounced dead 10/27/67.

CPL Dissinger, Gary Frank, USMC 2121407
Cause of Death: Explosion/Hostile
Ground Casualty
Date of Birth: 10/19/48
Died of Wounds: 10/27/67

I would be willing to sign any release form you require.

My request has the approval of my friend, Dr. S. Ward Casscells, Assistant Secretary of Defense for Health Affairs.

Thank you for your attention to this matter.

Sincerely,

John A. Parrish md

John A. Parrish, M.D.

Cc: Lewis Barger, III, MAJ, MS
Ward Casscells, M.D.

His name was Gary Dissinger. He was from Pennsylvania, a lance corporal, and had been in the service for a little more than a year. He and I shared the same birthday, and we had arrived in Vietnam on the same day. One week before his death, he had turned nineteen and I had turned twenty-seven. We had both been in the war for eighty days. Another teenaged boy took his place. What had he accomplished?

Now that I knew that, I thought it would be relatively easy to locate his family. It was not, but at length I found the name of someone I believed might be his mother. Her name was on one of the "casualty cards."

October 4, 2007
Mrs. Gloria F. Achenbach
PO Box 102
Fredericksburg, PA 17026

Dear Mrs. Achenbach:
I am a physician who served in Vietnam during 1967. One of my patients was LCPL Gary Frank Dissinger, who died around October 26, 1967. Are you a family member of LCPL Dissinger? If not, do you know how I can get in touch with a family member?

I do not wish to be intrusive in any way. I would simply like to pay my respects to the family of one person I treated.

I would like to call you in a few days. I wanted to send this letter to let you know about my interest. Making contact with you is important to me, but I do not want to disturb you with unwelcome reminders of loss and grief. Is there someone else I might call instead?

My address and contact information are on my letterhead

above should you wish to contact me. My assistant's name is Mary Beth Nolan, and she can find me at any time.

If I have written you in error, please accept my apology and let me know of my mistake.

Thank you for considering my request to contact you.

Sincerely,

John A. Parrish md

John A. Parrish, M.D.

A week or so later, I found the letter in my mailbox. It had not been opened.

ADDRESSEE NOT KNOWN
RETURN TO SENDER
UNABLE TO FORWARD

A few weeks later I received a reply to one of my earlier requests for records from the National Personnel Records Center:

November 5, 2007
RE: Veteran's name: Dissinger, Gary

Dear Sir or Madam,

Thank you for contacting the National Personnel Records Center. In working to fill your request we noted that your inquiry did not include the signed consent of the individual whose record is involved and must be returned without action. The Privacy Act of 1974 provides for the release of record only with the written consent (signature) of the individual to whom the record pertains . . . [or] the written consent of next of kin.

Sincerely,

Phyllis Patton

Archives Technician (4D)

I stopped searching, but I could not and would not forget. More information becomes available online every day, and through my involvement with Home Base I also had access to people who were better at searching for someone than I was.

From his hometown newspaper the bare bones of a biography began to be created. I read an account of his fourth birthday party, and a year later his fifth. He had an older brother, Joseph, and a younger sister, Kathleen. He attended Henry Houck Junior High, played tackle for the football team, and played Pony League baseball. He was once sent to the emergency room with a cut hand. His parents divorced. He enlisted in the marines at age seventeen in late 1964 and was at Parris Island in February of 1965. Before being sent to Vietnam he was stationed in the Aleutians.

He was squad leader, Group F, 2nd Battalion, 1st Marine Regiment, 1st Marine Division. His name appears on Panel 28–East Wall–Line 81 on the Vietnam Memorial in Washington. He was wounded by a land mine in Quang Tri and died on Friday, October 27, 1967 in 3rd Field Hospital, Saigon.

His obituary was brief—soldiers in Vietnam were dying all the time in 1967. They ran a photograph, a head shot in his dress uniform, the same picture they used in a brief story when he completed basic training. He is smiling. On Memorial Day the year after he died his mother placed a wreath at the base of the local war memorial.

For a few years his name appeared in the paper each Memorial Day along with the names of other local deceased veterans. Then nothing.

From these accounts, I was able to accumulate a large list of names of people who should have known him—teammates, friends, and relatives—and my secretary spent days trying to track people down. All of the individuals whose names matched were unrelated. We contacted the local police and fire departments, local cemeteries and funeral homes, and his schools, dozens of people and entities, but none of them knew Gary Dissinger.

I know more about how he died than how he lived.

Finally, in response to one of my many letters, I received a phone call from the Lebanon Valley Chamber of Commerce. The woman on the phone had recognized the name of someone who had attended Gary's fourth birthday party—a friend of her husband. She was kind enough to track him down and give me his phone number. The man I reached had been a boyhood friend of Gary Dissinger and had served with him in Vietnam. He did not know how to find any family members. This man told me he had served two tours in Vietnam, one during the time Gary Dissinger and I were there. He had been wounded and was partially disabled. He was now getting care for cancer at the local VA hospital.

He felt lonely and mostly just wanted to talk to someone who had been in Vietnam. We spoke for a long time.

CHAPTER 29

April 14, 2011
Dear Alex,

It was a powerful experience for me to attend your Valedictory Lecture at Duke. Although I am not a historian and, in your opinion, I am unable to master linear, logical thinking, I understood all that you said and I was absolutely captivated for the full fifty minutes! It was an excellent lecture. I am pleased that my contribution to the Duke History Department helped make the event possible.

At the reception and dinner I spoke with many of the forty former students who came from all over the U.S., and to a man (I only met one woman), they told me that looking back from their present high positions in academia, government, and business, they realize what a pivotal influence you, Professor Roland, played in their career growth. It also reminded me again what a privilege it is for me to be a close friend of a giant in the field of the history of war and technology. I am grateful that you share your forty years' experience with me and tolerate my relentless sophomoric invasions of your orderly mind.

Barbara and I enjoyed spending the weekend with you

and Liz in your exceptional retirement home in the mountains. While I still flounder to maintain enough self-worth to operate my life, you have known for decades what you want and what you need and have it. Congratulations!

On the plane ride home, my head still full of your elite academic world, I formulated five questions. Most are old questions, part of my relentless assault on your stable mind. However, I am now in a better position to understand your answers.

Question One: At my request, you taught a course at Duke entitled "What Is the Meaning of Vietnam?" I took the course and wrote a term paper. I learned much about U.S. use of force as a tool of politics in the 1960s. I read essays, books, editorials, and testimonials by many scholars, soldiers, historians, politicians, theologians, and students about the meaning of the American War in Vietnam. You rediscovered the absence of meaning for you and confirmed your theory that all observers, victims, perpetrators, and U.S. citizens decide their own meaning and use it to reinforce their own stories. I understand you have taught the course five or six more times and that it has become a popular course at Duke.

What is your present position on the meaning of the American War in Vietnam? What was the major "take-away" message for your students? For you? For our government?

Question Two: How do you put the American wars in Iraq and Afghanistan into historical and political perspective? In terms of execution, and outcomes, how do these wars fit into your global view after a lifelong study of technology and war? How do these wars connect to and compare with the American War in Vietnam? What is the meaning of our two present wars (to you)? What do U.S. reactions to the present violence in Libya say about American militarism and diplomacy, and how does Vietnam influence that?

Question Three: What is the future of warfare?

Question Four: Your lecture, "Between Ten Cultures: Confessions of an Agnostic Historian," was a clever combination of the story of your professional life and a critical perspective on American policy since WWII.

Can you summarize the central message left for your academic legacy? Looking back, what does it all mean to you?

Question Five: I'm sitting at a bar and a bright, savvy longstanding good friend sits down on the stool next to me and says, "I have often come across the name of Duke professor Alex Roland. Who is he? What has he done?" I respond by saying, "Oh, Alex Roland, I'm glad you asked. He is the man who . . ." What would you wish my answer to be?

I beg you to answer. Then, maybe I can stop being such a pain in your ass.

Love,

John

April 18, 2011

Dear John,

In answer to your questions:

Question One: What is the meaning of Vietnam to me?

1. It does not have much meaning for me, in the sense that I do not think about it much. For me, personally, as a participant, it was something I did and then put behind me. I think that most Vietnam veterans feel this way about it.

2. Historically, I think of it as a classic instance of the human predicament. Individuals and groups (up to, and including, states) move through life pursuing what they perceive to be their self-interest. From time to time, this behavior brings them into conflict with other individuals and groups. There

ensues a conflict of wills, in which each party tries to have its way. When the parties are states, the strong do what they can, as Thucydides put it so trenchantly, and the weak do what they must. But even then, as history has demonstrated over and over again, out of the conflict of wills emerges a result no one had willed. The American War in Vietnam was a war no one wanted. The North Vietnamese nominally won, but they paid a higher price than the United States and they are losing the peace. This leads to my third meaning:

3. The American War in Vietnam was a tragedy. Neither side realized a benefit commensurate with the cost. Neither side enjoyed a preponderance of virtue or guilt. North Vietnam imposed its will on the United States, but it did not achieve the result it had willed.

4. For me, personally, Vietnam was where I lost my best friend (Michael Wunsch) and discovered my new best (male) friend, you.

Question Two: What is the meaning of the wars in Iraq and Afghanistan?

It is too soon to tell. They are different undertakings, and yet they have become inextricably intertwined. I suspect that historians will view them as part of the same enterprise.

Afghanistan began as a hot pursuit of criminals who had attacked the United States. Before it could succeed, American military resources were redirected to Iraq, a discretionary misadventure that served the purposes of the terrorists who attacked us more than it served our purposes. Relatively small numbers of Americans have died in the two operations, and most of the monetary costs have been passed on to future generations. So neither undertaking is as unpopular as it should be. If the Iraqi people and the Afghan people end up better than they were before and less of a threat to their neighbors and the world, then the cost will probably be seen as acceptable. Failing those outcomes, I expect the two operations will be seen as mistakes of a hegemon grown intoxicated with its own wealth and power.

The impact of Vietnam on Iraq and Afghanistan is profound. First, the U.S. Army went to school in Vietnam. The Petraeus doctrine has its roots in Vietnam. Most importantly, our generation—yours and mine—views Iraq and Afghanistan through the lens of Vietnam. Our parents viewed Vietnam through the lens of Munich. You and I and our contemporaries were willing to go into Afghanistan to punish al Qaeda after 9/11, but we were reluctant to invade Iraq and we remain skeptical about staying in Afghanistan. You may recall when you and I revisited Vietnam in 2008, I concluded that the United States would have been better off getting out of Vietnam much earlier than we did and leaving the Vietnamese to do whatever it was they were determined to do to each other. I am inclined to believe that the same is true of Iraq and Afghanistan.

Question Three: What is the future of war?

This is a virtually unalloyed good story. In our lifetime, war has all but disappeared statistically as a significant cause of human death. Among noncommunicable diseases, cardiovascular, cancer, respiratory, digestive and neuropsychiatric diseases, diabetes, genitourinary and endocrine disorders, and "other" all account for more deaths every year than war. Among communicable diseases, STD/HIV/AIDS, diarrhea, TB, childhood cluster, malaria, and meningitis all account for more deaths every year than war. Respiratory infections, perinatal conditions, maternal conditions, and nutritional deficiency all account for more deaths every year than war. Among deaths by injury, traffic accidents, falls, drownings, poisonings, fires, other accidents, suicides, and nonwar violence cause more deaths every year than war. Deaths from war, both in absolute numbers and as a percentage of world population, have been falling consistently since the end of World War II. If you wanted to devote your life to reducing human suffering and death, there are dozens of fields in which you could invest your efforts more productively than war. Over a hundred thousand people die every year from war, but that is .3% of the world's nonnatural deaths. It is .00185% of the world's population. War is still a scourge on humankind, but it is no longer the nightmare of your imaginings.

Question Four: What does it all mean to me?

The central message of my "last lecture" was that I tried throughout my academic career to keep my politics and ideology out of my teaching and research. I resisted the penchant of my generational cohort to use the bully pulpit of the academy to advance some political or ideological cause. My motives were partially self-serving—timidity, careerism, indecision, perverse independence—and partially principled. I wanted to teach my students how to think, not what to think. I wanted my books to tell stories as I understood them, not as they fit into some larger political or ideological scheme. I wanted my readers, like my students, to draw their own conclusions. My purpose was to inform those conclusions, not determine them. I never tried to get on the right side of history, because I never found the right side of history manifest.

Question Five: Who am I?

Alex Roland was a content, self-contained teacher/scholar who conquered ambition, partially by failing and partially by choice. He wrote, co-wrote, or edited two hands-full of good books that few people ever cared very much about. He taught more than his share of undergraduate and graduate students at Duke University. And he administered a bureau-full of academic organizations and committees.

What he came to cherish most in his public life was wisdom. Everyone gets wise in their way. Historians have the opportunity to get wiser than most, because they spend their careers poaching on the hard-earned experience of others. But they grow wise only if they listen to the history. If they try to bend it to their political or ideological purposes, they will be deaf to its revelations. Roland listened well.

Love,
Alex

CHAPTER 30

Somewhere in an old, worn briefcase, I have ribbons, medals, citations, an oath, and a copy of the warrior creed.

My oath: "I, John Parrish, do solemnly swear that I will support and defend the Constitution of the United States against all enemies, foreign and domestic; that I will bear true faith and allegiance to the same; that I take this obligation freely, without any mental reservation or purpose of evasion; and that I will well and faithfully discharge the duties of the office on which I am about to enter. So help me God."

The warrior creed: "I will always place the mission first; I will never accept defeat; I will never quit; I will never leave a fallen comrade."

During the American War in Vietnam my job was entirely focused on fallen comrades—sick, wounded, and dead marines and army soldiers. I did not have the training to be a confident first responder in the acute care of trauma. At times, my best was not the best possible care. My training to be a warrior consisted of twelve days of lectures and light exercise.

My ability to do my job in Vietnam required a stoicism I did not know I had. I discovered and created the discipline, resilience, endurance, and toughness I needed to bring my emotions under enough control to do my job. It was the greatest of honors and the greatest of horrors to be placed into a war. Taking care of wounded warriors was a privilege, but the sense of wasted life and limb broke my heart. The nearness of death and danger caused significant psychological trauma.

Several weeks after I began my assigned one-year tour in Vietnam, I turned down an opportunity to leave the battlefield. I am proud that I remained at my post. However, a full year in the war left me unstable. My ability to connect to people and be nurtured by family and loved ones was seriously compromised. I was angry and sad and felt a sense of national and personal shame, all made worse by the recognition that the suffering I witnessed would never be redeemed.

The American War in Vietnam is in me forever. I cannot think of myself for very long without thinking of Vietnam. During the past forty years, my connection to war was both an involuntary compulsion and an act of will. As participant, perpetrator, victim, observer, survivor, and student, I tasted enough of the poisonous elixir of war to become addicted to its emotional and physiological surge. The toxic rush is followed by surrender. My lifelong grapple with war results from having had too much of war. My refusal to let go is because I have not had enough of war.

At times I think of my own "disorder" as my "invisible badge of courage" because I was affected by it in much the same way a superficial head wound affected Henry Fleming in Stephen Crane's *Red Badge of Courage.** I have used my pain for gain. In a clumsy attempt to avoid or combat my feelings of shame and loneliness, I learned to use my PTSD symptoms to manipulate others, using the more noticeable signs of psychic distress to save me from a deeper, more primitive

---

*Henry Fleming was eighteen years old when he volunteered to join the North against the South in the American Civil War. During his first encounter with the enemy, he panicked and fled. While lost, he got into a scuffle with another soldier, who hit him on the head with his gun, causing a minor but bloody injury. When Henry found his regiment, his colleagues assumed he had been wounded in battle and welcomed him as a hero, instead of a coward. In the next several weeks, Henry matured, gained perspective, and became a brave soldier.

pain. Have I magnified and exposed my inner war to create a false badge of courage? By wearing the sackcloth and ashes of a victim or apologetic perpetrator, I could avoid responsibility. I have used staged, stoic silence and reluctantly told stories that become more noble with time and retelling. I have used my own forms of transparent suffering and poorly disguised wounds to seek opportunities for recognition. By making war a massive object of hate, horror, and sorrow, I could obscure and maintain my attraction to it. The American War in Vietnam has been my stage, a place to wrestle with childhood trauma and human angst. At times, it has been a convenient platform to express the torture of a failing denial of my biology and death. I could use my war experience to explain my depression and failed relationships. I had a pulpit and a story.

Am I a selfish child driven by the need for some authority to say "thank you for your service" or "welcome home" or "you are a good boy"? Am I an advocate or an impostor seeking the approval of generals and the camaraderie of grunts?

During my career, the major source of funding for my research has been the U.S. Department of Defense. When it was helpful, I used my war experience to gain favor with the appropriators of funding. I suckled at the breast of the mighty military-industrial complex. Like so many others, I profited from war, perpetuating the very destructiveness that so impacted my own life. While trying to make a difference in the care of soldiers, I sold out to the power, excitement, glory, and money of the military and defense industry. I submitted to the lure of the inner ring of power and made sure I was on the winning team.

Then again, at times, I feel I would be more concerned about myself if I were not altered forever by my war experiences. Components of humanness and humanity require susceptibility to the impact of horror and death. Now I spend a great deal of time trying to help warriors overcome the stigma that prevents them from seeking help. I share with them some of what I have learned. We try to convince warriors that seeking help is actually the brave thing to do. Considering family and comrades, it is also the generous thing to do. The brain of every human can be rewired by trauma in a specific setting. To a certain point people can be trained to cope with stress and adversity, but still everyone is susceptible to having long-term consequences of stress. The threshold for prolonged stress reaction differs from person to person. Resilience is more of a process than a trait of an individual and can be learned. An injury is not the same as a disorder. Being unlucky is not the same as being dishonorable or weak. Even well-trained athletes can be physically injured and require rehabilitation guided by experts. Congruently, even the most resilient warrior may have psychological brain injury and require rehabilitation guided by experts.

Do I carry a right or an obligation for penance, retribution, or absolution? In order to better bear witness, do I have a moral obligation to prevent my own healing? As long as I remain damaged, I may cry out. Then, there is a chance my testimony will be heard and I can still make a difference. To heal quietly may be dishonest and selfish. The major lies supporting war are lies of omission. Silence is a form of complicity.

I have tried my best to understand war, and I have failed. War is something I cannot comprehend. It is such a major force in history—a constant human habit. I have studied war in anthropology, sociology, history, biology, and evolutionary psychology textbooks. I have waded through long diatribes about tribal behavior, prides, mating rights, territorial imperatives, herds and troops, social contracts, and a nation's right to kill and demand sacrifice. No logic, emotion, clusters of justifications, or theories provide me with a lasting comprehensive explanation. I just cannot get it. My intelligence, perspective, reasoning, and vocabulary are inadequate. The words of war poets spark teasing glimpses of insight, but I cannot hold them or name them or integrate them into my consciousness.

I do not have the expertise, experience, or clout to advise our national leaders about preparing for and making war. Reluctantly I accept that being prepared to go to war may be necessary to keep peace. I understand that America and its democratic allies must strike a difficult balance between exemplifying freedom and actively spreading democracy and capitalism by economic pressure or by force. It is alarming when war making requires lies and control of the press.

My personal biopsy of war has great limitations. Although I have purposely absorbed elements of the military culture, I was never trained to have "Battlemind."* I never killed anyone or destroyed anything. My family and property were never directly threatened. My observations of junior and senior warriors are limited to those warriors I happened to encounter. My personal interactions with them occurred in two wars that frame the forty years of my preoccupation with the human element of war. In Vietnam, I worked with physicians unwillingly removed from civilian life (and a few career medical officers) to care for highly committed marine and army volunteer warriors and heroic and hostile army draftees.

In the present American wars, I have met with generals who proudly tell me that their job is to make the military better at killing people and breaking things. Because PTSD and suicide are part of the cost of doing business, they explain, the military needs to get better at avoiding susceptible ("weak") people and train the troops to be tougher: "Get rid of people with psychological issues, or at least keep them out of my command."

I have also met with senior military and civilian leaders in Veterans Affairs and the Department of Defense who are very bright, articulate, and thoughtful and driven by concern for the physical and psychological health of their troops. I meet with warriors with major injuries, including amputations, who are committed to returning to the battlefield because "that's my job; that's what I do." I work among

---

*Battlemind was created for the U.S. Army by Colonel Carl Castro, Ph.D., of the Walter Reed Army Institute of Research. The word is an acronym for the different mental skills and mindset required to survive during war: Buddies, Accountability, Targeted aggression, Tactical awareness, Lethally armed, Emotional control, Mission operational security, Individual responsibility, Nondefensive driving in combat, Discipline and ordering.

men and women who are grateful for the confidence, self-discipline, ambition, and team skills acquired from their military experience. I also meet angry, disillusioned, or lonely warriors severely compromised by the psychological wounds of war. For some, their denial and their protective mechanisms are so strong that only their families know the magnitude of the pain they carry and inflict on others.

I was given the template of a damaged, passive, extremely naive boy. When Jesus, *Playboy*, and the Hollywood version of the soldier fought for my soul, I made a Faustian bargain with the Muse of Academia and almost lost everything, including my family, my sanity, my inner moral compass, and my self-respect. Although heavily burdened with shame, I expose my sins partly to openly assume responsibility for my actions, but mostly because I believe the behaviors and attitudes I demonstrated are the raw materials that make me susceptible to the God of War. I have terminal ambivalence. If I had not been to war, I would want to go.

My perspective may have components that collectively have unique or universal lessons. I am a physician and a full-time academician. All the men in my extended family went to war. I gradually moved from the poor white uneducated fundamentalist Christian Deep South to liberal Massachusetts and Harvard. I have lived in the USA during its seventy years of militarism and growing dominance by the defense industries. I observe that war is big business, a racket in which most of the profiteers are safe, powerful, and comfortable. I have lived among and worked with warriors who bear the greatest costs of and may have the least benefit from American wars.

In 1972, I published my unprocessed experience of war. Now, I have another chance to remind others of the human costs of war. If there is a minuscule chance that my testimony can add value to the voices that argue or beg for a longer pause before our leaders go to war, I must witness again. War is a learned behavior and must be seen as a confession of failure of diplomacy, negotiation, common sense, and leadership.

My view of the world is greatly influenced by the mythological destiny of the warrior. I admire and wish to emulate the brave, manly, and heroic qualities of discipline, stoicism, self-reliance, honor, respect for authority, and commitment to comrades, mission, and a higher cause. The trained warrior must also be able to call upon the will and skill to kill, but this power must be controlled by the morality, wisdom, and commitment to avoid killing. In training for war, killing is a central mission. Years of military training evoke the warrior ethos to support the instincts and motivation to kill and take the risk of being killed. Hypervigilance, controlled fight-flight hormone surge, and efficiency in neutralizing the enemy are teachable skills. Basically, the survival skills and fighting techniques used in battle parallel the symptoms of PTSD.

Some of the military trainees are very young and may not have the motivation or sophistication to carry back to their families and community the benefits of the hero ethos without killing-machine components harmful to the warrior and his or her family. The maturity and skills needed for reintegration also require training. I believe the military has been slow to put adequate energy and time into teaching the required resilience and coping skills and broadening of perspective. Presently, many warriors cannot successfully carry their warrior ethos into peaceful civil life. Or they remain alone. Multiple tours by too few warriors compound the problem. Our soldiers are tired. We need less war or more soldiers.

What war does to human beings doesn't change with time. Considering stress-induced psychologic injury of war, war fighters may be the canary in our foreign policy coal mine. They are among those most exposed to the human cost of military intervention. Whether bystanders, victims, or perpetrators, their proximity to carnage sensitizes vulnerable individuals to the horrors of war and the helplessness of civilians. Selection criteria for recruitment of service members make it unlikely that most soldiers have the rhetorical skills or platform to bear witness in ways that influence people of power. Military training and culture make it difficult for them to express the emotional burden caused by experiencing the brutality at the end of the spear. Suicide is one form of political protest.

Because we have not done enough to facilitate reintegration and to honor and serve the returning warrior citizen, the warrior pays an even greater price for our nation's foreign policy. Patriotism, mythologies, images of mental and physical fitness, and camaraderie go a long way to recruit volunteers and to bring the warriors to the battlefield, but these forces cannot keep them there and successfully reintegrate them into society unless they are sent to war by leaders who earn their respect and successfully articulate why the warriors must go to war and why they should pay a disproportionate amount of the costs.

I am an older and wiser man, and the albatross around my neck has become much smaller since I acknowledged its presence. I wish to mourn the sorrow of war, and I believe grief is best endured in community. The writing of this book is an attempt at connection by sharing. To my own life now, I am trying to apply the same morality test I wish my country to apply to wars like the American War in Vietnam: Does the action alleviate more human suffering than it causes?

At the time of maximum mental illness, my father decided to will himself to die. I have decided to will myself to live.

I am unfinished, but I do have a plan. I will focus on the invisible wounds of war and try to make a difference. I choose to try to help identify those warriors who are in need, motivate them to seek help, and point them to the best available care. I choose to explore new ways to support their families. I choose to identify and facilitate research that leads to improvement in the treatment of warriors with physical and psychological wounds of war.

I will most likely wrestle with my addiction to war until I fade away.

I carry on. The present missions of CIMIT and Home Base will probably bring me as much peace as I can find and likely more than I deserve.

Despite the pain I cause, very special people love me. Within my limited repertoire, I try to be worthy of it and find ways to express my love to each.

I choose to have hope and then struggle to justify it.

POSTSCRIPT

In July 2011 I had the opportunity to visit seven military bases in Afghanistan and to observe the in-theater care of soldiers with traumatic brain injury (TBI) and severe battle stress. I was the guest of General Peter Chiarelli, vice chief of staff of the army, who has been relentless in raising the awareness and improving the care of such soldiers. We were accompanied by other high-ranking military officers and my colleague, a physical medicine and rehabilitation expert and leader of the Home Base TBI Program, as well as General Chiarelli's senior staff.

I was overwhelmed by the magnitude and sophistication of the American military presence. The facility footprints and the amount of equipment are enormous. The U.S. Army supplied protective gear and I elected to wear the U.S. military-issue jungle boots I wore every day during my tour of duty in the American War in Vietnam. Everyone was part of a common culture, working toward a common goal. Nothing challenged the uniform world view. I met no Afghanis. The mostly male, no nonsense, slightly anxious ambiance combined with the oppressive heat and sleep deprivation felt disarmingly familiar.

I was amazed by the modern facilities used to care for wounded Americans. If forced to choose, I would prefer being seriously wounded outside the wire near an American base in Afghanistan than on the streets of most U.S. cities. We met with many military and contracted but nonmilitary psychiatrists, psychologists, occupational therapists, and other members of multidisciplinary teams working to individualize the care of soldiers with TBI and posttraumatic stress. Their skill, commitment, and teamwork were most impressive. My Boston colleague and I were given several opportunities for private interviews with soldiers being treated in newly established Concussion Recovery Care Centers. Based on these encounters, I believe that the protocol for treating concussions in the Centers is better informed than those employed at most organized scholastic or professional sports activities in the United States.

At Landstuhl Regional Medical Center (LRMC) in Germany we visited many ambulatory and hospitalized wounded warriors, triaged there from the Middle East because of their more severe physical and/or psychologic injuries. Each one told his or her personal story to General Chiarelli. Each warrior was given a special coin by the general, a traditional recognition of his or her service dating from the Civil War. No matter how serious their injuries, most men and women wanted to return to duty in Afghanistan. The soldiers we met seemed to believe in what they were doing and to feel a strong commitment to their fellow soldiers still on the front lines. Told to kill certain Afghanis and to win the hearts and minds of others, they did their jobs and returned to the relative safety of the base and the fellowship of their units. They were proud of their service, devoted to their comrades, respectful of their officers, and part of a proud tradition. We ended our tour by visiting the mortuary at LRMC where soldiers work under the direction of skilled and caring morticians, preparing soldiers for their final trip home.

The brief tour reinforced my decade-long opinion that we have the resources, talent, and will to take excellent care of our troops while they are in uniform. I was comforted to observe that, in contrast to my own war experience, the cumulatively devastating effects of killing and death on solders were acknowledged. The stigma of experiencing and expressing emotional pain has diminished over the past two years partly due to General Chiarelli's enlightened influence.

Members of the modern all-volunteer armed services are trained to survive and succeed. Some have grown from boys to men in the military and have embraced its well-defined culture. But when bad things happen to them and around them, when because of their injuries or their exhaustion they leave this black and white world, these admirable men and women may return to an alien environment where their values and coping mechanisms are suspect.

When I put these observations in the context of my personal history and what I have learned in recent years about the care of veterans, I realize we, the American people and our institutions, must increase our willingness and capability to support our troops when they rejoin us as civilians. Thankfully, and in contrast to earlier wars, Americans now distinguish the war from the warriors. Whatever their feelings about the rationale for invading Iraq or Afghanistan, or mounting the Surge, they can admire and appreciate those who sacrifice so much for our country. Yet even a heart-felt expression of gratitude to our active duty troops is not enough for discharged veterans. Their challenges are enormous. They may have seen and perhaps done unspeakable things. Their preparation for social reintegration is often inadequate and their care is inconsistent in selected parts of the United States of America. For many warriors, the invisible wounds of war are deep indeed. Their healing is our collective responsibility. They volunteer to be used but should not be discarded.